Combat Bandsman

Combat Bandsman

*Memoir of a Tour in
Vietnam with the
9th Infantry Division, 1969*

ROBERT F. FISCHER

McFarland & Company, Inc., Publishers
Jefferson, North Carolina

LIBRARY OF CONGRESS CATALOGUING-IN-PUBLICATION DATA

Names: Fischer, Robert F., 1945– author.
Title: Combat bandsman : memoir of a tour in Vietnam with the 9th Infantry Division, 1969 / Robert F. Fischer.
Description: Jefferson, North Carolina : McFarland & Company, Inc., Publishers, 2016. | Includes bibliographical references and index.
Identifiers: LCCN 2016037556 | ISBN 9781476664811 (softcover : acid free paper) ∞
Subjects: LCSH: Fischer, Robert F., 1945– | Trumpet players—United States—Biography. | Vietnam War, 1961–1975—Personal narratives, American. | 9th Infantry Division Band.
Classification: LCC ML419.F57 A3 2016 | DDC 959.704/37—dc23
LC record available at https://lccn.loc.gov/2016037556

BRITISH LIBRARY CATALOGUING DATA ARE AVAILABLE

ISBN (print) 978-1-4766-6481-1
ISBN (ebook) 978-1-4766-2444-0

© 2016 Robert F. Fischer. All rights reserved

No part of this book may be reproduced or transmitted in any form or by any means, electronic or mechanical, including photocopying or recording, or by any information storage and retrieval system, without permission in writing from the publisher.

Cover photographs taken by the author in Vietnam in 1969

Printed in the United States of America

McFarland & Company, Inc., Publishers
  Box 611, Jefferson, North Carolina 28640
  www.mcfarlandpub.com

To Jane,
the last woman I shall ever love

"They lied to us."—Larry D. Wolf,
formerly United States Army, Republic of Vietnam

Table of Contents

Preface	1
Introduction: The Orchestration of War, 1945–1969	9
1. Screw Up and You'll End Up in the Infantry	19
2. Forget Everything You Learned in Basic Training	35
3. Republic of Vietnam, January 1969	58
4. Republic of Vietnam, February 1969	77
5. Republic of Vietnam, March 1969	95
6. Republic of Vietnam, April 1969	121
7. Republic of Vietnam, May 1969	148
8. Republic of Vietnam, June 1969	174
9. Republic of Vietnam, July 1969	198
10. Republic of Vietnam, August 1969	218
11. Back in the USA	225
Glossary	229
Chapter Notes	235
Bibliography	243
Index	245

Preface

In every human's existence there is a time that cannot be forgotten. For some it may have been an event, a tragedy, a love, or perhaps a memorable adventure. For me it was a war, a politically vile, particularly nasty, morally controversial war. It had been like that for my father, but his memories of war intruded upon his reality only after senile dementia returned him to the trenches of the Champagne forever. Unlike my father, my memories have never faded. They are, and always have been, the semipermeable membrane through which I filter all I see, hear, smell, and otherwise perceive.

America's involvement in what would become *my* war began the same year I was born. Oddly enough my birth occurred at a time of great national rejoicing. The jubilation, however, had absolutely nothing to do with me other than the elation felt by my parents for having created such a cute nine-pound bundle. The national happiness was for world peace. It resounded across the land in the aftermath of the century's second and most devastating global war. After six long years of bloody fighting (1939–1945) the Allies had finally broken the will of the Axis European Fascist and Asian Imperialist to continue their quest for world domination. The cost in lives had been staggering, estimated to be 50–70 million human beings, most of whom were civilians who had borne the brunt of the Axis Powers' invasion and occupation wrath, not to mention the incessant bombings of civilian population clusters by both sides.

The seeds for my war germinated while I was still nursing at my mother's bosom. Three seemingly unrelated events transpired prior to my first birthday that would later influence the direction of my adolescent years and ultimately impact how I perceive myself, my countrymen, and my government: (1) a colonial Asian empire of France and wartime ally of the United States declared itself an autonomous democracy; (2) a cold war tempered by the threat of nuclear holocaust erupted between former allies; and (3) the population of the United States exploded in a heretofore unheard of boom of baby births. These events helped propagate one of America's most culturally tumultuous decades and set the stage for a politically devastating war that extinguished the lives of an estimated 1–4 million people,[1] including over 58,000 U.S. servicemen.

The tragedy and futility that have become the legacy of my war can be encompassed in a single word, *Vietnam*. Mere mention of Vietnam to almost anyone who experienced the social turbulence of the 1960s can reawaken all of the bitterness and anger felt by a youthful generation of Americans who had been incited to action and rebellion by misguided politics and whose antigovernment ideology infected a nation's mainstream population by fragmenting its normally complacent, silent, middle-class majority into vehemently opposing factions. It is generally agreed among historians that the *conflict* in Vietnam[2] began in 1965—the year *conventional* U.S. ground troops were first deployed to the Republic of South Vietnam. For all intents and purposes, however, active U.S. military intervention in Vietnam's political affairs began a decade earlier in 1953 when the French withdrew their forces from Vietnam. The United States reacted by sending military advisors to assist the newly formed Republic of Vietnam government in stopping North Vietnamese communist aggression.

The war in Vietnam became my reality precisely one year after I'd been drafted into the Army. I received orders assigning me to the United States Army, Republic of Vietnam. I set foot in South Vietnam during the first week of January 1969 when the war was entering its fifth year. Although the administration of President Lyndon B. Johnson had continuously and vehemently proclaimed its military success in containing communism in South Vietnam, an alarming percentage of Americans had become skeptical. After five years of nightly news televising graphic film footage of American boys being killed and maimed while conducting what appeared to be senseless missions, the specter of doubt concerning the government's credibility had arisen like a phoenix from the morass of political ineptitude. The down and dirty style of guerrilla warfare American troops faced in Vietnam, characterized by close physical contact with the enemy and the prolific use of ambush tactics and booby traps, was all too reminiscent of the dreadful jungle fighting encountered by island-hopping U.S. Marines during World War II. After 36,736 U.S. fatalities in Vietnam by the close of 1968, neither victory nor an end to the fighting was in sight.

Public support for the war had been irreversibly damaged in 1968 after the communists launched a massive country-wide offensive catching both U.S. and South Vietnamese military forces completely off guard. Although the offensive failed at great cost to the enemy in terms of causalities, its timing had effectively undermined the credibility of the U.S. government, having come only months after the American public had been assured of a victorious and imminent conclusion to the war. In spite of the reality that the enemy had suffered horrendous losses compared to U.S. losses, the magnitude and viciousness of the attacks irrefutably confirmed what people had already deduced from watching the nightly news—the war was far from being over.

Compared to the stateside army the army in Vietnam was unruly, unkempt, and verbally disdainful of its commanders and the tactics employed by them to defeat the enemy—a condition not at all difficult to understand in view of the political situation America found itself in at the beginning of 1969. The ongoing failure of the military hierarchy to fully grasp the nature of the enemy's resolve had given rise to overt political dissention on the home front and increasing discontentment within the ranks of soldiers fighting in Vietnam. The enemy was determined, elusive, and extremely confident defending their own soil. After five years of bitter combat the tactics employed by the U.S. military mimicked those of the defeated French army—troops operating out of fixed defensive positions, mounting numerous small patrols, scouring familiar territory in search of an enemy who had become all too effective at blending in with the environment and civilian population.

My first impression upon viewing Vietnam through the Plexiglas window of the military-contracted commercial airline flight delivering me to war was South Vietnam's verdant lushness. Given the perspective of distance, the terrain in the Mekong Delta where I was to finish the remaining ten months of my two-year military service obligation was unmistakably tropical, vividly green, and undeniably beautiful. Up close, however, the beauty was compromised by thick, gooey rice-paddy muck, razor-sharp grasses, venomous snakes and plants, stinging and biting insects, belligerent critters of all sizes, and overgrowth so thickly entangled every inch had to be vigorously hacked away to permit passage. Off of the roads and trails the soggy ground, the countless branching waterways,[3] and the dense foliage defied efficient movement. It was unquestionably the domain of the mosquito, the leech, the snake, and—in 1969—the Viet Cong. Add ambushes and booby traps galore and you had one hell of a good place to avoid.

Throughout my days in Vietnam I had been keenly aware of my participation in the making of history. I was seeing things I would never see again. So as not to forget the experience I took numerous photographs and recorded events I found notable. Now comparing what I experienced to how others have portrayed Vietnam in literature and cinema, I find few similarities. I can't recall ever having encountered crazed, indifferent, drug-addicted U.S. soldiers wantonly slaughtering Vietnamese civilians. If this did happen, it wasn't the norm where and when I was in-country. Our orders had been an emphatic *do not fire unless fired upon!* Friendly *irregular* local and regional Vietnamese forces carried rifles and wore the same black-pajama dress as the enemy. Most of the American soldiers I knew were reasonably disciplined young men instilled with mainstream American values concerning the sanctity of life and the value of private property. Although belittling the enemy with racial slurs such as dinks, slopes, gooks, zips, and worse, was common parlance among soldiers, it was merely one way to distance oneself from the brutality of war, by psychologically dehumanizing the enemy. The taking of a human life remains an inherently abhorrent and abnormal act, difficult to comprehend, let alone execute, but destroying something inhuman such as a dink, a slope, a zip, or a gook is not. Although prolonged exposure to the stress of combat can, and for many soldiers *did*, redefine the parameters of individual morality and emotional tolerance it was never to the extent of murdering the innocent.[4] During 1969 the around-the-clock insurgent warfare as conducted by the enemy and the inane policies of the U.S. military resulted in an army somewhat frayed on the edges but not one that was especially murderous or mutinous.

From the perspective of statistical evaluation, viewing Vietnam as one *ten-year* war compromises an accurate understanding of how the prolonged duration of the war affected the composition and morale of the U.S. Army. It is more meaningful to consider Vietnam as a succession of ten individual *one-year* wars. At the onset of the war the U.S. Army predominately comprised volunteers and career soldiers[5] who had trained together in cohesive units. These soldiers believed in the nobility of their cause, the sanctity of their government, and the invincibility of the U.S. Army. Their unit identification and morale were high. The relatively slow overseas waterborne transportation initially utilized to dispatch entire units to Vietnam permitted soldiers ample time to solidify their camaraderie and unit identification by discussing their fears and concerns among themselves. Representing the cutting edge of America's political will, they were confident in their mission of halting the spread of communism in Southeast Asia.

When these earliest Army units landed on Republic of Vietnam soil, it was with the blessing and support of an appreciative American people. Over the years, the appreciation waned, as did the rate of volunteering, which resulted in the ratio of volunteers to conscripts steadily skewing more toward the latter. For most replacement troops arriving in Vietnam after 1966 the morale-bolstering effect of camaraderie through association became almost nonexistent. Unlike their predecessors, who had been deployed as members of complete units, replacement troops were air expressed to Vietnam as individuals aboard commercial airline flights. The transition from safety to the frightening unknown of combat was approximately 18 hours. These later arrivals had insufficient time to psychologically acclimate themselves to the change.

Upon my arrival in Vietnam I had immediately perceived a profound difference in the military attitude of combat soldiers as compared to their stateside counterparts. The U.S. Army in Vietnam functioned in a hostile environment fraught with mortal terror and without hope of victory or cessation of hostilities. They existed in harm's way 24 hours a day, *every day,* and performed without the confidence and reassurance that comes from appreciating why they were fighting. Most soldiers didn't know or understand what their government's objectives were in Vietnam. I can't recall ever having discussed the political rationale of the war with any of my comrades, leaders, or commanders while serving in Vietnam. For the average soldier engaged in combat, survival concerns took precedence over intellectual matters. Everything within the parameters of a soldier's mortal existence was on the sacrificial altar of America's political will, done through executive power without the approval of Congress or the unanimous support of friends, peers, and neighbors at home. As a consequence, the majority of the soldiers I encountered focused their entire existence on the day they would get out of Vietnam.

My year of war, 1969, had been—in addition to being the midpoint of the war—the high-water mark of U.S. troop commitment, with almost 550,000 servicemen in-country at the end of April 1969. The year ended statistically as the second highest for casualties, surpassed only by the previous year. It's little wonder morale suffered. To the average American male conscripted and sent to Vietnam in 1969 the experience was more akin to a ritual of passage than a patriotic duty. Although most soldiers didn't comprehend the reason why they were fighting, it had been a commonly held notion it no longer concerned defending America. Many of us believed we were risking our lives and limbs in a foreign land to uphold the morally questionable government of an alien culture no one seemed to understand.

It had come as a great surprise when the Army decided I would best serve their needs and the war effort as a musician. In noncombat postings, musician was a choice military assignment not normally extended to draftees. I was flown from the replacement battalion at Long Bình southward to the Mekong Delta, where I learned of my assignment with the 9th Infantry Division Band. This placed me in a relatively autonomous and somewhat elite organization charged with the twofold mission of promoting esprit de corps and assisting the division in its civilian pacification efforts to win the hearts and minds of the local populace. If I had to choose a theme song for the mission it would have been "The Impossible Dream."[6]

Initially I had no reason to doubt I'd lucked out. Ever since fourth grade, making music had been an important aspect of my life, so much so that I'd brought my old beat-up E.K. Blessing trumpet along with my other personal articles to my first duty station at Fort Stewart, Georgia. Maintaining my musical skills through practice had meant as much to me as avoiding service in Vietnam had meant. I, however, eventually learned that, like Hollywood's bugle-tooting version of Rudyard Kipling's Gunga Din, in war even musicians are not immune from the tentacles of combat. The location of the 9th Infantry Division's Đồng Tâm headquarters, the base camp from where the band operated, was situated deep in Viet Cong–controlled territory. South of Đồng Tâm there had been absolutely nothing but trouble and a few friendly outposts manned by U.S. special troops and South Vietnamese irregulars.

Throughout the pages that follow I have endeavored to present a *factual* account of my military service, as well as a *factual* account of the 9th Infantry Division's final months in Vietnam. My effort, while sincere, has been undoubtedly distorted by the perspective of hindsight—not to mention the many years that have separated my recollections from real time. It must also be understood that my attitude toward America and my fellow countrymen evolved during turbulent times when being a Vietnam veteran was not highly regarded by many Americans, their having mistakenly associated soldiering with the policies of government. Although I have attempted to downplay this personal aspect of my experience, the scars and bitterness remain as festering emotional wounds.

All of the events I have described happened and all of the soldiers I've named are, or were, real people.[7] In reflection I now wish I had possessed the foresight to have reported more of events in my letters home than complaints about my dissatisfaction with the Army. The many letters I sent to my loved ones are replete with negativity about the Army and the war. Much to the horror of my parents, on occasion I did describe certain traumatic events as they occurred. Boredom, terror, destruction, and despair had become so much a part of my environment I thought nothing of the effect my candid and dispassionate reporting of tragedy, disaster, and anger might have on those who loved me and were deeply concerned for my safety.

Throughout the many decades that have elapsed since my departing Vietnam I have read enough accounts of other soldiers' experiences to conclude that as a literary genre the "Vietnam Experience" is, by default, defined as the plight of the infantryman and typically relates to *his* personal hardship, horror, destruction, death, sorrow, desperation, valor, and so on. Viewed from the perspective of what the typical "Vietnam Experience" actually was, the drama expressed in these accounts rings somewhat atypical in that it does not reflect the experience of the majority of soldiers who served and fought in Vietnam. Most U.S. soldiers dispatched to South Vietnam participated in combat support roles, the ratio being approximately 7–10 support troops to one directly engaged in combat.[8]

Combat in the sense of personal hardship, horror, destruction, death, sorrow, desperation, and valor was absolutely not the exclusive domain of the infantryman. Unlike previous wars in which America has participated, the primary yardstick of success had been the taking and occupying of enemy-held ground. No such defining measure existed in Vietnam, for the ground war was fought almost entirely within the Republic of South Vietnam, where no traditional combat demarcation lines of fronts and rears existed. The entire country was a battleground of one sort or another. It hadn't been at all uncommon for support soldiers to engage in some form of combat, whether ducking incoming enemy mortars or rockets, defending perimeters against ground attacks, being sniped at, being ambushed in convoys, or being exposed to booby traps. All soldiers risked their lives in Vietnam but in different ways and to different degrees of hardship, and therein lies the difference between combat and combat support in the Vietnam War—*the degree of hardship, not the exposure to risk.*

When I spoke of the 9th Infantry Division Band as having been an *elite* organization, it was from the standpoint of its mission.[9] Whereas most infantry and combat support troops operated within defined areas, the band journeyed far and wide throughout the division's entire operational area, often traveling by truck, river craft, helicopter, and fixed-wing aircraft. One of the more frightening events that occurred when I was a division-level bandsman was the time, when performing outside of Đồng Tâm, the band had been entirely responsible for its own security. The Army Table of Organization and Equipment did not authorize a radio for communication for division bands; if attacked we were expected to defend ourselves without support of the superior firepower the infantry was so dependent upon. In the bush, bandsmen went about their mission independent of any division combat assets. We were literally on our own. This reality had continuously escaped the notice of quite a few of my fellow musicians who were under the misbegotten belief our commanders would never place us in harm's way.

The sense of well-being that permeated the mentality of so many of my fellow bandsmen was a frightening reality to behold. My apprehensions about being ambushed while traveling over unsecured roads or performing in a remote location were adequately summed up in the words of a late arrival to the band, an infantry sergeant with airborne wings who shared my concerns. On one memorable alcohol-inspired occasion he revealed his fear about being engaged in combat with a bunch of silly musicians. Judging by what I remember of the overall combat readiness and attitude of the band, we both had good reason for concern. Over the duration of the division's approximately 970 days in Vietnam, Headquarters and Headquarters Company and Band suffered seven fatalities, of which six were hostile deaths, not a great number by combat standards but more than enough to dispel any notion about the safety of the nonexistent "rear."

Dealing with sudden terror was the ubiquitous nature of survival in the Mekong Delta, an insidious place with or without war where soldiers lived, labored, and died among their enemies—after often confusing them with the friendlies—and engaging in combat that took many different forms where only the truly fortunate were exempt.

Introduction: The Orchestration of War, 1945–1969

The seeds for America's participation in the Vietnam War were inadvertently sown in the aftermath of an earlier war. Although the legacy of World War II was supposed to have been universal freedom from tyranny and oppression, the inheritance had soon proven to be dichotomous. A new type of fear born of the Atomic Age and nurtured by a succession of vicious limited wars of containment pitted two diverse political ideologies against each other. Communist doctrine openly disclosed its goal of world domination. The defeated, vehemently anticommunist Nazi socialist of Germany and black shirt fascists of Italy had, in addition to having terrorized Europe with their armies, also contained the spread of communism. At the end of World War II the now unchecked march of the "red menace" had crossed Eastern Europe and entered Northern China. It spread rapidly, like a malignant cancer, metastasizing to infect noncommunist nations. Espionage and cold war tempered by the threat of nuclear annihilation replaced the bayonets and bullets of the vanquished Axis powers.

While the noncommunist free world was realigning itself through treaties of mutual defense and the redeployment of their armies, a thunderhead of nationalism had swept across Southeast Asia. The peoples of Burma, India, Indonesia, Indochina, and the Philippine Islands passionately longed for the unalienable right of self-determination. They had valiantly fought the Japanese oppressors alongside their British and French colonial masters and now demanded sovereignty. Their participation in World War II had provided them with the military training, combat experience, weapons, and national dignity to force independence if necessary. After seven years of war[1] the financial resources and manpower of both France and Great Britain had been drained. The time for independence had arrived.

To insure a peaceful resolution to the question of postwar colonialism, Asia turned to America. The United States, keenly aware that not to help would only promote anarchy, set an international paradigm in 1946 by granting independence to the Philippine Islands. In 1948 Great Britain reluctantly followed with Burma and India. Although the Dutch remained hesitant to relinquish their holdings in Indonesia, by 1949 pressure from the United States had undermined their resolve. French Indochina remained the only colonial empire remaining in Southeast Asia.

For almost a century the French had prospered from the extracted wealth and servitude of the Orient. Vietnam was one of the world's primary sources of raw rubber. The French industrial giant Michelin & Company owned and controlled vast tracts of rubber-tree plantings in the southern section of the Vietnam Peninsula. Although the French eventually withdrew their forces from neighboring Laos in 1947 and Cambodia in 1953, they adamantly refused to leave Vietnam.

France had been involved with Vietnamese affairs for approximately 100 years. During the 19th century they had assembled what they labeled the "Indochina Union" from the ancient dynasties of Laos, Cambodia, and Vietnam. Of the three, Vietnam was the richest in natural resources and by far the dominant country. Over a period of years commencing in 1858, the French had conquered, annexed, and merged the borders of these separate countries into one. Vietnam's national identity had been purposely obliterated when France split it into three separate regions: Cochin China (southern Vietnam—1863), Amman (central Vietnam—1883), and Tonkin (northern Vietnam—1883). These regions, including the protectorates of Cambodia (annexed 1863) and Laos (annexed 1893), collectively formed the colonial empire of French Indochina. After the French suffered a stunning defeat in June 1940 at the hands of Nazi Germany, Japan—the primary ally of Germany—occupied French Indochina and governed the union through Vichy, pro–Nazi, French colonial officials.

In May 1941 a mushrooming, 11-year-old, Vietnamese Communist Party established the Vietnam Independence League to organize anticolonial forces within Vietnam. To the international community they would soon be known as the Vietminh. The Vietminh established a communist training base for guerilla warfare near the Chinese border in Vietnam's remote northern Cao Bằng Province. The nationalistic posture and anticolonial goals of the Vietminh attracted large numbers of Vietnamese who, while unwilling to proclaim themselves communist, desired independence. The Vietminh, led by Vietnamese patriot and communist Nguyen Ai Quoc (born Nguyen Tat Thanh), became the most powerful anticolonial organization in Indochina and would eventually prove more than a match for the French.

Consistent with their nationalistic policies, in 1941 the Vietminh joined the United States-backed Chinese nationalist Vietnam Liberation League. The ideology of the two groups, however, soon clashed. Nguyen Ai Quoc's political intentions had become suspect to the Chinese and he was imprisoned. Without his guidance the Vietminh lost their effectiveness against the Japanese. From prison Nguyen Ai Quoc convinced the Chinese to let him organize, train, and lead Vietnamese guerrillas against the Japanese in China. The Chinese, desirous of his assistance but apprehensive of the possible negative effects his communist reputation would have on the Americans, insisted that he change his name. Thus the heretofore unknown Ho Chi Minh, the communist who would later gain international notoriety as the archenemy of the United States in Southeast Asia, spontaneously materialized into world politics during 1943.

Early in World War II President Franklin Delano Roosevelt had made United States policy clear toward the independence of Indochina. He and his cabinet had repeatedly acknowledged that after nearly a century of French colonization the Vietnamese were worse off than before.[2] This sentiment from the leader of one of the most powerful nations in the world had endeared Ho Chi Minh to America. During the later years of World War II Ho Chi Minh worked closely with the Office of Strategic Services (the predecessor of the Central Intelligence Agency) to rescue Allied servicemen from the Japanese. Ho Chi Minh's pro-Western attitudes and political brilliance was admired and well documented by the Office of Strategic Services.

On March 9, 1945, the Japanese violently ended French colonialism. They arrested Vichy French political leaders and attacked French military outposts. Many French units, caught completely unaware, surrendered. Others fought. Those survivors who escaped the vicious treachery of the Japanese found refuge with the Vietminh, who honored a promise to help any French soldier willing to fight the Japanese. By 1945 the Vietminh had a superb organization in place to rescue and shelter downed Allied airmen. They now allied with their former French masters to defeat the Japanese in Vietnam.

After Japan's unconditional surrender in August 1945 Indochina was left without a government. Ho Chi Minh sized this opportunity to declare the formation of the Democratic Republic of Vietnam. In a September 1945 declaration to the world community, Ho Chi Minh employed the immortal words of Thomas Jefferson's Declaration of Independence to declare Vietnam's independence. The United States had a blatant admirer in Southeast Asia who, unfortunately, was by reputation also a communist.

Vietnam's independence was short-lived. British and Chinese occupation forces arrived to accept the surrender of the Japanese and to insure the political stability of Indochina. Although there had been no political unrest, the majority of the Vietnamese population supported the nationalist stance of the Vietminh. To bolster the ranks, the British utilized defeated Japanese soldiers. The incredulous insensitivity of the British both insulted and infuriated the Vietnamese. It was all too obvious Britain and China were there to pave the way for the return of France.

In response, throughout 1946 Ho Chi Minh appealed several times to the United States for assistance. Their political benefactor, President Franklin D. Roosevelt, had died in office near the end of the war and the administration of the new president, Harry S. Truman, was not sympathetic to the nationalistic demands of the communist Vietminh. The chill of cold war hysteria had gripped America's leaders and rendered them fearful of communist aggression. Ho Chi Minh's communist background overshadowed all favorable analyses concerning the Vietminh's political motivation prepared by the Office of Strategic Services and its successor, the Central Intelligence Agency (CIA). The leadership of America desired a noncommunist buffer against China in Southeast Asia. Ho Chi Minh's pleas were ignored. The world's greatest arsenal of democracy turned its back on Indochina. The century-long oppression of the people of Vietnam was doomed to continue, and the seeds of America's future involvement with war in Asia were sown.

French forces began returning to Vietnam in 1946. Although they initially attempted to reestablish control in Cochin China, pockets of local resistance effectively compromised their rule. Throughout the year, relations between the French and Vietminh steadily worsened. By the end of 1946 an uneasy peace collapsed. The Vietminh attacked French forces in Hanoi on December 19, 1946, heralding the beginning of the First Indochina War.

In 1949 the French established the State of Vietnam and installed a puppet regime headed by Bao Dai, a Vietnamese national. To win support of the Vietnamese people, the new government espoused a nationalistic political platform. All of France's allies, including the United States, supported Bao Dai's government. In response, Ho Chi Minh's Democratic Republic of Vietnam turned to communist-bloc nations for financial aid and military supplies. Both governments in the North and the South claimed to represent all the people of Vietnam. This resulted in open hostilities and bitter violence directed not only at French colonists but also Vietnamese nationals.

The slaughter continued into 1954 when, in April, representatives from each faction, including their benefactors (United States, Soviet Union, France, Great Britain, China, Laos, and Cambodia), met in Geneva to discuss a peace settlement. The direction of the conference was dramatically altered in May 1954 when French military forces were resoundingly defeated at the battle of

Điện Biên Phủ. As a result, on July 21, 1954, Vietnam was temporarily partitioned—for a period of two years—to permit time to develop an acceptable unilateral political solution for the reunification of both Vietnams. The Vietminh and other communist supporters settled in North Vietnam, and French sympathizers and Catholics went to South Vietnam. Future elections, to be held in 1956, were planned in order to reunite all of Vietnam under one government. Bao Dai continued to head the government in the South and Ho Chi Minh in the North. After the humiliation at Điện Biên Phủ the French had had enough, and their century of dominance in Southeast Asia came to a bitter end.

As the French Tricolor was unceremoniously lowered for the last time in Hanoi on October 9, 1954, the Central Intelligence Agency—operating under cover of the American embassy in the same city—implemented a cold war policy of psychological warfare and sabotage against the Vietminh. Although a French presence lingered until 1956, the United States had effectively assumed control of Vietnam's destiny. From the perspective of the Vietminh, a powerful new colonial leader had replaced a less powerful older one. The die for United States military involvement in Southeast Asia had been cast.

The legal and moral justification for western intervention in South Vietnam had already been established earlier, on September 6, 1954, with the formation of the unilateral defensive pact called the Southeast Asia Treaty Organization, or as it was better known, SEATO. This broad-spectrum alliance was designed by the United States for the sole purpose of containing communist-bloc aggression in Asia. Although SEATO's mandates were vague, it permitted the use of arms to defend Asia, specifically South Vietnam, Cambodia, and Laos. Although the United States, Australia, New Zealand, the Philippines, Thailand, Britain, France, and Pakistan were all parties to this treaty, the latter three wisely declined any active intervention in the affairs of Southeast Asia.

In 1955 the people of South Vietnam replaced Bao Dai, who had been universally branded as flagrantly morally corrupt, with Ngo Dinh Diem, who established the Republic of Vietnam and installed himself as its president. Ngo Dinh Diem rejected the Geneva mandated elections of 1956 on the assumption that the communists would corrupt the vote. Vietnam remained divided.

President Ngo Dinh Diem's discriminatory policies against the poor farmers of the Republic of Vietnam led to rebellion in the South during 1957. The rebels, known as Viet Cong, were openly supported by Ho Chi Minh's government in the North. In 1960 the Viet Cong were organized into the

National Liberation Front. The expressed purpose of this political and military organization was to lead a revolution in the South. From this time onward hostilities in Southeast Asia would dramatically intensify, drawing the United States and several other free world nations into "limited conventional warfare" by 1965. The contemporary free-world thinking of the era was exemplified as a domino cascade of small, noncommunist, rice-bowl nations that had to be checked before the red menace infected all of Asia. In response, the United States clenched its political teeth and planted its colors in Saigon.

Thus began the Second Indochina War, as the communists called it, or the Vietnam War, as it was known in the free world. To the youth of the United States, however, it would be referred to simply as Vietnam. Reflected in this single word would all of the erupting frustrations and dissatisfactions with its government of an entire youthful generation be catalyzed into social upheaval and domestic anarchy. The legacy of their progenitors' hope for a peaceful existence and a hopeful world had been hollow. In slogan and anthem the youth of America repeatedly advocated not trusting the words and wisdom of anyone over 30 years of age. *The times they were indeed a-changin'!*

During the administration of President Lyndon B. Johnson the United States entered into one of its historically most prolonged and morally devastating military conflicts. Throughout an entire decade of fighting there would be no great battles or occupation of enemy soil. Although there had been costly and enduring clashes such as the tenacious defense of the besieged Marine fire support base at Khe Sån and the vicious urban infighting surrounding Tết 1968, the primary strategy of the United States military remained limited to a conventional reaction to unconventional enemy insurgency. The strategic combat mission of the United States Army in Vietnam was politically defined as "seeking and destroying the enemy within the Republic of Vietnam, preventing the enemy from crossing at the borders, establishing and securing lines of communication and transportation, destroying enemy base areas, securing key installations, and encouraging and supporting rural development."

To satisfy these political criteria in South Vietnam, the United States Army—which had been conceptually organized and trained under the principles of *fire and maneuver*—found itself tactically required to slug it out from fixed enclaves with a highly elusive enemy.[3] It wasn't until the closing years of the Vietnam War that U.S. forces aggressively pursued the enemy across borders,[4] but by then it was little more than an ill-timed incursion that resulted in many hostile and friendly causalities. The incursion did little to break the resolve of the enemy or end the war. Experience gleaned over the years in South Vietnam revealed that the enemy that American soldiers faced could be everywhere and nowhere. Finding and closing with the Viet Cong or North Vietnamese Army was a morale-eroding task. In reaction the Army mounted daily small-size reconnaissance patrols to scour the paddies, forests, mountains, valley, plains, jungles, and waterways of South Vietnam. Missions were categorized into three operational tasks: *Search and Destroy; Clear and Secure; Maintain Security.* Back in the early 1950s the threat of nuclear holocaust had relegated the massed troop formations of previous wars to antiquity. The ultimate world legacy of the Los Alamos whiz kids[5] was Armageddon. The Atomic Age had, inadvertently, furnished a deterrent for conventional warfare. Now the militarily weakest of all nations, if allied with an atomic power, could strike out and destroy both adversary and planet. An unconditional surrender demand could evoke massive nuclear retaliation. The time-honored measures of victory and defeat—the taking of ground—had changed to a measurement of corpses counted in piles. The era of the "Body Count" method of defining victory began to flourish in Vietnam. Its prolonged effect on traditional North American culture and values, not to mention the United States military, would be devastating.

The majority of the 2.5 million servicemen sent to Vietnam were born after World War II. The evil forces their parents' generation faced had been defeated at a horrific cost in humanity, money, and material. The universal pledge to the children of the 1950s had been world peace and the promise of a life better than that of their parents. Although the world had remained essentially nonbelligerent, the fearful creep of communism negated the lessons of history and of common sense. Old allies grew suspicious of each other's global ambitions. New battle lines were formulated delineating zones of hostility. Cold war had become an international political institution. Instead of world peace, postwar children, who had been dubbed Baby Boomers, were nurtured in an environment of cold war hysteria. Public schools routinely instructed students to save themselves from aerial bombardment and nuclear firestorm by sticking their heads in metal wall lockers or hiding under classroom desks.

On television Buffalo Bob[6] *never* displayed violence or bad language, and good guys wearing white hats always prevailed over bad men in black hats. Post–World War II children grew up in an idyllic era of rapid advances in technology, regional suburbanization, a growing economy, and an emerging middle class—all symbolized in the media by a Hollywood inspired John Wayne-ish morality and heroics.[7] Yes, *She Wore a Yellow Ribbon* and, by God, the enemy never broke a cinematic square.[8] But in actuality many hypothetical squares had been, and would be, broken. Far worse, the core of traditional American values began shrinking, replaced by an emphasis on self-awareness and a corresponding liberalization of social mores. The youthful army America deployed to Vietnam ultimately represented the rear guard of a society whose cultural values had been rapidly changing. The moral values of America's once dominant agricultural heartland were being challenged by outspoken liberalism. The burgeoning neophyte socioeconomic middle class was already in flux. Those generations who came after World War II would find it increasingly difficult to understand and accept the sacrifices their parents and older brothers and sisters had made. For them, and for most Americans, Vietnam was a faraway land culturally as alien and geographically distant to them as the stars in the evening sky.

* * *

By the time the whirlwinds of war in Southeast Asia swept me to Vietnam, the 9th Infantry Division had already served over 800 days in combat. Advance elements of the division had arrived three years earlier on October 19, 1966. This initial element, the 15th Engineer Battalion, had immediately started construction of a division-size base camp on a former 1st Infantry Division site named Camp Martin Cox (in Bien Hòa Province north of the hamlet of Long Thành, approximately 20 miles northeast of Saigon). Additional units had arrived by air the following December 8. The bulk of the division, deployed aboard United States Navy transport ships, arrived on December 16, 1966, when then division commander Major General George S. Eckhardt ceremoniously landed the division colors along with 5,000 troops on the beaches of Vĩnh Long. Of the seven infantry divisions deployed to Vietnam, the 9th Infantry Division would be the last to arrive and, ironically, the first to be withdrawn.

The 9th Infantry Division consisted of 20,000–25,000 troops divided into seven major commands, which included three brigades of infantry and four combat and combat support battalions (aviation, reconnaissance, artillery, and division). There were also several attached lesser combat and support units as well as nonattached units that directly supported 9th Infantry Division operations throughout the Mekong Delta region. During 1969 the division's headquarters base camp was at Đồng Tâm, a combat enclave situated on the north bank of the Mỹ Tho River in Dinh Tuòng Province. Also headquartered at Đồng Tâm was Navy Task Force 117, the Mobile Riverine Force. This unique unit was composed of specialized Navy vessels and crews, plus the 9th Infantry Division's 2nd Infantry Brigade.

Although the 9th Infantry had historically operated in 23 of Vietnam's

44 provinces throughout I Corps Tactical Zone (the Demilitarized Zone), III Corps Tactical Zone (the Saigon Area), and IV Corps Tactical Zone (the Mekong Delta southward), by 1969 division military operations were confined to just a few provinces in III and IV Corps Tactical zones. During 1969 one of the Division's primary military responsibilities had been keeping National Route QL-4 open to traffic. This critical artery of commerce linked the fertile rice-growing provinces in the south to Saigon and the northern provinces. To deny the enemy their objectives, the division utilized three maneuver brigades of infantry. Major elements of the 1st "Recondo" Brigade were positioned along Route QL-4 in a string of fire support bases stretching westward from Đồng Tâm, along the southeastern edge of the Plain of Reeds, to the ferry crossing on the Tiền Giang River. The 2nd "River Raider" Brigade was housed aboard U.S. Navy barracks ships and operated with great nautical mobility along the numerous waterways and inundated areas south and east of Đồng Tâm. They also maintained a complex of small bases collectively known as Tiger's Lair east of Trúc Giang (Bến Tre) in Kien Hòa Province. Elements of the 3rd "Go Devil" Brigade were deployed in fire support patrol bases north of Đồng Tâm in Long An Province at the eastern edge of the Plain of Reeds. Units from all three infantry brigades were routinely rotated into Đồng Tâm and other smaller defensive enclaves in the surrounding area for stand-down, or to provide security beyond Đồng Tâm's perimeters.

The final year of the turbulent 1960s became the high-water mark for U.S. troop commitment in Vietnam. Since 1967 America's taste for victory in Southeast Asia had steadily soured. Beginning in July 1969 the great Army of the 1960s began systematically being withdrawn. Although the war was far from over, domestic politics demanded the Army be disengaged before anarchy collapsed the home front and mutiny infected the rank and file. Sadly, during the next three years more soldiers would be sacrificed in a widening conflict (Cambodia and Laos) that by 1970 most Americans wanted to forget.

1

Screw Up and You'll End Up in the Infantry

An astute observer once commented that the Army was designed by geniuses and run by idiots—a harsh indictment and possibly an unfair one. Yet for those intimately familiar with the sociological and hierarchical aspects of the military, the observation resounds with aphorismic truth, for in any highly structured organization founded upon social order and discipline the very nature of its regimentation invites human frailties. In deference to the astuteness of the author, however, the Army is *not* run by idiots; it's run by lunatics—the major difference being idiocy is a constant mental condition characterized by low intelligence, while lunacy is an intermittent mental condition characterized by foolishness.

My involvement with the military began during an era of youthful free-spirited social and civic irresponsibility hyped by advocates of *that* kind of lunacy as "The Summer of Love." For me the summer hadn't lived up to its billing. I graduated from college in June 1967 and as a consequence lost my Class 2-S student draft deferment. The ink was still wet on my diploma when friends and neighbors on the local Selective Service Board reclassified my draft status to 1-A—*prime cannon fodder*. It would be only a matter of time before I was conscripted into the Army, so I consequently spent the early weeks of summer fretting about the inevitable call to arms. It still hadn't arrived by August when a Vette-head acquaintance of mine suggested we play out a latent Tod & Buzz *Route 66* fantasy by driving across the country in his 1965 Corvette.[1] He was in the same predicament as I was: *no job—no future—no deferment,* so we added *no destination* and took off for points unknown. After a month and a half of living in close proximity to each other and viewing what seemed like every spectacular natural wonder America had to offer, we could no longer tolerate the other's company and plotted a direct course back to New Jersey.

When I got home it was waiting for me on top of my bedroom dresser.

I slit open the envelope with mournful resolve. The message inside began in a friendly enough way with the salutation GREETING; but then it turned nasty: YOU ARE HEREBY ORDERED FOR INDUCTION INTO THE ARMED FORCES OF THE UNITED STATES, *et cetera et cetera et cetera.*

It wasn't that I was upset about being a soldier. I wasn't. I'd followed organizational rules and worn uniforms of various sorts from Cub Scouts through Boy Scouts, school marching bands, and two official years in the junior Green Machine Reserve Officer Training Corps (ROTC) at Jesuit-

When conventional ground forces were first being deployed to South Vietnam in 1965 I was in my sophomore year of college playing trumpet with the Seton Hall University ROTC marching band. A family subscription to *Life* magazine kept me apprized of the growing conflict in Southeast Asia (courtesy Albert Fischer).

1. Screw Up and You'll End Up in the Infantry

inspired Seton Hall University, plus an additional *off-the-record* year playing trumpet with the perpetually undermanned ROTC marching band. The unofficial year excused me from attending the weekly theology class required of students of Catholic faith, which, considering my limited academic tolerance for the vagueness of apostolic dogma, was a very good tradeoff. Inasmuch as familiarity can often breed contempt, it can also nurture stupidity. I became so enamored with ROTC that in my sophomore year I joined a gung-ho military fraternal order called the Triphibian Guard, an involvement that put huge dents in my spare time as well as my intellect. All things considered, I ultimately came to the conclusion that while it might be fine for others, military life just wasn't for me.

Looking back I can now admit my primary motive for attending college, other than my parents' incessant demands that I do so, was to avoid the draft and being sent to Vietnam. My college education commenced at about the same time the Pentagon was putting their final touches on elements of the first regular Army combat division to be deployed to Vietnam.[2] Never in my wildest imagination did I anticipate a limited war of containment waged against a microscopic third-world country would continue beyond the time of my graduation four years later. Apparently neither had our government. It had taken only four years following America's entry into World War II to defeat the fascist Nazis and imperialist Japanese, and they had been modern, well-equipped and well-trained military powers. Nevertheless, I resolutely accepted my fate and the notice to report for induction. At the appointed hour I morosely boarded the chartered bus that would deliver me to the United States Army Training Center—Infantry, Fort Dix, New Jersey. I was now in the clutches of the Green Machine. The die representing my own future and fate had been cast by strangers.

COMPANY A, 3RD BATTALION, 3RD BRIGADE, FORT DIX. The Army called Fort Dix THE HOME OF THE ULTIMATE WEAPON. I called it crappy—a bizarre mix of musty old wooden shacks heated by archaic coal stoves requiring round-the-clock fire watches mixed in with a smattering of contemporary brick and metal buildings thermostatically controlled with central heating and cooling. I quickly learned warmth was a very important commodity at Fort Dix. The eight-week Basic Combat Training (BCT) cycle transforming me from a *civilian* into an *ultimate weapon*[3] occurred between November 1967 and January 1968, very cold months in 1960s New Jersey.

As I mentioned earlier, inductees were transported to Fort Dix by bus. Upon arrival we were immediately greeted with a harangue of verbal and physical unpleasantries spewed out by the drill instructor (DI) staff. I assumed their performance was intended to frighten the arrogance out of us. My personal abuser, Jerry Reynolds, was a burly career sergeant first class (SFC) who was a bit shorter than I and a bit wider in girth. He wore his authorized Smokey Bear DI hat (known as a campaign hat in formal circles) at a rakish forward angle that nicely complemented the mirror image "U.S." brand burned into his cheek. The scar intrigued me. I envisioned torture at the hands of some dastardly enemy of the United States, but as he later explained after we came to know each other, the unique scar was the result of a childhood accident; he had fallen face first against the side of a hot coal stove. The raised lettering of the stove's manufacturer, the U.S. Stove Company, left a partial reverse imprint seared into his cheek! SFC Reynolds turned out to be not only a first-class platoon sergeant but also a first-class human being. He was a Korean War veteran who understood conscripts were not really soldiers, just civilians with guns. It was bad luck that at the time of my arrival he was training his replacement, SFC Randolph Engelbert.

Among the more effective threats DIs spewed out to keep the attitude and behavior of trainees in line with the expectations of the Army was this one: *"Screw up and you'll end up in the infantry."* This particular threat was issued often enough to impart a kind of gospel significance. I actually never really cared for the term infantry; its all too obvious etymology evoked a puerile association with crawly creeping things. Using the infantry as a threat indicated precisely where ground pounders ranked in the Army's Military Occupational Specialty (MOS) hierarchy. The threat didn't work for all recruits, but it certainly worked for me. I strove to do my best while in the Army and endeavored to never ever screw up.

Platoon Sergeant Reynolds' replacement, SFC Engelbert, was one of those lifer-oriented types who took his job quite seriously. Regardless of who or what a trainee had been in the real world prior to his being fed into the Green Machine grinder, SFC Englebert excelled at giving the impression he viewed all trainees as just another pound of chopped meat being prepared for combat consumption. A black fellow of impeccable military appearance whose uniform creases had creases, he was the quintessential subaltern indoctrinator who took his charge of overseeing the heavy hands-on process of turning high school kids into warriors very seriously—perhaps in his case too seriously. Although his experience in combat had been limited to rifle ranges and infiltration courses, he was an outstanding example of an Army drill sergeant—not too intellectual, not too friendly, and not too ambitious. Despite these personal attributes that some people might consider shortcomings under other circumstances, he was, obviously, tops in uniform and tops in memorizing and reciting instruction manuals. It was indeed unfortunate for him that his credentials as a warrior were regularly challenged by several of the training company's youthful Vietnam returnees, assistant DIs who took it upon themselves to routinely remind SFC Englebert of his lack of combat experience with peanut gallery–type catcalling. The collective attitude of these returnees, while reproachful to SFC Engelbert, was compassionate to trainees, many of whom were destined to be sent to the hell from whence the assistant DIs had recently returned. Unlike SFC Engelbert, these junior drill sergeants *knew* what lay ahead, because they had *been there—seen it—done it*. They were combat soldiers who, again unlike SFC Engelbert, were experienced in the ways of survival and killing. These Fort Dix critics were my first up-close contact with soldiers who had seen combat in Vietnam, other than my once having observed a bunch of young amputees attired in Army Class A dress (a formal uniform consisting of shirt, tie, slacks, and jacket, colloquially known as Greens for its color) being wheeled off the elevator at the Playboy Club in Manhattan during my still-a-civilian 21st birthday celebration.

    Despite the gloom, I did, however, enjoy some good fortune at Fort Dix that fanned an ember of warmth in my suddenly frigid life. My otherwise useless ROTC training and *sometimes* useful physical size (in this instance slightly larger than the other trainees) garnered me an on-the-spot promotion to platoon guide, which among other benefits entitled me to pin a snappy two-stripe, yellow on black corporal's armband to my field jacket sleeve. My appointment to platoon guide gave me a shred of dignity in what was otherwise a highly abusive environment. The goal of Army training doctrine of the 1960s was to psychologically reduce a trainee's pride and temperament to the level of excrement and then rebuild him in desired Army fashion. I soon discovered being a platoon guide coupled its micron of dignity to a ton of responsibility. In addition to specific leadership duties, I also functioned as liaison between the unreasonable and the oppressed. I quickly learned the value of information and the subtleties of leading those who did not want to be led. One had to deftly play each end of the stick against the other, but what was best of all, my new position entitled me to a billet in one of the toasty-warm modern barracks. Being close to the source of power *definitely* had its advantages in the Army, though I feared the tip of my nose might tinge to brown if I continued favoring the oppressors. Playing the middle against the ends was a tenuous position that demanded politics over deftness to maintain equilibrium. One had to keep one's head out of one's butt at all times, or at least give the prevailing powers in charge that impression.

    The eight weeks of BCT took on what seemed like epic duration. Exercising, or PT (Physical Training), as the Army called it, was a daily occurrence interwoven *before, during,* and *after* indoor instruction classes covering healthcare, survival techniques, military history, combat tactics, inspections, and outdoor jaunts for shooting lessons, throwing hand grenades, detonating explosives, marching, and the like. One memorable indoor class I have never been able to forget concerned frostbite. I can still vividly recall the repulsive sight of doctors peeling off soldiers' blackened frostbitten toes. Feet are important appendages in the Army and their care cannot be taken too lightly. Because the Army had no training film covering the immersion foot encountered by troops in tropical Southeast Asia (called trench foot in a much earlier war), a Korean War vintage film about frostbite had to suffice. In all fairness to Army logic, the prevention of both afflictions is similar and essentially entails keeping your feet dry by changing socks often. If when viewing one of these Korean War vintage films you disregarded the snow, ice, and bundled-up winter dress of the soldiers then stretched your imagination to infinity, you could almost envision the rice paddies of Vietnam.

The final ordeal before becoming an ultimate weapon was passing an outdoor infiltration competency test, which like the Korean War frostbite film further disassociated whatever Vietnam-orientated combat indoctrination we were supposed to be undergoing. The course consisted of advancing against an enemy position under machine-gun and mortar fire on one's belly using a squiggly technique called "low-crawling." To simulate actual combat conditions the Army fired live machine-gun rounds about seven feet overhead and detonated explosives in raised pits strategically positioned along the course. The exercise was perfectly safe but jarringly noisy and also a little bit scary, which was the Army's intent—to simulate the discombobulating hellish nightmare of combat.

The day my group took the test the temperature had dropped to an absolutely frigid degree after the warmth of a relatively sunny day. The snow-covered course had partially melted during the day and then slowly turned icy as the sun disappeared in the west. The sky changed to overcast, making dusk as dark as SFC Engelbert's naked butt. One couldn't see one's nose, toes, or the fellow ahead of him. The harsh weather conditions had effectively slowed the pace of late afternoon training classes cycling through the course. By the time our turn came, the foulness of the weather had become fully ensconced over the infiltration course. To enliven matters the low-crawling activities of previous groups had created hard-packed trails in the snow, which by the time we arrived had frozen into icy troughs. We negotiated the course on our bellies by propelling ourselves with our rifle butts, using them like poling sticks in a speedy fashion that would have impressed an Olympic bobsled judge. To the man we crossed over the finish line in record-shattering times. Needless to say, our individual scores were adjusted downward to reflect more believable results. Negotiating the course had felt more like a thrilling amusement park ride than an exercise in simulated combat!

Undergoing BCT between November and January encompassed three important holidays—Thanksgiving, Christmas, and New Year's Day. Although the Army had magnanimously prepared nice Thanksgiving and Christmas dinners for trainees and their invited guests, and even permitted those residing in New Jersey and nearby out-of-state localities a Christmas leave, the holidays added a miserable two weeks to the overall schedule, which extended my time at frigid Fort Dix well into the third week of January 1968. Despite the cold weather and the several days I spent as a patient in the base hospital (recuperating from an upper respiratory infection that had been complicated by a near lethal injection of penicillin administered by an eagled-eyed Army doctor who failed to notice the bold red ALLERGIC TO PENICILLIN stamped across *each page* of my medical records), I graduated with my class on January 18, 1968. I was now officially an ultimate weapon and thoroughly acclimated to combat in a cold-weather environment.

The last step before out-processing from Fort Dix was an interview with a personnel management specialist whose function approximated that of a military guidance counselor, in this instance one wearing the eagles of an SP-4 (Specialist Four). He asked me what I wanted to do in the Army. My initial reaction to his question had been surprise tempered by skepticism. I honestly thought he was joking. Had I known he wasn't, I would have given his inquiry more serious thought. I instead foolishly blurted out I had always wanted to learn how to type. After four years of college I was still using two fingers. He said, "Fine," and off I went to clerk-typist Advance Individual Training (AIT) at Fort Leonard Wood, Missouri.

Upon my completion of Army BCT and AIT I found myself superbly trained in cold weather combat and conventional warfare. I was now psychologically prepared to take my place in the battle line of America's defense ... *as long it wasn't in Vietnam!* (author's collection).

COMPANY C, 3RD BATTALION, 5TH BRIGADE, CLASS 28A, FORT LEONARD WOOD. Fort Leonard Wood was in the Ozark Mountains and gave this native son of New Jersey a new appreciation for the word C-O-L-D. The cadre troops in the garrison called the place Little Korea, and no wonder; the daily winter temperatures ranged from a minus 20 degrees to plus 20 degrees. Being on the minus side didn't make all that much of a difference on the discomfort scale; the humidity in the air coupled with the wind-chill factor kept soldiers in a constant state of motion lest they freeze in place. It was one of the few postings within the continental United States where headgear lined with fur and tie-down flaps was issued along with heavy greatcoats with zip-in fur liners. Had you pinned a red star to the front flap of my cap I could have passed for a North Korean or maybe even a commie Cossack!

Most of Fort Leonard Wood's training facilities were dedicated to AIT in combat engineering. The lesser clerical school and Adjutant General Corps billets were confined to a cluster of World War II–vintage wooden buildings interconnected by drafty enclosed walkways. The complex once had served as the base hospital, and inside the billets, which had once been patient wards, the windows were still adorned with cheerful red and white patterned curtains! It lent a homey touch to an otherwise stark environment.

The covered walkways were a functional concession to military asceticism. In order to avoid patient and medical staff exposure to the cold, the hospital's architects had interconnected all wards and examination rooms with enclosed and marginally heated walkways. The building that housed the typing class I attended, however, was physically isolated from the clerical school area and required a chilly walk along a short stretch of base road in order to reach it.

The AIT DIs, like their BCT counterparts, also spewed a favored verbal threat to keep trainees in line. Instead of the familiar *"Screw up and you'll end up in the infantry,"* these DIs turned up the heat somewhat by bellowing, *"Screw up and you'll end up in Vietnam."* This modification of threat implied Vietnam service was even more frightening than being in the infantry, which, considering the momentous event that occurred in Southeast Asia at the end of January 30, 1968, certainly made it seem so. In the early hours of that morning the North Vietnamese Army (NVA), in conjunction with Viet Cong (VC) irregulars, kicked off their Tết, Year of the Monkey Lunar New Year, celebration in the South. The festivities included a variety of lethal fireworks directed at Vietnamese and U.S. facilities in over 100 Republic of South Vietnam cities and towns. The attack came after communist politicos had agreed to a 48-hour ceasefire. Needless to say, the ferocity and scope of the deceit caught the United States and South Vietnamese armies completely off guard, as well as dissipating all hope that the ongoing peace talks in Paris would lead to a cessation of hostilities. The Vietnam War began its fourth year with no end in sight. While I froze my butt off pecking at a typewriter, half a world away American soldiers were being killed and maimed in increasing numbers. Ending up in the infantry was certainly undesirable, but ending up in Vietnam was a far more frightening proposition. I didn't want to be killed or maimed anywhere, let alone in Southeast Asia; so I kept my boots and military decorum spit-shined and my Army attitude so gung-ho positive I might have been easily mistaken for a lifer.

Although the Army typically favored military personnel for instructors, the typing class I attended was taught by a civilian who looked and sounded like actor/singer Burl Ives. He was a local fellow and undoubtedly appealed to the Army because of his quasi-military, homespun style of instruction: "All rightee, class, sit up, take a deep breath, and begin typing. And ah-one, and ah-two, and ah-three, and ah...." Other than his Ozark backwoods persona and his repeated use of the term, "all rightee," he was a good instructor. As hard as I tried, though, I couldn't harmonize with the rhythm he set in class to establish the typing pace. The Army tolerated only three strikeovers per page (no erasures permitted!). I couldn't type a sentence without making a mistake. I think the syncopation of all those typewriter keys banging in unison clashed with my artistic musical sensitivity. Perhaps if I had spent my adolescent years as a drummer instead of a trumpeter my typing performance would have been better. I barely passed the typing exam. Another fellow and I, however, did ace the written test (the *clerk* part of being a clerk-typist), and as a reward the Army selected both of us for further AIT in personnel management at the U.S. Army Adjutant General School, Fort Benjamin Harrison, Indianapolis, Indiana. We traveled from Missouri by bus and arrived in Indianapolis on March 24, 1968.

It was snowing.

COMPANY B, SPECIAL TROOPS, PMS 23, FORT BENJAMIN HARRISON. Of all the bases the Army ever sent me to, and there were quite a few, Fort Benjamin Harrison was *the* place to be. Army scuttlebutt called it "Uncle Ben's Rest Home." The fort, if it ever had been one, didn't even look like an Army base. Military decorum and courtesy were downplayed. Uniforms were worn only for ceremonies. Trainees from all branches of the U.S. Army and other friendly nations were treated like students, regardless of their rank. Our job was to learn. My roommate was a full-bird colonel (a colonel superior in rank to a lieutenant colonel and one grade below general) from Liberia. We got along fine. There were plenty of female students at Fort Benjamin Harrison, too. The Army called them WACs (pronounced "wacks"), for Women's

Army Corps, which was a good acronym; a gal had to be a little wacked to volunteer for Army service at a time when most males were trying to avoid it. Although classes were co-ed, male students were under strict orders not to get too friendly with the gals in green, especially in the rack. That didn't bother most of us; the base was overrun with enterprising civilian females looking to earn a night's pay or to hook up with an officer. Instead of hanging out on the street corners, they hung out at the base service club, which was open to soldiers over 21 years of age regardless of rank. With all of the free study time the Army made available everyone eventually got a shot at female companionship—even my high-ranking, wife-back-at-home, Liberian roommate. I was beginning to think *this* was what the recruiting posters meant when they advertised THE NEW ACTION ARMY, and not that Old Grumpy Army I had left behind at Fort Dix, the one that unreasonably disparaged your ancestors, humiliated you in public, and then gave you unpleasant work details.

Needless to say, the weeks I spent in Indiana passed quickly. I graduated on April 23, 1968, a full-fledged 71H30 personnel management specialist.[4] Another fellow and I were unexpectedly rewarded with an accelerated promotion, jumping over the rank of PFC (Private First Class) to the rank of SP-4 in recognition of our academic achievement and class standing. It hadn't taken much effort to be a standout in the largely conscripted army of the late 1960s. The prevailing attitude of the troops hadn't been all that gung ho back then, even those at lovely Fort Benjamin Harrison.

By the end of May 1968 I was still biding my time, awaiting receipt of the inevitable orders sending me to Vietnam. The suspense of the delay in my posting was, for lack of a better adjective, *maddening*. When my orders finally did arrive, I, however, learned I wasn't being sent to Vietnam. Instead I received orders assigning me to the Army Flight Training Center at Fort Stewart, Georgia. This was good news. I had spent the first seven months of my two-year active service obligation at one training facility or another, and, considering that Army duty station assignments typically lasted a full year, for the first time since high school I was beginning to think I would not end up in Vietnam.

It was a very good feeling.

HEADQUARTERS COMPANY, UNITED STATES ARMY GARRISON BATTALION, FORT STEWART. Fort Stewart had the nickname Camp Swampy. It was alleged to have been the setting for the Beetle Bailey comic strip series. I wouldn't argue the plausibility. Fort Stewart exuded a primordial back-in-the-swamp aura. The chronic stench of decaying vegetation and the vile odors released by nearby turpentine distilleries could bring tears to a pig farmer's eyes. This aura was enhanced by a predominant military architectural style that could best be defined as Tobacco Road—a preponderance of old, creaky, wooden buildings set atop concrete pilings. To muck up the overall *it ain't worth rebuilding* atmosphere, a contemporary brick dormitory and mess hall rose in stark contrast.

Fort Stewart was a sleepy, Old South military installation that had been established during another war to serve the needs of an earlier brown shoe Army.[5] Back in 1968 it was the hallmark of a less-than-elite stateside posting. The permanent garrison was small, which generated a kind of emotional intimacy among the cadre. We found ourselves far out of the mainstream of military priorities. Our spirits united in the brotherhood of backwater servants who merely went through the motions of being soldiers. Each day, we didn't go on duty, we went to work. The obligatory six-month physical proficiency test that could ruin a soldier's career in the military was a sham of its creator's intent. The test was taken, beer in hand, with predetermined scores. There were no Air-Borne Rangers at Fort Stewart, just a handful of disillusioned Vietnam returnees running out their remaining time in service, some tired old lifers who needed a rest, and a few draftees—*lucky bastards like me.*

Despite its antiquity and sometimes foul smell, Fort Stewart was the Army's largest installation east of the Mississippi River. It encompassed approximately 280,000 acres of Georgia costal lowlands, swamp, and piney woods. Earlier in its history it had served as an artillery training range. Two years after the first air mobile troops of the 1st Cavalry Division landed in Vietnam, the Army's accelerating need for helicopter and fixed-wing pilots eclipsed the training capabilities of both its existing aviation schools at Fort Rucker, Alabama, and Fort Walters, Texas. It was during the summer of 1966 that the HQ of the U.S. Army Aviation School Element was established at Fort Stewart and charged with the task of training fixed-wing pilots as an adjunct of the two existing schools.

In April 1967, after the U.S. Air Force base at Hunter Airfield in Savannah became available to the Army, the headquarters of the school was relocated to Hunter Airfield and the installation renamed Hunter Army Airfield. In July 1967 the combined facilities of Hunter Army Airfield and Fort Stewart were redesignated the U.S. Army Flight Training Center, and the task of training both fixed- and rotary-wing pilots commenced. Although Fort Stewart had its own small airfield, most of the aircraft were housed and maintained at Hunter Army Airfield. Part of Fort Stewart's vast acreage was used for a helicopter gunnery range and in the summer months another part for an armor-training facility used by National Guard and Reserve Army troops. The small garrison assigned to Fort Stewart maintained the base's infrastructure and provided administrative and financial services to the flight training center and National Guard when the latter was on the property.

Although not an idyllic posting (Fort Benjamin Harrison had been idyllic), Fort Stewart was a nice place for a middle-class kid from New Jersey to serve his country while honorably and lawfully avoiding Vietnam service. I was so confident of remaining stateside I acquired a slightly used 1967 Corvette (which my elderly parents found, purchased, registered, and then personally delivered from New Jersey to Georgia!) and several items of domestic comfort. I had plenty of spare time to enjoy the sights and antiquity of Savannah and the beauty of Georgia's many beaches and coastal barrier islands. Still, I was impatient to complete my active service in the Army and get on with my life. I got bored waiting. To help fill the days and eliminate the doldrums, I auditioned for the 80th Army Band, which was stationed at Fort Stewart. A neighborhood friend, Stuart Crawley, had served his enlistment in the 80th and asked me to look up his old commander, which led to my auditioning. Although the bandmaster said he had all of the trumpet players his band was authorized, he offered me a bugler's job that entailed TDY (Temporary Duty) with the U.S. Third Army Funeral Detail. Being assigned TDY to the funeral detail relieved me of all unpleasant work details other than standing guard at Fort Stewart every now and then.

The funeral detail I was attached to was staffed by a spit-shined group of exceptional troops whose proprietary mission was to render final honors to deceased soldiers at military funerals in Florida. Although I didn't appreciate it at the time, the honor guard was my first direct link to the tragedy of Vietnam. To the unfortunate soldiers of the war and their families the funeral detail represented the final aspect of their involvement with the military. Throughout my days in Georgia when I had trod the trampled guard path around Fort Stewart's mock Vietnam village, I never intellectually related what I was guarding to the horrifying reality on the other side of the world. My full-time job had been to administrate the personnel records of Fort Stewart's enlisted cadre above the pay grade of E-5, occasionally toot Taps in Florida, and not cogitate about the plight of young, transient, warrant officer pilots being trained for service in Vietnam. I was stateside permanently, or so I thought.

As I've already mentioned, guard duty was the only detail my TDY bugler's job couldn't get me out of. One night I was ordered to guard the office building used by the National Guard paymaster. It was an easy guard mount, requiring I only remain alert and awake. There was no walking involved. The guard had to stay inside the office building and protect a safe full of money, the stash necessary to fulfill a State of Georgia requirement that National Guardsmen on active duty be paid in cash. Unlike the other guard mounts at Fort Stewart, this one required bullets for weapons. I was given a magazine loaded with three rounds for my M-14 rifle.

The magazine must have been ancient, because the brass shell casings had corroded into one lump; still, they were bullets and the chance of anyone robbing an Army base full of ultimate weapons exceeded the realm of plausibility, except that at around ten o'clock in the evening I heard unusual rustling and scraping sounds outside. After ascertaining that the doors were locked, I nervously dialed the officer of the guard to inform him of my situation. *The telephone line was dead!* Fearful of an intruder, I inserted the magazine into my weapon and pulled back the bolt. No matter how many times I ran the bolt back and forth, a round would not chamber. This wasn't supposed to be happening, leastways not to me. The scuffling outside continued and for a moment I felt the relief of thinking it might be a dog sniffing around the foundation pilings. My relief was short-lived; I heard the unmistakable sound of footsteps on the front-door steps. I grasped my otherwise useless rifle by the barrel thinking it would make a splendid club.

The doorknob rattled!

In accordance with the Army Code of Conduct, the dilemma I found myself in was this: I couldn't leave my post unguarded and by my natural temperament couldn't remain cowering in the dark—after all, I was a trained ultimate weapon. I readied myself, clicked off the lock, and flung open the door in one swift motion! I stood my ground in the doorway, faithful to the both the Army Code of Conduct and myself. I was poised like a jolly green Casey at the Bat. The intensity of the moment was, however, thoroughly defeated by the presence of a man in telephone company attire complete with leather tool belt. He, having been surprised by the door being flung wide open in his face and the incongruous sight of an adrenaline charged guard brandishing a rifle held by the wrong end, stepped backwards and in the process fell off the low riser onto the dirt walkway. I, having regained my military decorum, authoritatively croaked the standard guard challenge, "Halt, who goes there!" The suspected prowler, responding in a high-pitched, fear-tinged voice, inquired if the telephone was now working.

A feeling of nausea overcame me for what I had been prepared to do. For whatever reason, the officer of the guard had foolishly authorized a civilian worker to make a repair in the dead of night on the outside of a building full of cash guarded by an armed soldier without having first alerted the guard of the impending visit! The old axiom about there being a *right way* to do something and the *Army way* rang, at that moment, resonantly of truth. The incident was merely a precursor of things to come.

While at Fort Stewart I was fortunate enough to have been included in two separate circles of friends, one group from the general community of soldiers living in the barracks and the other from the office where I worked. The latter circle actually consisted of only one fellow, a Vietnam returnee from the Midwest who just happened to own a Corvette! SP-5 Peter Lindenberger and I had hit it off immediately and for entertainment we often drove to Savannah Beach in search of female companionship. He eventually latched onto a Georgia peach who had a single-parent girlfriend desiring male companionship for herself and her juvenile son. A blind date was arranged. I eventually discovered my blind date worked as a prostitute in order to pay the rent and feed her son, as well as to feed her drug and alcohol addictions. Oddly enough, with all of her shortcomings she wasn't that bad a date, what with her being both attractive and well attuned to the intricacies of male behavior. I didn't have sex with her, though. The prospect of disease and emotional involvement with a spaced-out hooker grated on my middle-class Catholic upbringing. After all, I was just an innocent kid from suburban New Jersey. Despite her morally questionable lifestyle, her son was well-mannered and appeared to be surprisingly well-adjusted. After several dates, though, I could no longer tolerate her unpredictable behavior (nor she my predictable behavior). I found it personally offensive that she felt the need to drug herself into la-la-land before going out with me. I wasn't all that unpresentable, even for a soldier.

Fortunately for my male sensitivity my pals from the barracks were not as carnally motivated in their pursuit of entertainment. Most of the soldiers in this group were happily married men and consequently focused on wholesome pursuits like sports, literary discussions concerning what books they had read, or participating in an occasional fun-in-the-sun weekend jaunt to Jekyll Island, a vacation resort situated on a barrier island across from Brunswick, Georgia. All went well with our group until one of them received a Dear John letter from his wife announcing she had found another and wanted a divorce. Some of the other married fellows became gripped by paranoia and each day anxiously awaited mail call. The intellectually stimulating times we had enjoyed together dissipated into wife worries.

Jody, Jody, don't be blue, your old lady's gonna cheat on you.

Nearing the end of September 1968 I was dispatched to Fort Benning, Georgia, THE HOME OF THE INFANTRY—*I am the Infantry, Queen of Battle ... blah, blah, blah*—to attend the Service Rifle and Service Pistol Instructor Clinic. The commanding general at Fort Stewart desired to form competitive pistol shooting teams to promote morale (?) among the garrison troops. In civilian life I had been a member of a police-sponsored pistol team that competed with other police teams in the art of accurately punching tiny round holes in paper targets with special-purpose bullets called wad-cutters.[6] My participation had been noted in my 201 File—a soldier's personnel record that follows him from one duty station to another. I made the journey to Fort Benning with Fort Stewart's only other designated pistol instructor trainee, an affable captain of artillery. He had just returned from a tour in Vietnam and was still adjusting to being back, as he phrased it, in "The World." I made the trip in his personal vehicle at his invitation, and we had plenty of time to chat. After we established some rapport he ordered me to call him Charles, but only in private. He then gushed about how Vietnam was a real mess and that something was very wrong with the way we were fighting the war. All of this meant nothing to me. I listened and nodded at the appropriate times in respect of his rank but gave little credence to what he said. The Army had been *his* career choice. I didn't even know where Vietnam was. If the lifers had messed up the war, it wasn't my problem. There were no war or war-related hardships at Fort Stewart, other than enduring the stuff reported in the news or the occasional local crap from war protesters. I had just played Taps at a funeral detail in Jacksonville, Florida, for the other kind of Vietnam returnee.[7] Despite the grief borne by that soldier's family, they were still proud their son had sacrificed his life for our country. At this point in my military career I didn't want to hear how the war was all messed up. A lot of people believed in what we were doing in Vietnam and a lot of people were paying a high price for their beliefs. My impression of the war at this stage in my career was confused. I viewed it as a cultural rite of passage for an unfortunate few, a ritual concocted by our politicians and promulgated by the war lords of the Pentagon. Rendering last honors for our country's fallen gave it an obscene disenfranchised reality. Although the war was a great career boost for lifer types, from the perspective of this middle-class college kid from Jersey Vietnam essentially sucked!

I was one confused troop.

My TDY bugler's job had a bittersweet aspect to it. Beating the Army out of nasty work details was spiritually uplifting, but participating in military funerals was psychologically a downer. Music and the trumpet had been a part of my life ever since Mr. Popovich first taught me to play the instrument in the fourth grade at Battle Hill Elementary School. Then I played my trumpet all the way through Burnett Junior High and Union High School and in the ROTC band at Seton Hall University. Playing the trumpet had been second nature to me. I even brought my old tarnished E.K. Blessing Co., Inc., trumpet to Fort Stewart, which I later used on funeral details.

Under less tragic circumstances being a musician in the Army would have been a rewarding experience, not that getting away from the doldrums of Fort Stewart in itself wasn't a reward. I didn't have to travel or billet with the funeral detail. The band clerk made arrangements for me to fly to assignments, rented cars for me, and secured my overnight sleeping accommodations, while the infantry guys in the funeral detail rode to ceremonies in uncomfortable, olive-drab, Army buses and had to double up in motel rooms. I didn't even have to be in uniform. Army protocol of the era dictated that Taps be sounded from a concealed position, the music resonating across the cemetery from a phantom source. This was fine by me, except I *always* wore my Class A uniform with my brass insignia polished and shoes spit-shined to a high gloss. In appearance I was just as STRAC (Strategic Army Corps)[8] as any other soldier on the honor guard. I won't be so bold as to attest to being psychologically as STRAC as the honor guard members, as I never knew their respective states of mind, only my own. I, however, profoundly understood that it was my duty to pay homage to a fallen soldier and his family for the sacrifice they all had made. Anything less would have besmirched the honor and tradition of the United States Army, *and I wasn't about to do that.*

Near the end of October the 80th Army Band sent me to the west coast of Florida to play Taps at two funeral details—four days apart.[9] In typical Army fashion I was ordered to remain in Florida until both assignments were completed. The transportation officer secured a billet for me as a guest of the University of Tampa in downtown Tampa. The room I was assigned was on a vacant floor in the girls' dormitory wing, one floor above where the cute little lassies slept!

After having performed my duties as a soldier faithfully and to the best of my ability, on November 1, 1968, without warning or presumption, I received orders reassigning me to the USARV (United States Army, Republic of Vietnam). The orders materialized out of nowhere, *suddenly,* like a dark gray raincloud on an otherwise clear day. I should have known it would happen, for I had been in the Army precisely one year *to the very day!*

2

Forget Everything You Learned in Basic Training

The news of my assignment to Vietnam had come during working hours. It was delivered by my office supervisor, a WO-3 (Chief Warrant Officer Pay Grade 3). His name now escapes me, but he validated the old lifer expression "Read it and weep." His eyes actually watered when he delivered the bad news. As I mentioned earlier, the cadre at Fort Stewart were a close-knit group, emotionally bonded through swampy association. His emotional outpouring, while tender and caring, may have had something to do with the fact his uniform's ribbon rack didn't display the familiar yellow, green, and red Vietnam service decoration. His tears may have been partially for himself because his time in Vietnam still lay ahead of him.

As horrific as the news was, I didn't get that chilling internal flash that typically accompanies this type of news. I suspect it was because Vietnam had long loomed on the horizon of my future. Although I had beguiled myself into believing I'd dodged the bullet, on some level of negativity I had never entirely accepted the plausibility of my *not going*. Throughout the span of my adolescent years Vietnam had lurked in the shadow of my existence like a portent of vile fate to the extent that my future inclusion in the war had clouded my days with solemn inevitability. Oddly enough, I felt compassion for my boss, who was taking the news harder than I, for he had a wife and children to consider. I consoled him with the false assurance that going to Vietnam was no big deal, a reassurance that neither of us truly believed.

Still, I couldn't avoid thinking I must have screwed up: *why else would the Army be sending me to Vietnam?* Wasn't that the threat of the lifers at Fort Leonard Wood? *"Screw up and you'll end up in Vietnam."*

My WP (Will Proceed) date to USARV was in six days. With this in mind, I immediately requested all of my accumulated 45 days of leave and any future leave I was entitled to. Soldiers bound for Vietnam were permitted to do this. It made no sense to get killed with unused leave time on the table.

I then cashed in a few past favors I had performed for the fellows across the hallway who cut personnel travel orders and requested mine read I would *drive* to the Vietnam embarkation station at Oakland, California, instead of to the closer embarkation station in New York. It was indeed fortunate for me that logic rarely entered the minds of the Green Machine. Since I had a registered automobile on base, this highly questionable juxtaposition of embarkation stations gave me validity for an additional seven days of travel time, which I did not intend to use driving; instead I would fly and enjoy the extra days at home with my family. I was able to shave two whole months off of my one-year Vietnam tour of duty, a juxtaposition that may well have saved life or limb.

After the shock of learning I was going to Vietnam had dissipated, I hunkered down to my fate. I decided the AIT instructors at Fort Leonard Wood had been wrong about Vietnam; you didn't have to screw up to be sent there, you just had to be damn unlucky. *Unlucky like me!*

There were four holidays left in 1968 for me to enjoy with my family and friends: Thanksgiving, my 23rd birthday, Christmas, and New Year's Day. What could be finer than a last holiday fling at home? Armageddon may loom ahead, but it was still two months in the future. As circumstances developed, I wasn't good at eating, drinking, and being merry. Although this should have been the keynote of my existence at this juncture in my military career and life, it wasn't. The approaching horror of Vietnam service soured my stay of execution. I became morose and reclusive, turning not to the joys of companionship but to introspective speculation concerning the nature of my existence. I sought and found consoling wisdom in the literature of the ages. I had to prepare myself psychologically. Would I be afraid, would I be a coward, *would I, would I* ... all questions that cannot be answered accurately under theoretical circumstances. One had to nose up to one's demons to really know and mine were still far away on the horizon, blocked by the lofty majesty of distant mountains painted of purple patriotism or whatever.

BUILDING 5, UNITED STATES ARMY OVERSEAS REPLACEMENT CENTER, OAKLAND, CALIFORNIA. Early in the morning of January 3, 1969, I left my New Jersey home to fly the friendly skies of United Air Lines across the wide expanse of the continental United States to the very edge of the Pacific Ocean. I spent the evening in San Francisco at the Airport Holiday Inn and the next morning reported, as ordered, to USAOSREPLCTR (United States Army Overseas Replacement Center) at Oakland, California. I had been an ultimate weapon for a little over a year and would now have the opportunity to use what I'd been taught at Fort Dix. Combat was the warrior's ultimate challenge, the essence of being a soldier. I prayed my essence was up to the challenge.

The few days I spent at Oakland Army Base as a transient en route to

2. Forget Everything You Learned in Basic Training

Vietnam are now mostly a blur in my mind. I do, however, recall the stress of the unknown I experienced entering this military portal to man-made hell. I arrived without the companionship or consolation of sharing my fears with a familiar face. I felt very much alone in spite of the fact the timing of my arrival in Oakland was during President Johnson's massive and final troop buildup in Vietnam and there were many, many soldiers in transit—both coming and going. We were all strangers unto ourselves and couldn't take comfort in the trusting brotherhood of warriors, for we were not warriors—having not been tested in battle ... yet.

The processing at Oakland Army Base consisted of assignment to a transient company, receiving all necessary immunizations—mine a booster shot for cholera, exchanging uniforms, performing demeaning work details such as floor sweeping, policing the grounds for cigarette butts, KP (Kitchen Police) and enduring total boredom, which was occasionally agitated by the apprehension inherent with waiting to be pulled out of ranks with the inevitable flight orders to Vietnam. The overall experience gave me an understanding of the fear cattle must sense while crowded into slaughterhouse pens enduring the doom of the unknown.

After relinquishing my winter, Class A, dress uniform,[1] my snazzy saucer cap, three sets of fatigues, and two pairs of standard-issue leather combat boots, the Quartermaster Corps issued me three sets of jungle fatigues and two pairs of tropical-combat boots. Unlike the standard-issue Army cotton fatigues, jungle fatigues were made of a lightweight synthetic fiber. The tunic top, or "jacket," as the Army called it, was worn outside the trousers to promote ventilation. Its long sleeves could be worn either rolled up above the elbow or in the buttoned-down position. Unlike the all-leather, smooth-sole combat boot, the tropical counterpart had uppers fabricated from canvas, with metal drain grommets in the lower arch area. The soles were thick rubber and imbedded with steel wire mesh to help protect feet from puncture by sharp objects. Inside the boots were removable nylon pads that mimicked Dr. Scholl's comfort inserts in appearance but were actually airy spacers to promote quick draining and drying. The soles of the jungle boots were embellished with deeply cut treads that could have been designed by Firestone for off-road motor adventuring. All reclaimed personal clothing not authorized for Vietnam service was shipped by the Quartermaster Corps to each transient's declared HOR (Home of Record). I kept my two Army-issue baseball caps, field jacket, several sets of underwear, multiple socks, Class B Khakis uniform, and foldable garrison cap (colloquially referred to as a "piss cap" or by another name too exceedingly offensive to the female anatomy to mention).

My embarkation orders came the next morning, January 4. I and my duffle bag of personal items were summarily ferreted away to be sequestered in a huge warehouse that served the base as a preflight staging area. Numerous folding Army cots filled the vast expanse of open warehouse floor. The cavernous space literally swarmed with noisy, squirming, khaki-clad humanity. Had Lucifer first been consulted, the experience couldn't have been any more distasteful. My flight to oblivion was scheduled for the morning of January 5. My group of fellow travelers and I were brusquely rousted at 0200 hours, that's 2:00 a.m. in civilian time, by a dick-headed lifer NCO (Noncommissioned Officer) blowing a whistle. I hadn't slept a wink.

After breakfast and a final roll call, a small fleet of olive-drab Army buses arrived to deliver us to nearby Travis Air Force Base, where a waiting government-contracted World Airways commercial jetliner would take us to where—from an Army perspective—the proverbial action was. In obscurity—without ceremony, fanfare, or public notice—we left the comfort and security of the United States. We were on our way to war and nobody seemed to care, not even the now-absent hippie war protestors we had been warned waited outside the base's gate to shout obscenities and spit at departing soldiers.

Traveling to war on a civilian-contracted flight was a bizarre experience, to say the least. We were approaching Armageddon in the comfort of plush reclining seats with headrests, pretty stewardesses, coffee, tea, and juice. After traveling about 20 hours, which included stops for refueling, we were finally in South Vietnamese air space.

90TH REPLACEMENT BATTALION, CAMP LONG BÌNH JUNCTION, BIÊN HÒA PROVINCE. From an altitude of 3,000 feet Vietnam looked like any other place I had ever been.... Well, perhaps it was a bit greener. Oakland and the USA were now two landings behind us. The plane had refueled in bone-chilling minus 14-degree temperature at Anchorage, Alaska, and then again—in a more temperate climate—at the U.S. Air Force Base in Yokota, Japan. At Biên Hòa Airbase, our journey's end, the jet jolted harshly as it settled onto the runway. Over the intercom the pilot casually announced,

> Welcome to Vietnam. Biên Hòa Airbase is presently under mortar attack. When the aircraft stops, gentlemen, you will have three minutes to exit the plane. The runway officer instructs that you stay calm and proceed to the drainage easements on either side of the runway. Remain there until the all clear signal is given. Your crew hopes that you enjoyed your flight and thanks you for flying World Airways.

I had barely cleared the edge of the runway when I heard the plane accelerating for takeoff. They would obviously refuel elsewhere. My initial impression of Vietnam was that the climate was insufferably hot and muggy, far more uncomfortable than that at Fort Stewart. I also noticed a spicy sweet odor in the air I could not identify.

Minutes later, what I assumed was the all-clear siren wailed and we were instructed to gather our gear, which had been haphazardly ejected from the belly of the aircraft onto the runway. We were told to wait under a large open-sided tent I hadn't noticed until now. Buses would be arriving to transport us to the 90th Replacement Battalion in nearby Long Bình. A group of soldiers in transit were already sitting on wooden benches under the tent. I selected a vacant spot alongside a rather scruffy-looking fellow sporting a large leather holster hanging from a web belt loosely cinched around his waist. I immediately noticed his faded jungle fatigue jacket displayed no identification or markings other than a subdued U.S. ARMY patch[2] over his right breast pocket (left side from my perspective).

As I settled onto my seat my scruffy neighbor casually glanced at my spotless, unfaded jungle fatigues and then looked away. He said nothing, no greeting, no personal inquiry. His bare head revealed a shock of hair far in excess of the regulation Army buzz cut. I suddenly felt uncomfortable in my all-too-obvious newbie attire.

An adorable Vietnamese kid wearing a New York Yankees baseball cap and carrying a wooden shoeshine box worked his way over to where we were sitting. My mute companion casually removed his weapon and, pointing it directly at the kid's nose, told him to "fuck off." After the boy scurried away he turned to me and said with a solemnity that may have been rooted in past misfortune, "Never trust the little bastards." And that was all he said, my first instruction and introduction to the *real* action Army.

After sitting in crowded silence for a while, a small convoy of noisy Army buses arrived. They were similar in appearance to stateside Army buses but differed in having their windows covered over with heavy steel-wire mesh. Not a good sign; it didn't bode well for motor travel along Biên Hòa's narrow streets. The implication was all too obvious: the locals liked to throw things, *like hand grenades,* through the open windows.

The bus ride afforded my first up-close glimpse of Vietnam. Many of the Vietnamese civilian men I observed along the streets of Biên Hòa wore either Army fatigue green or western-style clothing. The women stuck to the more traditional garb of black silk pajama bottoms and white tunics. Once outside the airbase the landscape transitioned into gentle rolling hills with swampy gullies and ravines. Although there weren't many trees, wherever vegetation grew it was thick and tropical and lush. Military vehicles abounded. They were parked in backyards, along streets, and in compounds. We passed many bunkered fortifications enhanced with multiple strands of barbwire fencing or spiral concertina wire. The soil was reddish and produced a fine powdery dust that clung to everything in sight.

Our destination encampment shared the same initials with our soon-to-be-relieved commander in chief of the military, President Lyndon B. Johnson, LBJ—Camp Long Bình Junction. It also shared initials with another nearby facility, Long Bình Jail, the central U.S. Army Military Police prison in the Republic of Vietnam. As the convoy of buses approached the entrance gate to the 90th Replacement Battalion, I could see many wooden buildings sprawled across a gentle rise. The facility overlooked a huge military complex consisting of offices, depots, and warehouses all bearing the official designation of Long Bình Post, but it was more commonly referred to by most U.S. troops as just "Long Bình." Long Bình Post was actually a U.S. military-controlled area contained within the city limits of Biên Hòa.

As the buses came to a stop at the reception area, I couldn't help but notice the similarity of Long Bình Junction to Army bases back home: mowed strips of grass, concrete sidewalks, paved roads, corner street signs bearing

The 90th Replacement Battalion was one of two facilities in Vietnam processing incoming and departing troops (the other was the 22nd Replacement Battalion at Cam Ranh Bay). The battalion was situated within the city limits of Biên Hòa, approximately 22 miles northeast of Saigon, and was part and parcel of a sprawling U.S. military complex collectively known as "Long Bình Post" (author's collection).

2. Forget Everything You Learned in Basic Training

The 90th Replacement Battalion offered all of the amenities of a stateside Army post: snack bar, post exchange, social clubs, barber, chapel, laundry, tailor, movies, medical clinic, mess hall, Red Cross and Veterans Administration offices, and an infrastructure that included concrete sidewalks lined by manicured grass strips and corner street signs (author's collection).

the names of U.S. states, a PX (Post Exchange) with Kwiki Lounge snack bar annex, wooden telephone poles, street lights, etc. Other than the sandbags neatly stacked around the base of buildings and the wire mesh covering windows, it could have been Fort Dix or Fort Stewart. The home of the 90th Replacement Battalion hardly conveyed the atmosphere of a combat posting, which made it feel surreal. This was, after all, Vietnam and a war. I had expected a less civilized environment, not one providing retail outlets where soldiers could fulfill their shopping needs or enjoy junk food snacks at a Kwiki Lounge while they awaited assignment orders. The clincher was a large sign in front of the Post Exchange that instructed anyone interested to LOOK SHARP—BE SHARP—SALUTE SHARP. *Right* ... how about: Look Sharp, Be Sharp, *Stay Alive!* Death, mayhem, and destruction lay just a few meters beyond the perimeter wire, but at the 90th Replacement Battalion they were worried about military dress, decorum, and courtesy.

Could Vietnam be another *lifer-land*?

The first order of business after reporting for duty and being assigned a bunk in one of the many wooden barracks was to exchange all U.S. currency for MPC (Military Payment Certificates). In compliance with MACV (Military Assistance Command Vietnam) Article 37–6 it was illegal to possess U.S. dollars and coinage in Vietnam—*except for pennies*. I never understood why pennies were OK, perhaps it was to enable troops to play penny poker during their slack times.

I couldn't help but notice there were many Vietnamese civilians on the base. It was bizarre to see people who resembled the enemy in physical appearance and dress lolling about everywhere I looked. Back in the USA the press had typically associated black-pajama-clad Vietnamese in conical hats with the enemy. Here at the 90th Replacement Battalion it was a common civilian worker's uniform of the day. It was my understanding Vietnamese laborers performed many of the tedious or nasty chores for very low wages. Things being what they were, my first impression of the Vietnamese was understandably negative. I didn't want to die for a noisy, backwards, poverty-riddled populous. I listened to the ethnic slurs and denunciations from my fellow soldiers and accepted what I heard as truth. I knew nothing of the ways of the Vietnamese, but I did notice they had a healthy respect for our trash, undoubtedly for personal, commercial, and, I assumed, *devious* uses. A fine example of their cleverness was the traction grip sandals they all wore and also offered for sale. The soles were cleverly fashioned from discarded motor vehicle tire treads!

Because of the 15-hour time difference that exists between Pacific Standard Time and Indochina Time, I arrived in Vietnam at approximately 2:00 p.m., January 6 (January 7 in the USA). I spent four days at the 90th Replacement Battalion, which may not seem like a long time, but considering that the quality and safety of my future hinged upon what was written on the next sheet of paper I would receive, it seemed like an eternity. The waiting had been made more unbearable by the many rumors circulating among transients—Black Horse had been overrun, the 199th Light Infantry had just been mauled, American[3] lost another company, the *Old Reliables* of the 9th Infantry Division were getting clobbered in the Delta, and the like.

The Green Machine, however, did its utmost to distract me from my fears by filling my fretting time with various make-work projects such as sweeping floors that were already spotless, scraping and painting freshly painted barracks interior walls, and washing clean windows and floors until I halfheartedly believed I might be in janitorial AIT, which if it kept me out of the infantry was OK by me. In view of the effort, time, and expense the Army had expended training me to be a personnel management specialist, I couldn't even imagine they would make me a ground pounder. I hadn't really been trained for that type of duty. I might hurt myself, or someone else, but this was the Army and they had oodles of taxpayer money to squander on unnecessary training. If USARV needed riflemen, I was going to end up humping the bush; in military logic it was as simple as that—the needs of the service superseded MOS training, and in truth, you really didn't need much advanced training to be a rifleman. Every day three formations were held for the purpose of roll call, issuing assignment orders, and doling out work details. Those who received orders left immediately. I lingered on.

One bright sunny afternoon while standing in a noisy queue of soldiers, I happened to notice the soil near the lineup occasionally erupted in a small geyser of thrown earth. At first I was not alarmed, thinking it some bizarre Asian insect burrowing a home. After more geysers at different locations gushed I became aware that a distant popping sound, barely audible above the chattering soldiers and passing vehicles, followed each geyser. A sudden chill swept through my body. Could it be gunshots? No one else in the line seemed to notice. I didn't want to embarrass myself. Several more geysers erupted in rapid succession. I anxiously tapped the shoulder of the fellow ahead of me and asked if he thought someone was shooting at us. He shook his head and contemptuously dismissed my concerns. At that precise moment a gaggle of three helicopter gunships swooshed overhead at low altitude and in unison launched a sudden attack directed at a distant, overgrown, swampy area barely discernible beyond several latrines. It was my first time under fire and both my companions and I in the queue *almost* had been completely oblivious to the experience! I decided then and there that henceforth I'd rely on my own judgment as to what course of action I'd take in the future and not consult with others. My life was too precious for me to place it in anyone else's hands.

RELIABLE ACADEMY, ĐỒNG TÂM BASE CAMP, ĐỊNH TƯỜNG PROVINCE. On January 9 I received orders assigning me to the 9th Infantry Division, the unit mentioned earlier as being clobbered in the Mekong Delta. The following morning at 0530 hours—that's 5:30 a.m. in civilian time, I left the 90th Replacement Battalion and Long Bình to depart from Biên Hòa Airfield in a military C-7A Caribou transport plane furnished by the United States Air Force (USAF). I had a ten-hour wait at the airfield, which was overrun by American soldiers and aircraft of all descriptions: military transports and fighters, civilian jetliners, and aircraft with unusually long engine nacelles lettered Air America.[4] Rock 'n' roll music blared throughout the terminal and soldiers in varying degrees and styles of military dress milled about, some clutching transistor radios or tape recorders or portable television sets.

Vietnamese civilians lurked everywhere, blatantly shining shoes for 50 cents without first asking permission, blatantly selling iced cups of Kool-Aid for 15–20 cents, blatantly offering sexual services from their sisters for nominal fees. It was all very blatant—not at all like I thought it would be in a combat zone. If it hadn't been for the occasional distant outburst of gunfire and the oriental appearance of the civilians, I wouldn't have thought Biên Hòa was in Vietnam.

The PA (Public Address) system finally announced boarding for the flight to Đồng Tâm and those of us embarking trudged through the gate, entered the aircraft, and flew southward to the 9th Division's Mekong Delta headquarters base camp. I learned its name, Đồng Tâm, was an American military contrivance meaning "United Hearts and Minds." Hmm ... well, anyway, the Caribou landed at Đồng Tâm in an unexpectedly steep descent, touching down at the extreme edge of a PSP (Perforated Steel Plate) runway; then it decelerated to a stop in a brake-smoking, reverse-prop pitch, seatbelt-restraining maneuver. I later learned the passenger-unfriendly landing was made to avoid sniper fire originating from the tree line across the river opposite the southern end of the runway. (I also learned the ten-hour wait at Biên Hòa Airfield was to allow the runway we had just landed on to be repaired after having sustaining damage in an overnight mortar attack.)

My orders specified I report to the 9th Adjutant General Administration Company, which I assumed would have the responsibility of finding a slot for me within the division's TO&E (Table of Organization & Equipment). The TO&E was the division's master plan of what unit got what and how much of it they got. My assumption had been incorrect about the division's finding a slot for me; they already had one waiting, having anticipated my arrival. Unbeknownst to me my career in Vietnam had been prearranged while I was still at the 90th Replacement Battalion. After deplaning, the group I was with received instructions to wait for transportation under a shady awning near the control tower—that is, all of us except yours truly. I was told to go around to the front of the airfield office and wait there. There was no shady awning. I had to stand in the sunlight.

Time passed. *Hurry up and wait.* My stomach was aflutter with butterflies of apprehension. I watched several small observation planes take off and land. It was a busy airfield. Then a quarter-ton utility truck that resembled a low-slung Jeep stopped in front of me. Its driver, a deeply tanned fellow with a black, subdued lieutenant's bar on one collar point of his jungle fatigue jacket, inquired if I was Fischer. He instructed me to throw my duffle bag in the backseat and climb aboard. No greeting or introduction. He said it in an affable tone, so I threw him my best pseudo-lifer salute. He looked over at me and said, "No need for that kind of stuff around here." I lowered my arm wondering what happened to *Look Sharp—Be Sharp—Salute Sharp.* Had he not processed through the 90th Replacement Battalion? If he had, perhaps he hadn't read the sign?

I hopped aboard and we drove out of the airfield area, turning onto an unpaved base road and in the process kicking up great clouds of dust. My initial impression of Đồng Tâm was that of a gritty environment faded into sun-bleached earth tones. Most of the buildings were the grayish beige of unpainted wood in varying stages of weathering. The soil was a granular tan. What little vegetation struggled in and along drainage ditches and at the foot of sandbag revetments was a pale yellowish-green color, similar in hue to the faded jungle fatigues worn by the troops we passed. The only contrast to the overall earthy tone of the camp's décor was that there were numerous signs posted along walkways and driveways leading into various administration buildings and unit compounds. These large, freestanding signs displayed bold black lettering and colorful heraldic unit insignias set against solid white backgrounds.

My highly overqualified driver (by rank) negotiated several turns, spinning the steering wheel expertly with an unauthorized death knob someone had clamped to its circumference and in the process casually waving off an occasional salute coming from what I could only assume were newbie arrivals like me. It was then that I caught a glimpse of the collar point *opposite* his lieutenant's bar. It was the crossed rifles of the infantry! What had I gotten myself into? What kind of unit sends an officer to fetch a mere SP-4? Advance RECON (Reconnaissance)? LRRP (Long Range Reconnaissance Patrol)? Snipers? Scary stuff filled my thoughts as the lieutenant made a snappy turn into an unmarked driveway.

We passed between two long buildings and came to a slow rolling stop in front of several bare-chested soldiers who were busily kibitzing with each other while filling sandbags and stacking them atop a dilapidated-looking bunker. It must have taken a lot of hits for it to be in such deplorable condition. Beyond the bunker and above the corrugated metal roofs of buildings I noticed numerous columns of thick black smoke rising high into the sky. Were they telltale signs of the aftermath of battle? If so, they were weird-looking, like powwow signals rising on the horizon in the old cowboy and Indian cartoons I used to watch.

The lieutenant said Ed Johns wanted to take a look at me. He instructed me to grab my gear and pointed to a building where I could find Mister Johns. My arm twitched several times, but I did not salute as he backed away in the utility truck. The laboring soldiers gave me no notice as I passed them. Not a friendly face among them. I quickly learned that new guys in Vietnam were held in some disdain. Brotherhood had to be earned. I entered a covered platform that resembled a low stage. A few rows of gray, metal, folding chairs with red backrests leaned against a side railing and numerous heavy-looking black metal music stands stood upright, filling a corner of the platform. It looked like a stage. Music stands? *It was a stage!* I then spotted two large, circular Octofoil signs nailed to the back wall on both sides of an open doorway. They each bore this inscription: 9TH INFANTRY DIVISION BAND IN CONCERT. I cautiously entered the doorway. An older-looking soldier was busily shuffling a pile of paperwork strewn about the top of a folding table. His degree of dress was the same as the soldiers outside filling sandbags. Sweat from his partially balding head ran down his face and dropped onto his hairy chest and papers; the sweat he mopped up with a soiled handkerchief. I had no idea who or what rank he was, so I stood silently in the doorway.

He settled on a piece of paper, glanced up at me, and asked, "You Fischer?"

I assumed he was Ed Johns. I didn't know his rank or how to respond to his inquiry, so I took the safe route and threw him a smart salute with an official, "Specialist Four Robert F. Fischer reporting as ordered, Sir."

The man gave me a look of incredulity that I hadn't yet seen in Vietnam. He mumbled something about not doing that kind of stuff around here and then asked if I played trumpet. I found the question provocative in view of my clerical MOS, but informed him I'd played trumpet since the fourth grade. He nodded and went into another room. He then reemerged with a trumpet and asked if I could read music, which I said I could. He handed me the trumpet and asked me to play anything I wanted. Bizarre, but why not? This was, after all, the Army, where anything and everything could happen. I removed the mouthpiece from the proffered instrument, grabbed my own well-used mouthpiece from my pocket where I always carried it (a trumpeter had to keep his armature in shape), blew into it out of habit, and then gently twisted it into the lead pipe of the trumpet *without* tapping it in place. I ran up and down the scales a couple of times to warm up and thought I might play a few bars of "Cherry Blossom Pink and Apple White" for Mister Johns' entertainment. It was a trumpeter's favorite because it offered lots of possibility for improvisation. I inhaled a large breath to begin playing, but he stopped me with the words, "Don't bother, you're in." He said I could leave my gear with him, but I had to report in at the Reliable Academy across the street to undergo an obligatory one-week indoctrination designed to familiarize incoming troops with the skill necessary to survive in-country. Indoctrination for survival sounded great to me.

"Tell them I said you're with the band, and they'll make your assignment official, but you still have to go through the processing cycle."

2. Forget Everything You Learned in Basic Training 47

I was confused; my MOS was 71H30, a personnel management specialist. I asked if I was going to be the band's clerk. He sighed and said *that* would personally be very useful to him, but the Army's TO&E didn't authorize a clerk for a division band. I'd have to settle for being a musician. He did, however, suggest I consider volunteering for the job after the Reliable Academy had finished with my indoctrination.

My assignment to the band came as a complete surprise. I knew when I had received orders sending me to USARV my future and fate were up in the air. The needs of the Army came before mine, and I suspected I'd end up an infantryman slogging in the boonies—an assignment, viewed from the perspective of my precious hide, representing a worst-case scenario. I, however, had no idea how critical a skill musician was to the Army. It was an MOS they couldn't teach in AIT. To be a musician you had to have talent and to have undergone years of training and practice. The habitually undermanned 9th Infantry Division Band had fewer musicians than their TO&E-authorized complement of 43. I made 35; the band was still short several musicians and would remain so throughout my tour. My 201 File must have been flagged back in Oakland, which may have accounted for the slight delays

The headquarters base camp of the 9th Infantry Division was situated in the Viet Cong-infested Mekong Delta on the north bank of the Mỹ Tho River. It was erected upon 600 acres of filled marshland. It was also homeport to Navy Task Force 116, the Navy component of the Mobile Riverine Force (author's collection).

The short 1,500-by-50-foot runway at the Reliable Fixed Wing Airfield was constructed using interlocking perforated steel plates coated with sand paint for adhesion. The runway was adequate to land the Air Force's De Havilland C-7A Caribou transport planes if the pilots stood on the brakes and quickly reversed prop pitch upon touching down (author's collection).

Newly arrived troops to the Division were given five days of *Vietnam style* combat training at the Reliable Academy. The class cycle was introduced with the phrase, "Forget everything you learned in basic training." The additional training was essential to introduce troops to the specialized weaponry and unconventional tactics used to fight the Viet Cong in the Mekong Delta (author's collection).

2. Forget Everything You Learned in Basic Training 49

During 1969 Đồng Tâm's primary defensive weapons were four 82mm mortars of the Four Deuces Mortar Platoon. The tubes were mounted on two barges berthed along the north bank of the turning basin and were manned by troops from the 3/60th Infantry Battalion (author's collection).

at each stage of my processing. The Army administrators had, apparently, been trying to determine which division band most needed a trumpeter.

My assignment to the 9th Infantry Division Band obviously came as the result of my having been a bugler for the 80th Army Band at Fort Stewart. To be a bugler, even a TDY one, Army protocol demanded that a soldier possess a 02B trumpeter MOS. Unbeknownst to me when I had passed the audition, I had automatically received a secondary 02B MOS. Unfortunately, no one had bothered to tell me about it.

I took my leave of Ed Johns, who, I assumed—for want of uniform insignia or introduction, was the bandmaster and I crossed the street and reported in to the Reliable Academy as ordered.

They were expecting me at the Academy. Well, they were actually *looking* for me. I hadn't been with the others on the academy deuce-and-a-half[5] and they were wondering what happened to me. I was greeted by a three-stripe SGT (Buck Sergeant), who demanded to know where the "fuck" I'd been for the last hour. I pointed my thumb over my shoulder and told him across the street. Fortunately, at that precise moment a second, more congenial NCO with a superior SSG (Staff Sergeant) rocker under his three stripes entered the office and in a matter-of-fact tone informed my inquisitor everything was cool. He said I was one of Mister Johns' people, which apparently explained everything.

I'd been with the division only for a couple of hours and I was already getting the impression bandsmen weren't viewed in the same light as other soldiers. Apparently being one of "Mister Johns' people" was a good thing. I didn't fully comprehend the why of it; but I did know from ROTC that a military band's mission was to promote esprit de corps by providing entertainment and upholding the ritualistic traditions of the Army through ceremony. This lofty musical mission gave the band an intrinsic autonomy that set it apart from other supporting elements whose missions were to furnish soldiers with the physical needs of combat. The nature of support provided by a military band was psychological, the primary goal being to promote morale, which in view of the average American's post–1968 Tết perception of the Vietnam War now bordered on the impossible.

I would later learn the hierarchical status of the band within the division was quite autonomous. Although the band was attached to the DISCOM (Division Support Command) headquarters company, which was commanded by a captain, it was directly accountable to the DISCOM battalion commanding officer, who was a full "bird" colonel.[6] The band's association with the headquarters company was for administrative and logistical purposes only. The headquarters company fed the band, maintained its personnel records, furnished adequate living quarters, and in broader terms provided all that was necessary for soldiering in a combat zone outside of the band's musical duties, duties which took precedence over all company work details except perimeter guard duty. Bandsmen, like all 9th Infantry Division support troops, were soldiers first. If, however, a company-assigned work detail interfered with a bandsman's musical duties, the music took precedence. This created some animosity towards the band within the command and ranks of the headquarters company. Luckily for the band, the commanding general of the 9th Infantry Division, Major General Julian Ewell, considered the band his personal property, to be utilized as he pleased for his own enjoyment and that of his subordinates and guests. I eventually determined that within the division's hierarchy the more astute treated us as the general's band, and woe to the one who did not recognize or accept this fact, which—of course—contributed even more to the overall animosity towards bandsmen.

The Reliable Academy began each five-day cycle with a formal greeting from the assistant division commander, Brigadier General Frank L. Gunn. Everyone got to shake his hand and then trundle off to receive their billet assignment and new equipment allocations and accomplish other administrative tasks. I was assigned the lower rack of an upstairs bunk in one of the

2. Forget Everything You Learned in Basic Training 51

several wooden barracks within the Reliable Academy compound. When I opened the metal wall locker assigned to my bunk, I found an M-60 machine gun, two M-16 rifles, belts of 7.62 caliber ammunition, hand and smoke grenades, battle harnesses with full ammunition pouches, and so forth. I needed the wall locker to secure my personal belongings, so I reported my find to the Reliable Academy CQ (Charge of Quarters), who advised me to ignore the stuff because it probably belonged to some visiting eleven-bravos (infantry) who were in from the field for the day. He assured me they would retrieve their stuff later.

The presence of weapons and ammunition in my wall locker was more confusing than disturbing. During the formal "Welcome to the 9th Infantry Division" introduction, which preceded the handshake from General Gunn and followed the "Forget everything you learned in basic training" introductory statement from the head training officer, we had been advised that live ammunition was *not authorized* for troops inside Đồng Tâm's perimeter. Its discovery could result in an Article 15, a disciplinary action administered at the company level that typically resulted in a reduction in rank or extra work assignments or both. Infantrymen in from the field must have been an exception to the rule.

While my group was still occupied with the orientation ceremony, the Air Force unleashed a ground-shaking aerial attack against Thới Sơn, an island in the middle of the nearby Mỹ Tho River. The river, which bordered the southern perimeter of Đồng Tâm, was one of nine diverting branches of the Mekong River that formed the alluvial Mekong Delta. The bombarded island was just a couple of klicks, meaning kilometers,[7] southeast of the base. The troops at Đồng Tâm called it "VC Island" and were fond of proliferating the rumor that it was where the enemy sent their troops for R&R (Rest & Recreation or Rest & Recuperation, depending on your state of mind). To my ears it was a stretch of the imagination to think the enemy maintained a rest area just across the river from a major U.S. combat installation, although I did consider it an ideal location for launching mortars aimed at Đồng Tâm. The R&R rumor may have had some validity, because the 9th Infantry Division's Mobile Riverine 2nd Brigade had just completed an exhaustive large-scale "search & destroy" sweep of the island as part of operation Water Trap, and the aerial bombardment was the Air Force putting their finishing touches on the operation.

After the day's indoctrination formalities were over and we were tucked in for the night, at around 2330 hours (11:30 p.m. in civilian time) the VC demonstrated precisely how effective an operation Water Trap had been by launching a mortar attack from the island. It came soon after the last giggly whispered joke had subsided in the barracks. The detonations of the mortar impacts awakened everybody on the floor and created instant pandemonium when one of the bulbous projectiles skittered down the metal roof above us. It apparently flew in on an angle that so complemented the pitch of the roof that it tracked in the trough of one panel's corrugated grooves. As it slid down the roof it made a terrifying noise that got everybody's attention—BIG TIME. It dropped off the edge and detonated ineffectively in the dirt strip between the sandbagged barracks and company HQ building. The horrific explosion set everyone in the barracks in motion, all haphazardly scurrying for the safety of the personnel shelters. The fellow sleeping in the bunk above me managed to cold-cock himself into oblivion when he panicked and smashed his head against a length of exposed roof truss. Another fellow jumped off the second-story stair landing and broke something when he hit the ground. Because of all the confusion and commotion, I hadn't been able to get to the personnel shelter until after the all-clear siren sounded. Both of the upstairs exits had been clogged in a panicked log jam of tangled bodies, flailing arms, and kicking legs. I didn't lose control of myself like many of the other soldiers; my fight-or flight-reaction time had been delayed by intellectual speculation concerning the reality of the situation. No one had ever tried to blow me up before and I found it emotionally distressing. My heart was pounding and it was difficult for me to breathe normally. I had to consciously block thinking about what could have happened if the trajectory of the projectile had been just a wee bit different.

The next morning, January 11, rumors circulated throughout the compound that there had been several casualties. No official mention was made of the injured soldiers. It was almost as if they hadn't been part of our class. Here today, gone tomorrow. I was beginning to learn that the reality of combat recognized no past and no future, only the present.

The day's indoctrination included familiarization with the many types of booby traps the VC were fond of setting. We saw visuals and demonstrations on how the traps worked and what to look out for to avoid tripping one. No mention was made of random bombs falling from the sky. Perhaps *that* subject would be covered on another day.

We were informed we could write letters home during our training at the Reliable Academy but should not expect to receive mail. No explanation was given, but I assumed it had to do with the brevity of our stay. By the time those relatives and friends we'd like to hear from received notification of our Reliable Academy mailing address it would be out of date, for we'd be gone, having received a permanent assignment to one of the division's many units. Not getting mail for a week or so was a downer in the morale department.

2. Forget Everything You Learned in Basic Training

There was a lot going on around us, none of it good. It would have been nice to read loving words of comfort from home.

What was a week in the 'Nam? *I was learning it was a damn eternity.*

Classroom topics the following day included health and hygiene in a hot, humid, unsanitary environment, and small unit tactics. We were emphatically instructed that under no circumstance were we to drink local water without first dropping in a few purification tablets. The Vietnamese were acclimated to the impurities and toxins in their water sources, but it could make a GI (Government Issue—World War II holdover slang for a U.S. soldier) very sick. Knowingly drinking unpurified water was grounds for an Article 15. The tablets made drinking the water safe but gave it an unpleasant chemical taste that some troops attempted to disguise with Kool-Aid. We eventually learned Kool-Aid didn't hide the chemical taste and its sweetness exacerbated thirst problems in the field. We were advised not to mix Kool-Aid with our canteen water.

Small unit tactics as developed in the Mekong Delta sounded downright scary. The concept necessitated the mounting of numerous squad-size patrols[8] to saturate an area in search of the elusive VC. The standing order for this type of combat was to locate the enemy and then destroy him with superior firepower, which meant artillery or airpower, not small arms. Sometimes the enemy found our patrols first, which gave rise to the last-man-in-the-squad genre that would later become so fashionable in Vietnam myth and prose. Occasionally gunfire could be heard far in the distance. While we lay snug in our bunks out in the boonies, other soldiers were fighting, perhaps for their lives. Troops in Vietnam had an expression to rationalize these kinds of situations: "It don't mean nothing." Experience taught that each and every one of us would eventually have a turn at one kind of terror or another. There were no rear areas in the Mekong Delta, hence no sanctuary from the Viet Cong. *Mister Charles,* or just plain *Charlie* (from the phonetic *Victor Charles* for VC) was always out and about looking for weakness in our defenses or slackness or indifference in our soldiers' awareness of their environment and circumstances.

After the mortar attack on the Reliable Academy compound, Mister Charles took a few evenings off. On January 12 my training group exchanged the classroom for a practical application exercise on the Đồng Tâm firing range. We each got to fire the M-60 machine gun, the M-79 grenade launcher, and the M-16 assault rifle on full automatic, and toss a baseball-shaped fragmentation grenade. The firing of a LAWS rocket (Light Antitank Weapons System) and detonating a Claymore antipersonnel mine were left to the instructors, which, considering the frighteningly deadly effectiveness of the devices, was probably a good thing. They were dangerous weapons to both friend and foe and not to be handled by NFGs (New Fucking Guys) unfamiliar with their use.

It was astonishing to see how large an area Đồng Tâm covered. The Reliable Academy compound was on the south side of the 600-acre base and adjacent to an area occupied by the U.S. Navy. A man-made harbor, or "Turning Basin" as the Green Machine designated it, was on the south perimeter along the Mỹ Tho River. The rifle range was at the opposite end of the base beyond the heliport that ran inside the length of the north perimeter. We rode in the open bed of a deuce-and-a-half past numerous unit compounds and supply depots. The road the driver followed skirted the east perimeter of the base for quite a distance. The elevated height of the truck bed offered an unobstructed view over the dirt berm of what lay on the other side of the perimeter. I saw a small village with several rustic-looking huts soldiers called "hooches," inundated grassy expanses that ended in dense tropical growth called "tree lines," and an occasional stone sepulcher that, if it hadn't been for the Vietnamese's inherent respect for their ancestors, would have been called "firing positions" for the VC.

The following morning, January 13, we were issued our M-16 rifles, flak vests, gas masks, steel helmets, canteens, and web battle harnesses that came with a small first-aid kit and attached empty ammo pouches. The first-aid kit included a couple of compress bandages for sucking chest wounds (gauze with an impervious plastic backing), a few small bandages, vials of sulfur powder, and a hypodermic needle loaded with atropine—a drug issued in conjunction with the gas mask to delay the effects of nerve gas. The Army apparently never forgot the horror of the poison gas used in World War I. We were also issued a supply of salt tablets (taken as needed), chloroquine primiequin quinine pills (taken daily), and quinine pills (taken weekly), the former to prevent dehydration and the latter two to prevent malaria.

Later on the same day we returned to the firing range to sight in our new rifles. Mine was stamped "Colt" and bore the serial number 859896. We were each given a magazine loaded with 18 rounds and instructed that, although the M-16 rifle's magazine was designed to hold 20 rounds, only 18 rounds should be loaded. Experience garnered in the field indicated loading 20 rounds would eventually cause the magazine's feed spring to lose its tensile strength and cause the weapon to jam—a highly undesirable occurrence in combat.

The M-16 was surprisingly lightweight and exotic-looking compared to the heavier and larger M-14 rifle I had been issued at Fort Stewart. While the M-14 was equipped with a wooden stock, the M-16 had a lightweight plastic one, a pistol-grip trigger assembly and a carrying handle that also served as a rear-sighting ramp above the receiver. Some of the fellows joked that the M-16 resembled a futuristic space ray-gun, humorously associating the weapon's manufacture with Mattel, the toy maker. It fired a small .223 millimeter caliber bullet that resembled the .22 caliber rim fire bullet used in small-varmint rifles, except the gooseneck brass cartridge of the M-16 was much larger. Because of the relatively small powder charge, firing the M-16 produced a *tat-tat-tat* sound compared to the authoritative *C-A-R-A-A-C-K* of the enemy's AK-47 rifle. This idiosyncrasy gave rise to use of the expression *popping caps* for firing the M-16. My weapon had the improved closed-ring flash suppressor instead of the earlier, open-prong, vine-snagging suppressor that field troops found so useful in opening large, metal-banded, shipping crates of C rations (insert the band into the prongs, twist the barrel, and *snap-o-pop-o* the band breaks!).

After we finished sighting in our rifles we remained on the firing range to eat supper and then, after nightfall, to learn how to use the Starlite Scope, an optical device that intensified ambient light to enhance vision at night. Upon completion of the demonstration we each had the opportunity to try it out. I hadn't yet had my turn when the class was interrupted by an NCO who arrived in a quarter-ton utility truck. He spoke briefly to our training instructor then drove away. We were told to take a break. While we were on our break a deuce-and-a-half drove onto the range. It came to a stop and a couple of Reliable Academy cadres I recognized from other classes jumped from the truck bed and unloaded several metal ammunition boxes. Each of the soldiers was armed with an M-16, which didn't seem all that unusual in a combat zone. But then my gaze wandered to the abandoned north perimeter berm behind us. Silhouetted along its top was a row of unevenly spaced helmets, *which was unusual;* they hadn't been there when we arrived!

The rifle range was in an area being expanded for rotary-wing aviation use beyond Đồng Tâm's original north perimeter. The new north perimeter berm was in place and defended by a string of new wooden shell- and dirt-fill bunkers (the old bunkers were constructed of sandbags and sections of PSP). Only a few of the bunkers were manned. The rest were still under construction.

I later learned a civilian informant had warned of a VC sapper[9] attack directed at the heliport, which was a favorite target of VC mortar men. The heliport ran the length of Đồng Tâm's north perimeter, just inside the old berm. If a ground attack actually materialized, my group would be given ammunition and moved into position on the new perimeter. The two Reliable Academy cadres who delivered the ammunition were now busily readying an M-60 machine gun. I wondered if this was real or just part of the training. It certainly looked and felt real to me.

The realization that the Green Machine was going to use *us* to fight the enemy hit me with the intellectual profundity of a wet towel whapped against my emotions. Why didn't the Army call in soldiers who were trained for this sort of thing? Speculation of this metaphysical nature ravaged my mind until the truth of our situation became all too apparent. Here in this place, at this particular moment in time, the buck stopped with us. It was *our* duty to engage the enemy; *we were the soldiers trained for this sort of thing*. The gravity of the situation was unnerving. Was I alone in my fears? I glanced at the young faces around me. Some looked visibly shaken, while others appeared oblivious to what was unfolding. A few were even kibitzing with each other and telling jokes. To my sensibilities, it was all very bizarre. We could die on this beautiful starlit evening defending a godforsaken country inhabited by an alien people. The impact of the realization left me quite unsettled.

Thank goodness nothing came of the alert; no ground attack materialized. But later that evening, after lights out, several mortar rounds sailed into Đồng Tâm. Most of the detonations sounded far away, probably where we had been at the heliport, but then some exploded nearby, which once again send us scurrying helter-skelter to the safety of the personnel shelters. Later, when the CQ made his bed check, he found all of us in the personnel shelter. In consideration of our harrowing experiences of the day before and earlier that evening he took the time to explain that the explosions we collectively judged as having been so near were actually created by friendly, outgoing, fire from Đồng Tâm's "Four Deuces Mortar Platoon," which was emplaced a few blocks away. He advised us to get familiar with the sound because we'd be hearing a lot more of it. Infantry units patrolling security outside Đồng Tâm's perimeters had been reporting increasing signs of VC activity. The Vietnamese Lunar New Year, "Tết," was imminent and if the little people celebrated the holiday like they did in 1968 it would soon be getting a lot noisier.

The CQ's prophesy of more noise to come became reality the next evening. During the first mortar attack of the evening the captain of the Reliable Academy HQ company suffered injury when a wooden, dirt-filled ammunition box torpedoed his leg, snapping the leg back like a dry twig. He must have been on his way to the personnel shelter when the blast from a mortar dislodged the box from the revetment surrounding the HQ building. It was said that his pained sobbing and moaning could be heard up until the medics gave him a shot of morphine and removed him to the 3rd Surgical Hospital a few blocks away. I hadn't heard a thing. It was rumored that not a single trainee had risked leaving the safety of the personnel shelters to help the captain.

Throughout the night sporadic gunfire could be heard along the north perimeter and there were two more mortar attacks, one at 0230 hours and the other at 0400 hours. A military policeman from the 9th MP Battalion, SP-4 Michael Archie Blakey, was killed and numerous soldiers were injured during the attacks.

"You're in the Army now...."

3

Republic of Vietnam, January 1969

HHC & BAND, DISCOM. Someone high up in the command hierarchy of the Reliable Academy made the decision that the hostile loss of several class members, including the HQ company commander, constituted sufficient disruption of the indoctrination cycle to forego the formalities of graduation day. Not many classes passing through the academy had a trainee who received the Purple Heart, let alone multiple awards of the medal. The Reliable Academy was supposed to be a place where newcomers to the division could make mistakes without getting hurt, not be blown to smithereens by VC bombs falling out of the sky. Although I was anxious to get out of the academy, relocating a couple of hundred feet away did little to relieve my anxieties. I later learned it hadn't been the academy the VC had targeted; they were after the Navy's river craft berthed in Đồng Tâm's turning basin and the Navy's repair facilities along the east and south edges of the harbor. The harbor area, along with the heliport, was number one on the VC hit parade of things to routinely blow up. To further increase my apprehension, the DISCOM compound was uncomfortably close to the aviation POL (Petroleum Oil Lubricant) storage area, the fixed-wing airstrip, and Đồng Tâm's battery of defensive mortars. Although not a prime target in itself, DISCOM was smack-dab in the middle of a choice VC target zone. It was DISCOM's misfortune the hit and run VC mortar-men had notoriously lousy aim; and as everyone in combat knows, with explosives the collateral damage inflicted by a near miss is as deadly as a direct hit.

It was, therefore, without fanfare or ceremony that on January 16, or as the Army favored recording it, "16 JANUARY 69," I was handed Special Orders Number 16 assigning me to HHC & Band DISCOM (Headquarters & Headquarters Company & Band, Division Support Command). While others from my class awaited transportation to their gaining unit, I merely trudged across the street and took a flying leap over the drainage ditch to land on DISCOM turf. I reported to the bandmaster's office, but like Macavity the Mystery Cat the bandmaster wasn't there. Instead a passing soldier in abbreviated fatigue attire consisting of faded trousers and scuffed jungle boots spotted me on the bandstand and correctly interpreted my forlorn look as belonging to one in need of assistance. I was apparently expected. He introduced himself as Pat Townley (I would later learn he was the band's first sergeant) and immediately placed me in the care of another similarly attired passing trooper, Wilbert West, whom he introduced as the leader of the trumpet section and the person who would get me situated in my new billet.

I followed West to the center of the DISCOM compound's parade ground, whereupon he, with an informative sweep of his arm ending in an extended forefinger, identified the location of the mess hall, company HQ (Headquarters) building, DISCOM commander's trailer, separate officer and EM (Enlisted Man) showers and latrines, DISCOM battalion HQ building, band barracks, the personnel shelters, a hand pump gushing water from a well he warned should absolutely never be consumed, a tank trailer of potable water that should be used instead, and the outdoor movie area. After my rapid-fire ten-second familiarization was over, he led me into one of the barracks, halting at a ground floor cubical he identified as being my "hooch."[1] He told me my new roommate, one of the musicians left behind to fill out the company duty roster, was in the mess hall on KP. West said his name was Denver and he was a French-horn player and former high school music teacher from Detroit, Michigan, which in my mind invited the possibility of future enlightened conversation.

My duffel bag lay on top of the hooch's double bunk bed. As the new guy, I was given the less desirable upper berth. Other than the obvious necessity of having to climb up to go to bed, the upper bunk was less desirable because the height of the mattress was above the protection of the sandbag revetment surrounding the building.

My new billet consisted of 64 square feet of partitioned living space— the size of an office cubical back in The World. A four-by-eight-foot sheet of plywood fastened horizontally approximately two feet above the floor on each side of the cubical offered the illusion of privacy, which was further enhanced by two facing metal wall lockers at the open end of the partitioned space leading to the barracks' center aisle. It reduced the opening to just a few feet. A strung-bead curtain made of multiple strands filled what was left of the makeshift entranceway, lending the hooch more a tropical ambience than a military one.

The overall décor was combat rustic with overtones of South Sea island tropics, just bare-bone essentials dusted by a fine layer of grit. What little furniture there was consisted of the aforementioned tubular-steel-frame bunk bed shoved up against one partition, a homespun pine-plank writing table accessorized with shelving extending from exposed wall studs, a single folding metal chair identical to the ones I'd seen on the bandstand, and two standard-issue Army wooden footlockers. A Japanese-manufactured "Teac" reel-to-reel tape player/recorder and an oscillating desk fan rested on the tabletop. Taking everything into consideration, including the reality that this was an active combat zone, the accommodations were more than adequate, perhaps even luxurious by the standards of field troops, who when humping the bush had only a rubberized nylon poncho and liner thrown on the ground to rest upon.

The plywood partition opposite the bunk bed was partially decorated with pictures of attractive black women, obviously extracted from girlie magazines. Some of the pictures were risqué by Army standards, but none were lurid or pornographic. I surmised that my roommate was black, a realization that did not dismay me but did evoke some discomfort. My knowledge of black culture was limited to what I'd seen on television and my experience with a few black kids I'd known in high school, the latter within the context of the classroom and playground. My discomfort lay in the racial tensions of the 1960s and my knowledge that preexisting anxieties could be exacerbated in a restrictive environment like an eight-by-eight-foot cubicle. My memory flashed back to the industrial relations courses I had taken at Seton Hall University and in my mind's eye I visualized tiny white mice crowded in a box viciously vying for survival. Our close proximity might prove trying for both of us.

Wilbert West had said I could have the remainder of the day off to unpack and acquaint myself with my new surroundings. Other than making up my bunk, stowing my combat gear and personal stuff, and hanging my uniforms in the empty wall locker, which I assumed was for my use, I didn't have much else to do.

While I was arranging my socks in the upper tray of my footlocker, a soldier with a neatly trimmed mustache poked his face through the beads and introduced itself as Larry Wolf. He asked if I was the new guy, which if this wasn't the Army would have been otherwise obvious. In keeping with the spirit of my new circumstances, I told him I was.

Larry turned out to be a neat fellow. He informed me the majority of bandsmen were away from Đồng Tâm performing at one of the division's fire-support bases. A few bandsmen had been left behind assigned to DISCOM HQ company work details. Pat Townley, the band's half-naked first sergeant, hadn't been able to make the performance because of his being a bit under the weather. Trumpet section leader Will West had been left behind to supervise the work details, which on this day, Larry informed me, were more numerous than usual. Larry was one of the band's saxophone players as well as the band's drum major when one was needed. He was also the only band member in possession of a military driver's license.[2]

Although Larry's primary MOS was 11B20 Infantry, he, just as I was, had been unexpectedly assigned to the band. As I later found out, snatching music talent from the ranks of other military specialties was a common practice for division bands.

Regular Army career musicians were mostly assigned to numbered Army bands and were typically kept out of combat zones. There was only one numbered Army band serving in Vietnam,[3] and they were in Saigon, which was about as safe a place as could be found in the Republic of Vietnam, with the possible exception of the Army R&R centers at Cam Ranh Bay or Vũng Tàu. All of the other Army bands throughout Vietnam were divisional assets.

Larry generously offered to show me around Đồng Tâm. He had most of the day off; he was currently functioning in his role of band chauffeur. His only duty assignment for the day was to be awaiting the return of the band with what he called "the bandwagon," the nickname given to their deuce-and-a-half truck, at the designated pickup point at 1550 hours—3:30 p.m. civilian time. He suggested I ride shotgun and kill two birds with one bullet: I would have the opportunity to meet the band as well as see the base. Although I was beginning to like Larry, I didn't much care for his clever epigram about bullets and birds—it struck too close to home.

Not long after Larry disappeared through the beaded threshold, a sweaty, fatigued-looking black fellow zipped in. A brief flash of surprise widened his eyes when he saw me, but I assumed his exhaustive state minimized his reaction. I got the distinct impression that at the moment he couldn't care less about who I was or what I was doing in his hooch. Over the past year I'd learned how 14 hours of nonstop KP can reduce one's wants to basic needs—in this instance, a shower and rest. He whisked past me, grabbed a bar of soap and towel, and curtly announced where he was going. As he disappeared back through the beads I deduced he could only be my new roommate.

Alone once again, I shrugged my shoulders and resumed unpacking my stuff. I noticed my roommate's foot locker and wall locker both had combination locks securing their contents. Stealing was a big no-no in the stateside Army and I wondered if there was a problem at Đồng Tâm. I made a mental note to purchase a couple of locks at the PX, not the combination kind like my roommate's but the old fashioned key-lock type. My memory wasn't all that good for numbers.

In short order my roommate returned from the showers. He arrived garbed in only an olive drab terrycloth towel tightly cinched around his waist. He was tall, slender, and of light complexion with tightly cropped hair that hinted of premature balding. His demeanor was not the happy-to-see-you outgoing kind like Larry's. It was more serious, with a deportment of intellectual intensity. I thought he might be my age or a bit older. He extended his right hand in formal greeting and politely said, "Hi, I'm Al Denver. Who are you?"

I told him my name and indicated Will West had assigned me to his hooch. He nodded in acceptance and said I could use half the desk and shelving for my personal stuff. He then said he was sacking out and asked me to try to keep the noise down. Before tucking himself in, he glanced at the partition wall of magazine photos and said with unabashed warmth in his voice, "Good night, ladies." Other than his being black and having an intimate relationship with photographs, I suspected Albert Denver and I had a bit in common.

As far as I could tell, the traditional acknowledgement of rank in the sense of military courtesy didn't matter much in the band. Everyone I had

All buildings and facilities at DISCOM were built around an open area called the "parade ground." In this view the DISCOM battalion commander's bunkered, air-conditioned, mobile home occupies the center of the photograph. A portion of the band barracks is visible at the left (author's collection).

3. Republic of Vietnam, January 1969

During daylight hours contracted Vietnamese laborers overran Đồng Tâm. They literally could be spotted everywhere. In this photograph two female laborers with parasols are cutting across the north side of the DISCOM parade ground. Having once been a candidate for mama san's stew pot, canine band mascot Bummer is ascertaining the ladies *leave* the compound (author's collection).

met seemed happy interacting on a first-name basis rather than adhering to the military protocol of stating one's rank before name, such as plain old Bob instead of Specialist Four Fischer. The combat Army seemed pleasantly more sociable than its peaceful stateside counterpart.

I didn't want to disturb my roommate's slumber, so I left the barracks and sat on a low bleacher erected near the bandstand. Beyond the shower, latrines, outdoor movie screen, and the rear wall of the DISCOM transportation pool maintenance shed I could hear metal being hammered and, farther off, splashy sounds similar to the sounds kids make when they're frolicking in a swimming pool. It was bizarre, but I knew there was a rational explanation. There had to be. After all, this was the Army.

I'd have to remember to ask Larry about it.

While I sat contemplating my strange new environment, across the way an open-bed deuce-and-a-half rumbled into the transportation pool compound. It screeched to a dusty stop. The driver jumped down from the cab with the engine still running and quickly disappeared, my view blocked by the maintenance shed. The truck carried a load of stacked lumber. I wandered

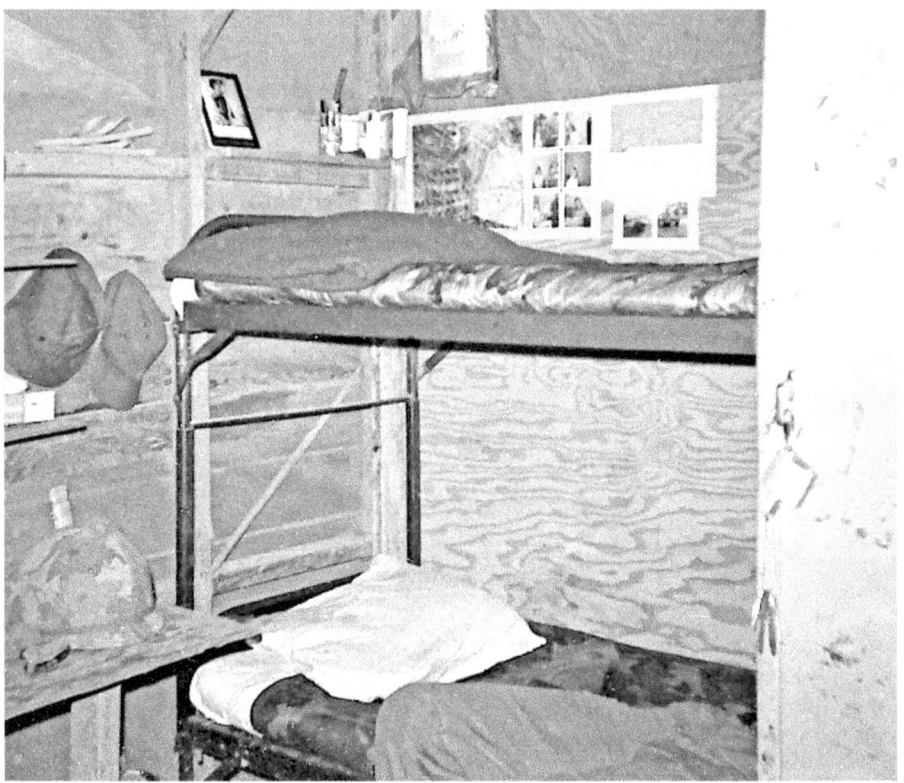

The interior of the band barracks was divided into semiprivate living quarters called "hooches." Bunk beds were double tier and made of tubular steel with interwoven sprung wire substituting for box springs. Mattresses were conventional, but only about four to six inches deep. Camouflage pattern poncho liners did double duty as blanket and bedspread (author's collection).

over to a wire fence separating DISCOM from the transportation pool area to gain a better viewing vantage. The driver returned to the truck, climbed aboard, rolled a distance forward and then slammed the gearbox into reverse and rapidly accelerated backwards. About halfway across the compound he jammed on the brakes and the momentum of the unsecured lumber sent it flying out of the truck bed. It landed neatly on the ground. A small cheer echoed from the maintenance shed—score one for the Army way.

  Just as I was turning away from the wire fence, a beat-up–looking deuce-and-a-half rolled into the DISCOM compound. My new friend Larry was at the wheel. He tooted the horn and waved and I went over to the truck. Its faded and weathered olive-drab finish exhibited numerous rust spots and jagged punctures in its thick sheet-metal hide. Both the cab roof and truck

A Boeing CH-47 Chinook medium-lift helicopter is about to set down with the 9th Infantry Division Band aboard. The outdoor engineering storage area was one of several pickup/landing sites for the band at Đồng Tâm (author's collection).

Enemy snipers often fired their weapons at targets over Đồng Tâm's perimeter berm. They climbed into trees to take their shots. In this view two Huey gunships are blasting snipers hidden in palm trees with rockets (author's collection).

bed canvasses were missing and " FTA" was stenciled in white paint on the front edge of the engine compartment hood. I'd noticed the same FTA marking stenciled on other Đồng Tâm vehicles, as well as inked on an occasional soldier's helmet cover. It didn't take much effort to deduce it meant FUCK THE ARMY. I couldn't fathom why the Green Machine tolerated such obscenities. Maybe the lifers thought it meant FOLLOW THE ARMY or FOR THE ARMY or even FIGHTING TOUGH ARMY, or perhaps they just didn't give a FF. Whatever their reasons for letting it slip by their scrutiny, it definitely meant fuck the army to every swinging dick without bars, pips, eagles, or stars on Đồng Tâm.

A cute white dog peeked over the upper edge of the cab door, its attention focused on my approach. I stepped up onto the running board, swung open the door, and took a seat on the passenger side, being careful not to sit on the pooch. Larry said his companion's name was Bummer and humorously referred to the little creature as a VC *chieu hoi*, meaning a VC political repatriate. The dog had been rescued from a villager's stew pot during a musical "win their hearts and minds" engagement somewhere out in the boonies by trumpeter Larry Corigliano. As it turned out, the dog was not only entertaining to the band but comforting as well, so the pooch was made the band's unofficial mascot.[4] I was to learn having cuddly animal mascots was common practice for most units in Vietnam.

On the drive to the prearranged pickup site, Larry pointed out Đồng Tâm's attractions. We passed a Vietnamese-operated gift shop he said was called "Charlie the Gook's Place," a high-fenced POW stockade, the 3rd Surgical Hospital, which Larry related was mostly underground, a PX, post office, a library, a snack bar, a Vietnamese-run barber shop and laundry, and a Red Cross office. I mentioned to Larry I thought I had heard splashing and happy sounds near the bandstand. Without answering he swung the vehicle around the next corner and doubled back on a street parallel to the road we had just driven. He then pointed out the EM club, with its large above-ground swimming pool alongside, a Class Six liquor store,[5] and a multidenominational religious chapel. He said there was a miniature golf course at the other end of the base. I marveled at how much Đồng Tâm resembled a huge hotel resort complex,[6] except for the sandbags, bunkers, barbed wire, and rather explosive night life.

We arrived at the PZ (Pickup Zone) just as a big Boeing CH-47 "Chinook" helicopter was touching down. Its whirling double rotors raised voluminous swirls of billowing dust from the loamy soil. Bummer let out a greeting yelp when he saw the first bandsman descend down the aircraft's rear unloading ramp. The trooper was a large black fellow carrying a big bass drum. Each of the drum's playing surfaces (known as "skins" in percussion parlance) were brightly adorned with the division's octofoil crest and bore the circular inscription 9TH INFANTRY DIVISION BAND "OLD RELIABLES."

The day was sweltering and as the group of musicians neared I could see their adherence to military dress code was far greater than that of other troops I'd seen on Đồng Tâm. Uniforms were sweaty, but they looked crisp and otherwise clean. I no longer felt out of place in my snappy new jungle fatigues. I didn't see any of the unauthorized uniform accessories other 'Nam troops favored, such as love beads, peace emblems, and disparaging (of the Army) helmet graffiti. Everyone was essentially dressed alike. The leather tips and heels of jungle boots were polished. Some bandsmen wore the regulation baseball cap,[7] while others had helmets on. Wide web belts cinched the waists of some and others had the belts draped over their shoulders. Each man carried a rifle and an instrument case. I could discern the rectangular outline of ammunition magazines in a few bandsmen's jacket and pants pockets. All walked with a tired gait born of heat exhaustion.

Although a few waved lethargically to Larry and me in greeting, no one said anything; they just tiredly hoisted themselves into the bed of the truck. Ed Johns climbed up into the cab beside me. I slid over to make room for him. Bummer obliged by scrunching up against Larry. Mister Johns' uniform displayed a subdued WO-3 (Chief Warrant Officer, Pay Grade 3) rank pin on the point of his fatigue collar. I said hello, addressing him as "Mister Johns," which was Army protocol for warrant officers. WO-3 Johns looked at me, wiped the sweat from his brow with what appeared to be the same handkerchief he had used when I was first interviewed and said, "Glad you made it through the academy in one piece, Fischer. Things aren't usually that exciting over there." That's all he said.

Larry drove us back to DISCOM.

* * *

I spent the next several days getting acclimated to my new comrades and their lifestyle. Back in The World, my roommate, Albert Denver, had been a public school music teacher with a bachelor of arts degree. He had been drafted around the same time I was, only in his case Uncle Sam's call to arms had come quite unexpectedly. Up until 1967 schoolteachers had been more or less off limits for draft boards. As the war escalated and public disfavor grew, the number of citizens volunteering for military service had declined and draft boards began filling quotas with members of professions previously passed over. Math and science teachers were still off limits, but all other categories of educator had pretty much been made fair game.[8]

During my initial acclimation period with the band the VC surprised everybody by not launching mortar, rocket, or ground attacks for a few whole days. Division was apprehensive about the inactivity and as a consequence placed the base on full alert. We each had to remain in the DISCOM compound with rifles and battle harnesses[9] at the ready to take to the perimeter to repulse a ground attack. The enemy's inactivity after so much nighttime hostility had everyone on edge. It was unnerving knowing they were out beyond the berm waiting for the opportune moment to strike. The Green Machine even issued warnings of a second Tết, the first Tết having been launched countrywide one year ago and having caught USARV completely off guard. Although the 1968 attacks had been quickly quashed, with the enemy suffering horrendous losses, the action had resulted in disastrous political repercussions on the home front and had been reputed to have convinced President Lyndon B. Johnson not to seek reelection.

On January 19 the first gig (band nomenclature appropriated from civilian life meaning a performance) I was to participate in was cancelled. We had been scheduled to play a Win Their Hearts and Minds public relations job at Vĩnh Kim, a village to the west of Đồng Tâm. Although the village wasn't all that far from the base, the Kinh Xàng Canal, which bordered Đồng Tâm's western perimeter, blocked direct access to the village, the nearest crossing being quite a few klicks northward on National Route QL-4. Earlier in the war the VC had blown up the old French bridge at the canal's outlet on the Sông Mỹ Tho. The bridge had connected Vĩnh Kim to the more direct Provincial Route TL-25.[10] The only way now to get to Vĩnh Kim by motor vehicle was the roundabout route using QL-4. Although division perimeter patrols used Vĩnh Kim as a base of operations, the area was saturated with VC, making the long drive potentially hazardous.

Had the gig not been cancelled the band would have set up around the communal stew pot and played a few tunes intended to encourage the villagers to forgive our having mowed down their kin with our bullets, burned their villages with our Zippo lighters, defiled the graves of their ancestors with our bombs, and ruined their crops and their health with our Agent Orange. It was, admittedly, a more benevolent approach to winning the war than our earlier and far deadlier "Search and Destroy" method. Now we were going to win their friendship by enriching their lives with Cole Porter and Irving Berlin show tunes, occasionally enlivened with a snappy John Phillip Sousa march, the latter to let them know we were, above all else, a military band.

The socioeconomic environment of Mekong Delta rice farmers was absolutely feudal. In every sense of the word they were peasants, dirt poor unfortunates who lived in poverty and worked land they did not own. Most

3. Republic of Vietnam, January 1969

of their dwellings were palm frond huts without electricity, water, or sanitation. Live music, or any music at all for that matter, didn't play into their lifestyles. Their primary form of entertainment was the euphoric high they enjoyed from chewing beetle nuts, which unfortunately also blackened their teeth, which in the big picture didn't matter much since they lost their teeth early in life due to nonexistent dental hygiene and medical care. In the Delta the typical 30-year-old peasant looked to be about 50 years old. They endured a hard lifestyle and U.S. military policy made it even harder for them.

So, instead of winning the hearts and minds of the peasants of Vĩnh Kim that morning, the band practiced on the bandstand. The session lasted an hour and a half, after which time those of us who didn't have a company work detail were free to do whatever we liked. The base swimming pool was close enough to DISCOM to be considered not off limits. Some of us beat the heat and tension by swimming. I hung around the hooch with Albert. He wrote letters and I prepared my short-timer's countdown calendar[11] so I could know how close I was to getting out of 'Nam each and every day.

As it turned out, nothing much came of the alert and the next day, January 20, the band flew to an engagement at Vĩnh Long. Vĩnh Long was beaucoup (French for mucho and pronounced boo-coo by GIs) klicks southwest of Đồng Tâm and a large city by Mekong Delta standards. It was situated on the south bank of the Cô Chiên River, or *Sông Cô Chiên* as the Vietnamese called it. Vĩnh Long was the site where Major General George S. Eckhardt had landed the initial contingent of 5,000 troops of the 9th Infantry Division back on December 16, 1966. The band had preceded the division ashore and greeted them with patriotic military marches as they disembarked from the Navy landing craft. Also on hand had been pretty Vietnamese girls who draped Hawaiian style leis around the necks of the troops as they waded ashore. The occasion had been recorded by the news media as having been festive—a colorful introduction to marching into the horrific grinder of guerilla warfare.

Vĩnh Long was a hub of U.S. military activity, being home to both U.S. Navy and U.S. Army aviation units. The band's gig was a concert for the entertainment of the Army's 114th "Knights of the Air" Attack Helicopter Company (AHC). They operated out of Shannon-Wright Compound, so named in honor of the 114th's first two combat fatalities: SP-5 Wyley Wright, KIA (Killed in Action) March 9, 1964, and Lieutenant Kenneth Arthur Shannon, KIA March 15, 1964.

A now fully clothed Sergeant Townley signaled our departure to the rotary-wing airfield with the unmilitary order, "Let's saddle up, cats." The size of the band needed for the performance at Vĩnh Long required the transport capacity of one CH-47 Chinook helicopter, a medium-lift aircraft that could accommodate approximately 23 musicians and their weapons and musical gear. My first Chinook ride turned out to be noisy, breezy, and uncomfortable. There were two open hatches in the fuselage, one forward and the other above the rear ramp. The former was the most interesting. It was cut into the floor in the center of the walkway and was large enough to pass the bulk of a clumsy or distracted bandsman. Retractable bench seats made of tubular aluminum upholstered with bright red webbing ran the length of the passenger compartment and offered a spectacular view to those seated on either side of the hatch. Whenever we crossed over an expanse of water, and there were several expanses to cross, the helicopter shook. It was scary until I realized it's what helicopters do over water.

Other than the ride, the gig was uneventful. Although it was my first exposure to helicopter flight and my first time outside Đồng Tâm's protective berm, I wrote my parents that the big event of the day had been my purchase of a quarter interest in a small refrigerator. Go figure! One had to get one's priorities straight in the 'Nam.

By January 22 I had pretty much settled into the routine of my new lifestyle. A typical day at DISCOM entailed reveille formation at 0600 hours, then after a few minutes standing in roll-call formation *rest* until time for police call[12] at 0715 hours (picking up discarded refuse in a designated area of responsibility), then after about 10 minutes of gathering tossed cigarette butts eat breakfast and *rest* until the Reliable Academy graduation ceremony gig at 0840 hours (only if assigned to perform and there was a class graduating), then *rest* until band practice at 0930 hours (every other day), then following 90 minutes of practice, *rest* until 1200 hours, then after 60 minutes for chow call, *rest* until 1600 hours—the official end of the workday. Dinner was served at 1700 hours. This schedule was adhered to each and every day the band didn't have an assigned musical engagement on or off Đồng Tâm. On the days there was no band practice or Reliable Academy graduation ceremony scheduled, rest was substituted. Being a member of the dance band combo or having bugler duty altered the routine a bit, but not enough to cause much stress or loss of *rest*. The killer was KP duty. Lasting 14 to 16 hours and under the complete supervision of unsociable, nasty Army cooks, it was a rather unpleasant, humiliating, and sweaty duty that ensnared everyone in the band below pay grade E-6 every 16 days. Still, it beat humping the bush, or so I was told.

Having so much free time was great but soon led to boredom. Reading, napping, and avoiding being volunteered for work details became my prime daily activity, which I occasionally integrated with a visit to the PX, a quick

3. Republic of Vietnam, January 1969

dip in the pool, or a stroll over to the harbor to examine the Navy boats. Writing letters also became a favorite alleviator of boredom. The temperature was blazing hot, which made fatigue a common ailment. Salt tablets were mandatory. I liked taking mine with Kool-Aid. I'd walk over to the mess hall outdoor seating area where the cooks typically set up two insulated marmite jugs on a table under an overhang of the roof, one filled with ice-cold water and the other with Kool-Aid. The DISCOM mess hall was named Cal's Place for an unknown reason and had the responsibility of feeding division visitors as well as transients and was, subsequently, a bit larger than most other mess halls on Đồng Tâm. Because of its dual function, it also required more KPs. During the day, the KP roster was supplemented with Vietnamese civilian laborers, mostly female. They arrived after breakfast and left before supper and functioned primarily as dishwashers and grease-trap cleaners.

It was surprising how many Vietnamese civilian laborers were employed on Đồng Tâm during daylight hours.[13] Every unit compound had several. In addition to supplementing the KP roster, civilians also provided maid and valet services for the officers, assisted with construction projects, cleaned company latrines, operated concessions on base, functioned as nursing assistants, or did just about anything they could do to earn a couple of MPC bucks.

I witnessed a memorable event involving a Vietnamese civilian one lazy afternoon on a return trip from the PX. I was walking along the DISCOM access drive when a couple of enemy mortars exploded nearby. I'd already learned when you can feel the concussion they're way too close. It was unusual for the VC to launch a daytime mortar attack (they didn't want to risk hurting the Vietnamese civilian works, some of whom were also their informers and, very likely, their comrades) and the blasts caught me completely off guard. DISCOM had recently lost a well-liked ARVN (Army of the Republic of Vietnam) interpreter to a random VC mortar that happened to explode near where I was walking at that very moment. The entrance to the Air Force weather detachment personnel shelter was just a few feet away. It bordered the driveway opposite the mess hall. In my haste to avoid becoming a statistic, I plowed into the baffled entrance of the bunker, careening off one sandbag wall into the other, and landed flat on my back inside the shelter. As my eyes adjusted to the dim interior lighting, an attractive Vietnamese girl, formally attired in a slinky purple silk dress materialized above me. A dozen or so candles illuminated her finely sculpted face and figure. As I rose to my feet a short-stemmed martini glass was thrust toward me accompanied by a deep manly greeting: "Glad you could stop in, relax and have a drink." The bartender wore the insignia of a light colonel. I assumed he was one of the weather pilots. I didn't have to assume much about the pretty Vietnamese girl. Her bearing and overall appearance were far too attractive and sophisticated to be a local peasant gal, so I surmised she was the live-in lady of the house—in this instance, of the barracks. She had probably been imported from Saigon. The higher up the chain of command the more flexible became the rules and the more luxurious the accommodations, or so it seemed.

After another evening of relatively light enemy activity, the alert status reverted to everything's OK, and life on Đồng Tâm returned to being as normal as it could be, given the circumstances of war. My first KP duty occurred on January 27. In anticipation of the dreaded event I arose at 0330 hours, a few minutes before the CQ's head popped through the beaded curtain to ascertain whether or not I was awake. He waved a silent greeting before his head disappeared back through the curtain. I was careful not to disturb Albert. He needed his rest to get through the boredom of the upcoming day. As per band protocol, I had reserved one set of jungle fatigues for musical engagements. They were kept clean, starched, pressed and ready for use in a moment's notice. I used a second set for casual wear around Đồng Tâm and a third solely for work details. Following the same logic and instruction, I maintained one pair of jungle boots in almost STRAC condition and wore the other pair the rest of the time. Spit shining wasn't a requirement for the 9th Infantry Division Band, hence the "almost STRAC" stipulation. Brush polishing saved a lot of time and effort, not that it mattered greatly, since the band's schedule didn't require that much of our time anyway.

I finished dressing and dutifully reported to the mess hall. The cooks were busily scampering around preparing for breakfast. I was a wee bit early and my presence was not immediately acknowledged, so I grabbed a cup of coffee. The oversight didn't last long. Eventually a scruffy-looking cook's assistant whose uniform resembled something nasty from the grease trap asked if I was a KP. He had to ask because however unlikely it seemed, I could have been a transient visitor in need of coffee. Although I was wearing my designated dirty working fatigues, they were still new enough to appear STRAC to the cook. Although he was momentarily confused by my appearance, I properly identified myself as a KP and he took charge of my activities for the day. Since I was the first KP to arrive, I was given my choice of jobs. The choices were narrow: work in the dining areas wiping down anything that didn't move; maintain the supply of beverages, trays, flatware, officer's plates, etc.; serve officers in their private dining room; wash trays, flatware, and dishes in the kitchen; or scrub pots and pans in the dingy, dark recesses of the backroom. Although the job I chose garnered a look of incredulity from my temporary supervisor, I opted for the pan scrubbing. It was nasty work most other KPs avoided, but I liked it. My logic was simple, based upon

3. Republic of Vietnam, January 1969

my experience in stateside mess halls—there were far fewer pots and pans to be cleaned than trays, flatware, and dishes. But most important, the job didn't entail sucking up to anyone. The cooks tended to leave the pots and pan scrubbers alone with their chores, which I appreciated. The motivation behind their benevolence was understandable: *you* do the nasty work and *we'll* cut you some slack. Sometimes one of the cooks would feel sorry enough for you to send back an unfortunate Vietnamese laborer to help out.

There was a Vietnamese mother and daughter team who always seemed to gravitate to the scrub room. They were appropriately nicknamed, "momma-san" and "baby-san." Momma-san was perpetually in some cycle of nursing and had plenty of spare mother's milk to squirt in the face of a KP who aroused her disfavor. Baby-san was an attractive teenage girl and momma-san discouraged flirtatious advances with a shot of her milk. If I remember correctly, her aim had been rather good.

I can't speak for all Army cooks, but the attitudes of the ones at DISCOM toward KPs reminded me of a DI or two back at Fort Dix. I suspect their hostility had something to do with the hot greasy conditions they labored under. It tended to make them a bit surly. KP started at 0400 and typically lasted until 2000 hours. That's 16 hours of heat and grease that also tended to make KPs a bit surly. I didn't like working in the mess hall and always preferred guard duty to KP. Some relief from the HQ company work roster would eventually come to me when Mister Johns *volunteered* me to the position of band supply sergeant and office clerk. I was exempted from all company work details, except guard duty and the dreaded KP.

In further regard to cooks and the chow they served at the DISCOM mess hall, it was usually too Latino-spicy for my taste. I ended up eating breakfast, which was OK, and stacked my own sandwich for lunch (foregoing the USARV-promised hot meal). I passed on supper, except for dessert, which was usually some kind of pudding, ice cream, or pastry. Thankfully the cooks weren't authorized to spice up the eggs, bacon, pancakes, toast, or cold cuts and cheese. On one occasion after the VC dropped a mortar round alongside the kitchen and shrapnel perforated every DISCOM pot and pan, we ate vintage Korean War–era C rations[14] packaged in olive-drab tin cans from the Greenland Quartermaster Supply Depot. The cooks dumped the tins into galvanized 32-gallon garbage cans of boiling water (the water was heated by portable propane heaters that hung inside each garbage can) and we ate our MACV-promised hot meal with melted cheese, melted chocolate bars, hot cookies, hot peaches, and hot whatever else was in the can. You know what? It actually tasted great compared to mess hall chow!

To complement meals the mess hall served several different beverages of varying palatability. Hot coffee, Kool-Aid, and ice water were available at all meals and throughout the day but tasted of chemical purification. The chemical taste notwithstanding, all three tasted better than the milk the mess hall served. The stuff came from Foremost Dairies, Inc., a mid-western U.S. agribusiness formed by retail magnate J.C. Penney to manufacture recombined milk products. They supplied the 9th Infantry Division with bulk milk packaged in cardboard-sleeved plastic bags designed for dispenser machines and quart sizes packaged in orange and white waxed-paper cartons. Foremost Dairies divided whole milk into anhydrous fat and nonfat solids at their U.S. plant and after removing the water shipped the solids to a Foremost Dairies plant in Japan[15] where the solids were reconstituted into whole milk by the addition of specially treated water. The liquid milk was then shipped on freighters to the Port of Saigon. Foremost Dairies-processed milk wasn't as tasty as real milk taken directly from cows, but their chocolate-flavored variety was acceptable.

One sweltering afternoon after having played a gig at some godforsaken place, the band returned to the DISCOM compound to face an overwhelming odor akin to that of decomposing flesh. It saturated the air in and around the barracks. Larry and I hopped into the bandwagon and drove around Đồng Tâm in search of the odor's source. We found it a few blocks away in a drainage ditch alongside one of the base roads. The ditch ran white, full of putrefying milk! It stank to high heaven. Someone had disposed of a large quantity of the stuff in the ditch, never considering the effect the heat would have on it or on the troops who had to breathe it. The smell eventually went away. I suspect the engineers pumped and flushed out the ditch.

As I've previously stated, I found the food served in the DISCOM mess hall too spicy for my taste. I did, however, enjoy the bread, which was freshly baked each day. The bread came from a local civilian bakery and was similar in taste and consistency to a French baguette but a bit thicker in girth. The crust was crunchy and the inner part soft and tasty. I enjoyed the bread without reservation until I learned the little black specs dotting the soft innards were *bugs!* Sanitation was not a big thing in the Delta. The Green Machine undoubtedly felt the high temperatures used to bake bread would kill off any harmful effects of baked bugs. I eventually accepted the yummy taste of the bread over the uncertainty of the bugs.

As bad as the week had begun for me with KP duty heading the activities, it began even worse for the 15th Combat Engineer Battalion. While I was feeling sorry for myself for having KP, two engineers lay dying on Đồng Tâm's perimeter.[16] They'd been operating heavy equipment near the rifle range, working on expanding Đồng Tâm's north perimeter, when they came under

3. Republic of Vietnam, January 1969

sniper fire from VC hidden in the trees adjacent to the construction site. The noise of their bulldozers had drowned out the gunfire and they were picked off one after the other until someone noticed what was happening. It had been a sobering event underscoring the dangers that faced every soldier on Đồng Tâm. The same fate could befall any one of us at any time, for we dwelt among our enemy deep within his territory.

At 0400 hours the next morning the lights unexpectedly went on and I was introduced to my first "shakedown inspection." For those unfamiliar with the term, a shakedown is a surprise inspection wherein the DISCOM HHC commander, accompanied by his first sergeant, rifles through one's personal belongings in search of illegal paraphernalia such as drugs, U.S. greenbacks, pornography, whiskey, unauthorized weapons, ammunition for authorized weapons, or anything else the Green Machine deemed objectionable at the time. They found nothing of particular interest among my things, except for the Greek inscription I had neatly scripted in black magic marker on the front of my wall locker: *Vitae Summa Brevis Spem Nos Vetet Incohare Longam.* The foreign words had piqued the curiosity of the first sergeant, who, pointing at them, asked what they meant. I told him they were from the introduction to Homer's first book of *Odes* and were translated as "the shortness of life prevents us from entertaining far-off hopes." The sergeant stared pensively at the inscription, rubbed the stubble on his chin, and said, "Oh." He obviously wasn't all that familiar with Homer.

The closing days of January played out as the month had begun, with a bang. The VC had resumed their nighttime routine of mortaring, three rounds each session. They must have been Dr Pepper fans, for they sent them flying into Đồng Tâm at 2200 hours, 0200 hours, and 0400 hours, 10–2–4, just like the old Dr Pepper slogan, but with a 12-hour time shift. The incoming mortars came with such punctuality several band members kept resetting their alarm clocks to go off five minutes prior to the anticipated times in order to avoid the rush to the personnel shelters in the dark amid the terror of exploding ordnance and panicked troops. On such extended occasions of enemy activity, others, like my roommate, Albert, who said he was superstitious, simply stayed overnight and slept on the shelters' wooden benches. A few of us remained in our bunks, victims of the debilitating daytime heat and the dreary existence that combined to induce a profound exhaustion of body and malaise of mind. My remaining in my bunk was not a defiant act of courage, nor was it foolhardy. I soon concluded that by the time one grabbed the required flak vest, helmet, and rifle and slipped into one's boots, the third round had already hit. Running to the personnel shelters was a panacea for those who didn't fully comprehend the reality of the situation. The VC fired their mortars quickly without specific targeting. Fate guided their trajectory, or maybe it was a Higher Power. Oddly enough, after having experienced 23 years of indoctrination in the Roman Catholic faith, which included a Jesuit-inspired higher education, only when engulfed in a nightmare existence of hellish proportions was I beginning to accept God's presence, not see Him, not hear Him, but *sense* Him. He was like a benevolent phantom patiently watching and caring in the shadows well beyond the limits of my understanding.

4

Republic of Vietnam, February 1969

The calendar rolled around to February with the VC continuing their sporadic *all or nothing* pattern of nighttime mortaring. The DISCOM compound was close enough to the Four Deuces Mortar Platoon that if the wind was right and you were paying attention you could hear the rounds slide down the tubes before the big 82mm mortars fired. The platoon consisted of four weapons mounted on two barges modified with sandbagged gun emplacements, two per barge, and bunkered living quarters for the mortar men sandwiched between the emplacements. During my time at Đồng Tâm, Four Deuces was manned by troops from 2nd Brigade's 3/60th Infantry Battalion. The guns were kept at the ready with round-the-clock crews billeted aboard the barges.

When the VC fired mortars into Đồng Tâm the paths of their incoming projectiles were triangulated by radar receivers mounted on three communications towers[1] and their reverse trajectory instantly calculated by computer to yield firing coordinates for Four Deuces' tubes. Typically you'd hear three LOUD bangs (incoming) followed by a succession of LOUDER bangs (outgoing) followed by the piercing wail of Đồng Tâm's alert siren. This occurred three times a night and made sleeping very difficult.

As I have previously mentioned, during the quieter daylight hours and on alternate days when the band had no musical performances scheduled we rehearsed on the bandstand for about 90 minutes and afterwards those of us not assigned to company work details were free to do as we pleased. There was always plenty of slack time to write letters home or dictate voice-mail tapes, visit the snack bar, go swimming at the EM Club, or shop at the PX. Once settled into the routine, daily life became rather humdrum. I had brought my old Ansco 35mm rangefinder camera with me and enjoyed snapping photographs of my fellow bandsmen, exotic-looking Vietnamese laborers, and any other subject I found interesting at Đồng Tâm. I initially shot only black and white film and for something more to do developed it myself at the base arts and crafts center, which had a photo lab available for troops who were into processing their own prints. My attempts in the darkroom proved rather feeble, so I quit trying and instead began utilizing the services of the PX, which offered black and white processing. When I eventually gravitated to color slides I used Kodak prepaid mailers purchased at the PX and had the finished slides mailed to my parents' home.

The prints processed by the PX were done locally and were always a bit too high in contrast, which resulted in their having a dark grainy quality more a black and white than a continuous gray tone. I suspect this was the result of processing the film and prints in a darkroom with higher than ideal room temperatures, which elevated the processing bath temperatures and made the chemicals difficult to manage, as well as quick to kick out of useful life. Many of the negatives the PX processed for me are marred by tiny white specks caused by the less-than-ideal laboratory conditions and chemicals pushed beyond their limits. Still, the PX prints were better than the ones I made at Arts & Crafts.

February 5 marked my first musical engagement away from Đồng Tâm where the band utilized ground transportation. One month earlier, on January 12, enemy sappers had blown up two spans of the old French bridge carrying National Highway QL-4 over the Kinh Xàng (Kinh is Vietnamese for canal) in the village of Long Đinh. QL-4 was known as the "People's Road" and was a vital military and civilian transportation link between Saigon and the Mekong Delta region. Erecting a new bridge had been a joint effort of Company E, 15th Engineer Battalion, and Company B, 7th ARVN Engineers. The damaged structure was removed and replaced with a standard, single-lane, 90-foot U.S. Army tactical Bailey bridge, which resembled something made from a kid's giant Erector set.[2] Long Đinh was close enough to Đồng Tâm to justify ground transportation,[3] so the band climbed aboard two deuce-and-a-half trucks and off we went. To reach the bridge, a roundabout route utilizing both paved and dirt roads had to be followed. It was unnerving to drive unescorted in what the infantry referred to as "Indian Country." Everyone carried M-16 rifles except Mister Johns, who favored a Colt .45 automatic pistol, and Larry Wolf, who preferred the M-79 grenade launcher, a weapon that fired either a 40mm explosive shell that armed itself after so many revolutions or a large-caliber shotgun antipersonnel round if the enemy got too close. I grabbed 15 magazines of ammunition (about 270 rounds) and stuffed some of them into my pockets, into a bandolier slung across my chest, into my trumpet case, and, for extra measure, a few single cartridges in the stretch webbing of my flak vest. I might have overdone it. Most of the bandsmen took only a few magazines and some others just the one they locked and loaded in their rifle. Before departing, SFC Townley had said we could take all of the ammunition we wanted. There had been a large stack of steel ammo boxes on the bandstand, and I just dug into them and took as much as I felt comfortable carrying.

The countryside we drove through was staggeringly beautiful, with a primordial antiquity no longer found back in The World. The terrain was dead flat and radiant in a panoramic explosion of brilliant green colors. It was an agricultural checkerboard of open grassy pastures and lush rice paddies crisscrossed by earthen dikes. Bordering stands of untamed tropical growth lined the fields and paddies, delineating ownership. Occasionally the route we followed pierced a dense stand of jungle that funneled the road into a narrow tunnel of vegetation. Most of the dwellings along the roadsides were homespun, made of branches and thatch that oozed tropical charm. If it hadn't been for the rampant poverty everywhere and the nauseatingly sweet stench that filled the air, one might have reasonably thought it a secular Garden of Eden.

During January 1969 enemy sappers blew up the old French bridge over the Kinh Xàng in the hamlet of Long Định. The crossing was vital in that it carried National Route QL-4, the "People's Road," over the canal. Working together U.S. and ARVN engineers replaced it with a 90-foot tactical Bailey bridge. The 9th Infantry Division Band performed at the dedication ceremony (author's collection).

The bridge gig at Long Đinh was my first road trip off Đồng Tâm and was, by no small measure, mentally harrowing. Driving along the rural back roads of the Mekong Delta through Indian Country frazzled my nerves, so much so I had taken over 250 rounds of ammunition with me! (courtesy Larry Wolf).

Upon arriving at our destination the band set up alongside one of the bridge approaches. We slung our loaded weapons over our shoulders and readied our musical instruments to play our national anthem. Speeches were made by military and local officials and afterwards we enlivened the lifer-rich atmosphere with a few morale-rousing John Philip Sousa marches. When the ceremony concluded we packed up our instruments and drove back to Đồng Tâm. I returned 14 magazines to the armory. I kept one magazine in defiance of the no-ammo-on- Đồng-Tâm rule. In typical Army fashion no one in the armory said a thing about the missing magazine, nor do I think they noticed or even cared. That's the way business was done in the 'Nam. The reports were submitted in triplicate, but the reality was what you wanted it to be.

4. Republic of Vietnam, February 1969

On the return trip from Long Đinh I not only had the opportunity to get a second close-up view of provincial life in the Mekong Delta but also to ponder the logic of Army rationale. The band had piled aboard unarmed and unarmored trucks and driven eight miles in each direction through VC-infested territory to play at a bridge crossing the enemy had recently blown up. We had no medic, no radio, and no plan in case we were attacked. We drove into harm's way passing heavily escorted convoys, groups of armed locals, shot-up hulks of previously ambushed vehicles, and barbed-wire defensive positions that bristled everywhere. The black silk pajama dress worn by the friendly Vietnamese peasants we passed alongside the road was identical to the dress of the unfriendly VC. From the perspective of appearance you couldn't tell the good guys from the bad, hence our standing orders not to shoot unless fired upon. It was an oriental version of the American Revolutionary War battle of Concord-Lexington, except in this contemporary version you couldn't distinguish who the enemy was. You had to either see into their hearts or risk getting shot.

Concerning the topic of the Vietnamese farmer, before experiencing Vietnam the concept of peasant was alien to my middle-class upbringing. I knew America hosted migrant workers, vagrants, and other indigents, but never had I encountered peasants. The Mekong Delta was predominately inhabited by rice farmers. Although I wasn't exactly certain what distinguished their labeling from their counterparts in America, I instinctively recognized them as peasants.

The peasant population in the Mekong Delta lived in home-built shacks U.S. troops called hooches, the same name we applied to our own living quarters. They constructed their crude dwellings from natural or recycled materials. One exceptionally distinctive hooch I remember seeing had been cleverly fashioned using homespun siding made of discarded metal Coca-Cola cans. The builder had cut off the ends, slit the cans lengthwise, flattened them out, and then nailed each flattened sheet to the walls of the hooch in the manner of overlapping shingles. It was an eye catching roadside advertisement for Coke, Coke, Coke....

The average Vietnamese hooch consisted of one room, a thatched roof made of palm fronds, a dirt floor, very little furniture, and an open hearth in the center. Their custom was to sleep on woven mats. In the Mekong Delta sanitation was not a big issue. Rice paddies were fertilized with human waste. The peasants just hung their butts out over the dike and dropped a load. Riverfront hooches not near rice paddies typically had a single plank dock built out over the river. Papa-san would squat while momma-san washed their rice bowls a few feet downstream. Peasants didn't enjoy long lives or good health. The putrid odor of the rice paddies combined with the stench of decaying fish gave the Delta a distinctive, spicy, sweet fragrance that permeated the region.

The conditions surrounding their lifestyle and economic circumstances made the Vietnamese peasant a natural forager. Their VC relatives created wonderfully frightening things with our refuse. To them our discards were a cache of intelligence data, parts for booby traps, and construction materials. Often a ramshackle hooch not much larger than one or two of our metal CONEX (Container Express) overseas shipping containers would have a quarter-ton utility truck or M-35 cargo truck decorated with U.S. markings parked alongside. To prevent theft, all vehicles on Đồng Tâm had to be secured with a padlock and heavy chain threaded through the steering wheel and cinched around the clutch pedal. During daylight hours Đồng Tâm hosted an army of civilian workers, some of whom were undoubtedly VC or VC-controlled.[4]

On February 8, VC mortars caught DISCOM unit supply specialist SP-5 Alvin Lee Shadwick out in the open. He was the first DISCOM hostile KIA to occur during my tour and his death made quite an impression on me. But after weeks of being pounded with mortars and rockets, the maniacal aspect of living in fear had lost some of its psychological edge. Mail call became more critical to my mental condition than fear of VC mortars and rockets. A day without a letter from home was as devastating as the mortar attacks were terrifying. The fact that someone in the real world remembered you and appreciated the morass your country had placed you in generated an indescribable euphoria when a letter arrived with your name on it—and the depth of depression when one did not. Although my parents were faithful in their correspondence, my girlfriend was not. I soon began experiencing the anger and despair of romantic abandonment.

During the second week of February, after a couple of days of relative quiet, the VC resumed their Dr Pepper schedule of mortaring. Once again sleep deprivation became an issue. Being kept awake dulled our senses and sapped little morale remained among us. Physical exhaustion had some of us on the precipice of emotional despair, which promoted irritability and carelessness. For some troops, whenever the mortars fell terror reigned and when they did not apprehension about when the next bombardment occurred. A few members of the band began displaying bizarre behavior. I won't mention any names, but one fellow spent his off-duty time screaming obscenities into a tape recorder and then playing them back; another listened to the same record over and over until someone on the verge of being driven to insanity said something to him about it, whereupon he, in a fit of rage, smashed his record player to the ground (this occurred a couple of days after he, a career NCO, gave an impromptu lecture admonishing us to keep our tempers in check). The VC, heat, boredom, and lack of sleep were making us hypersensitive to just about anything encroaching upon our intellectual or physical space. Each of us endured the psychological effects of prolonged exposure to terror and physical exhaustion in different ways. I channeled my apprehension into cynicism about the army and those who commanded us. The war had never had made much sense to me, and I felt trapped between a quagmire of political ineptitude and my conservative, perhaps in the case of Vietnam, *archaic*, sense of Duty-Honor-Country.

To escape the reality of my existence, I read novels, sometimes voraciously consuming up to three a week. I could have read even more, but I instead began spending an increasingly larger percentage of my off-duty hours simply napping, from exhaustion or depression or a combination of both. My letters home, which initially had been objective and informative, slowly eroded to trite topics of a more domestic nature, such as send more of this or don't send that or how is so and so doing? I wrote home more often and revealed increasingly less about the war, although my dissatisfaction with the army and my situation continued to be an underlying theme. The Army was stupid, my superiors were stupid, the war was stupid, etc., etc. I failed to realize that I was stupid. I was participating in the making of history and all I wanted to do was complain to my parents about it! Along the lines of stupid, every now and then I'd interject a brief mention of an attack, sometimes detailing destruction, death, or injury but always failing to recognize that combat-related occurrences commonplace on Đồng Tâm could sound horrifying to those on the home front, especially those who were desperately worried about the safety of their loved ones.

As the days passed I began degrading the Vietnamese in nonhuman terms. In my mind they had become objects, *things* that needed to be defended or killed depending upon the circumstances of the moment. My cold-hearted attitude may have reflected the attitude the Green Machine held toward its soldiers. We were *things* to be maneuvered and manipulated, to do or die trying. As far as the locals were concerned, I found it rather incomprehensible to interact with and respect a population that was friendly during the day and hostile at night. Nothing made much sense in the 'Nam, and I was beginning to fit right in.

* * *

Although the passage of many years now makes understanding my negativity toward the Vietnamese people difficult to fathom, let alone explain, I suspect my callousness was rooted in a normal human reaction in an effort to psychologically shield inner emotions from ongoing tragedy and horror. Little did I know at the time that my personality was actually undergoing a subtle transformation from civilian caring to military callousness. My emotional highs and lows were converging upon each other. The bowels of despair and the loftiness of joy I once felt as a civilian were losing their divergent impact. *The sole purpose of my being had evolved into that of survival.* Without any realization on my part, Vietnam had whittled away my intellect, my morality, and my respect for humanity down to animalistic proportions. I had crossed over the line of human compassion and now consider *anything* or *anyone* threatening my survival as the enemy.

When I first arrived in-country I had possessed all the sheltered naivety of an educated, middle-class, pre-baby boomer[5] nurtured in all the luxuries the rapidly expanding post-World War II American economy made available to families of modest means. I'd been blessed with loving parents and raised in Roman Catholic Christianity. I had little doubt the bachelor of science degree I had earned from Seton Hall University would one day open the doors of career opportunity to me. I was well read in the literature of the ages and a fairly competent musician. I cherished the synergy of words and music and how they could be melded into poetry and song. The promise of the future offered only the best possibilities for me. Vietnam, unfortunately, undermined much of this by altering my basic perception of morality and self. The meaning of life wasn't about satisfaction of career or the level of consumerism one attained, as I had formerly believed, it was about *survival*. Unlike the psychological *threat* of nuclear holocaust we children of the 1950s and 1960s were indoctrinated under, the threat of Vietnam was manifest: hell was 20 air hours from home, and I was stuck smack-dab in the middle of it.

My transformation from *who I had been to who I became* began the moment I arrived in-country and intensified throughout the months of January and February. It finally culminated on February 23. I use this date not because it is a fact of scientific measurability but because a landmark event occurred on that particular day that conveniently marked the change. Although I had initially been naïve in my understanding or acceptance that someone was trying to kill me (I had no desire to kill or hurt anyone), the inhospitable quality of the Mekong Delta environment, furthered by the presence of unrelenting fear and lack of adequate rest, had subtlety eroded my sense of morality to the extent that my perception of the boundary between right and wrong—*biblical Good and Evil*—had imperceptibly shifted from mainstream civilized to jungle predatory. After two months of exposure to the worst of my preconceived fears, I could kill or be killed without remorse because intellectually I had accepted the readjusted parameters of my own moral values. I had finally evolved into what the Army had trained me to be, an ultimate weapon. Perhaps because of my age, level of maturity, or education it just took a bit longer for this to happen.

In regard to ultimate weapons, and to amplify my observations, one day I encountered a familiar face cutting across the DISCOM compound. Jay Trichler had been one of the guys in my BCT training platoon back at Fort Dix. My having once been his designated platoon guide had made me partially responsible for guiding and monitoring his training. In the fashion of a mother hen recognizing one of her chicks, I immediately spotted him. He had evolved from the oppressed nervous kid I remembered from back in BCT to an ultimate weapon in faded jungle fatigues and floppy bush hat. The recognition had been mutual and he dallied briefly enough to inform me he was with one of the division's infantry battalions—a designation I no longer remember. Although his unit was on four-day stand down, he was looking forward to getting out of Đồng Tâm and back to the field where life was quieter and less hectic at night. When he learned I was with the division band his attitude turned aloof, as if I, a pussy-ass bandsman,[6] hadn't been dodging the same mortars and rockets as he had. His attitude was typical of infantry troops. Their despicable existence in the bush, which in the Mekong Delta included slogging waist deep through leech-infested rice paddy muck and mire, instilled within them a heightened unit esprit de corps that more often than not blossoms among those who communally endure adverse conditions. The phenomenon is universal enough to suggest it is part of the overall Human Condition. In a community such as a military unit, one's association and associates are viewed as being tougher or better than anyone else's. Although the infantry MOS is absolutely entry-level Army—meaning no specific skills required—it is officially hyped by those who are a part of it as "The Queen of Battle."[7] The process of BCT qualifies every swinging dick in the Army for the position of infantry rifleman and expects every soldier to perform as one if and when the need arises. Those of us with specialized skills, like musician, essentially had *two* jobs: perform what you were trained to do and also fight the enemy when necessary. This occurred during Tết '68 when support troops of the 9th Infantry Division, the only reserve troops immediately available at the time, were rushed to Saigon to engage the VC with the infantry at the Y Bridge over the Saigon River. In all fairness to the ground pounders, their primary mission is to ferret out the enemy and destroy him, while the type of combat that support troops typically engage in is more defensive in nature.

So, as I was saying, on February 23 my perception of reality was indelibly altered. The day had begun like any other day at Đồng Tâm—*crappy*. Reveille, roll call, work detail assignments, blah, blah, blah. Towards evening, after twilight descended and the stars were twinkling, Four Deuces fired several rounds—nothing unusual. My first clue there was a problem came when one of the shorter fellows (not height, but time left to serve in-country) inexplicably burst out of the barracks at full gallop attired in bed dress (underwear) and abbreviated combat gear (flak vest, helmet, unlaced jungle boots, and rifle). He swung out of the door in a wide arc so as to compensate for the centrifugal force effect of the speed he was running at in order to reach the nearest personnel shelter. This also was not unusual. At times, otherwise solid troops would lose their composure and freak out. This fellow was a short-timer; his behavior was completely understandable. This particular event transpired during a colorful display of perimeter activity. I was on top of the shower water tank platform taking photographic time exposures of the brilliant green flares drifting over the east berm and trying to capture the distinctive path of the green tracer bullets spewing out of the perimeter bunkers when SGG William Jenson, the band's el primo flautist, shouted up to me that we didn't use green flares or green tracer bullets.

The enemy was probing us!

In my intense desire to photograph the scene I had confused incoming mortar detonations for a fire mission of Four Deuces. Apparently the VC had launched a coordinated attack against Đồng Tâm. Then the entire east perimeter suddenly lit up, now ablaze with our *yellow* flares and our *red* machine-gun tracer bullets. Several more explosions striking nearby got me thinking maybe I should pack up my camera and tripod and abandon my highly exposed lofty position. There had been no warning siren, and I wasn't exactly combat-ready, being attired only in regulation OD (olive drab), boxer shorts and locally manufactured flip-flops (the ones cut from tire treads).

Things really heated up when the Navy's gunboats began firing their heavy weapons over the west perimeter, which was also lighting up with flares and machine-gun fire. The harbor was only a block away and I had a clear view of this highly unusual Navy action. Swept up in the unfolding drama to the west, I repositioned my camera and snapped a frame at the precise moment the Reliable Airfield POL depot in the southwest corner of the base blew sky high. A brilliant red ball of fire filled the western horizon, bathing everything and everyone within sight in an eerie crimson glow. Now convinced of the precarious nature of my position I hastily climbed partway down the water tank ladder and jumped. Upon landing I careened into a passing trooper on his way to the personnel shelter. The butt of his rifle smashed into my knuckles and knocked the camera and tripod out of my hand, leaving me with a painful memento of the evening. Had I remained perched where I was, I would have been fine.

Next morning Larry and I walked over to the airfield, which was only a few blocks away, to explore the damage. Two of the four huge storage tanks had received direct rocket hits that entirely destroyed them, and the two remaining tanks, which probably had been partially empty, imploded from the intensity of the surrounding fires. Rumor was that Đồng Tâm had taken over 100 hits and had suffered numerous causalities. The Arts & Crafts Center and multidenominational chapel had both been hit and now displayed walls pockmarked by shrapnel punctures and gaping holes where mortar rounds had penetrated their corrugated metal roofs.

Apparently Tết '69, or Second Tết, as the Green Machine called it, was underway. For several evenings VC rocket, mortar, and ground attacks pounded Đồng Tâm keeping the perimeter guards busy and billeted troops hopping between barracks and bunkers. The EM Club taproom[8] took a hit, as did one wall of the rubber-lined, above-ground swimming pool. It released a tidal wave of water that gushed across DISCOM and through the lower floor of the band barracks.

During the week following the ground attack I was placed on company bugle duty, a nonmusical gig that entailed the mechanics of playing prere-

During the night of February 23, 1969, an enemy barrage of 122mm rockets destroyed the fuel storage facility at Đồng Tâm's POL depot near the Reliable Fixed Wing Airfield. The evening sky was ablaze as thousands of gallons of aviation fuel burned out of control (author's collection).

Four out of the five fuel storage tanks at the POL depot were completely destroyed (author's collection).

corded bugle calls piped over Đồng Tâm by means of a PA system. On the first night of this duty, precisely at the moment I depressed the play button to sound Taps, a mortar round exploded so near the bandstand to where I and the tape recorder were positioned that I could hear wood crack and smell the odor of cordite.[9]

The advent of Second Tết summoned a new wave of insanity at Đồng Tâm. A quarter-ton utility truck passing on the road between the Reliable Academy and DISCOM rolled over on itself for no reason other than the driver jerked the steering wheel too harshly in response to a mortar detonation farther down the road.[10] A soldier wearing only fatigue jacket and combat boots zipped across DISCOM with three MPs (Military Police) and a major in hot pursuit! It seemed like every night at 2300 hours (11:00 p.m.) when I depressed the recorder button to sound Taps something went BOOM. After four nights of this Mister Johns relieved me from further company bugle duty. I thought it might have been because I played the incorrect call one morning (after a harrowing evening mortar/rocket attack I forgot to set up the tape recorder for reveille), but he told me that had nothing to do with it. It had been at the request of the battalion commander, who had suddenly become superstitious about a particular bugler and the timing of the mortar attacks. Participating in one less duty suited me just fine.

In regards to the DISCOM Battalion Commander, Colonel Arthur P.

Hanket, the enemy's tactics must also have been getting to him. His commands normally weren't as foolish as the one he issued to the band in the middle of February. He informed Mister Johns that Bummer, our precious morale-boosting dog, had to go and threatened that if we didn't get rid of it he'd have the MPs shoot it. Apparently one day when leaving the safety of his sandbag-bunkered air-conditioned mobile home he stepped in something nasty, which he attributed to Bummer. Now, in spite of the fact that we kept Bummer on a leash so he wouldn't sniff his way into trouble and also taking into account the numerous stray dogs roaming freely about Đồng Tâm (the stray pooches shared the edible contents in our mess hall dumpsters with our Vietnamese laborers), he still issued his decree. Many of us felt that maybe the colonel had to go and jokingly (I think we were joking) speculated how to get rid of him. One idea I especially liked was to drop pieces of paper outside the perimeter with artillery coordinates for his mobile home. Another less feasible proposition was to follow the more fashionable way and simply frag[11] him, but he hardly ever left Đồng Tâm and when he did it was usually by helicopter. To be a successful fragging it had to be executed in the confusion of battle. Mister Johns came to our rescue and solved the problem by

Two of the POL storage tanks took direct rocket hits. The raging flames from the ensuing fire created a vacuum in two partially full tanks, and they imploded from the intense heat (courtesy Larry Wolf).

bestowing the rank of SGT on Bummer and having him rotate home with trumpeter SP-5 Cary Mathews. Bummer spent his remaining days in the serenity of an upper New York State farm. For Bummer the war had finally ended. Lucky dog. I still had over 250 days to go.

Getting back to the subject of distasteful work details, everyone below the rank of SP-6 or SGT had to participate in shit-burning details. Fortunately the job required only two bodies and there were enough eligible troops in DISCOM to make this particular unpleasantness infrequent. The procedure entailed approaching the EM or officer's latrine from the rear (no pun intended) and swing up a hinged access door to expose a row of 55-gallon steel drums cut to a quarter of their original height with welded-on handles. If the latrine was occupied, fleshy cheeks with dangling scrotums were visible pressing through the circular openings above the drums in a most interesting spectacle of human anatomy and Army ingenuity. The drums beneath any occupied seats were not to be removed. After a couple of shit-burning details one learned to place an Out of Service sign across the latrine seat directly above a removed drum lest one be required to do a little extracurricular shoveling. Each drum was extracted by sliding it out and carrying it a safe distance from the latrine, dousing it with gasoline, and then igniting it. The burn period was conducted under the watchful gaze of the work detail, typically in a reclined posture from a nearby shady spot. After the fire had reduced the barrel's contents to ashes and the barrel cooled, it was dumped and repositioned in the latrine. This process was repeated until all of the drums had been emptied, a task that if properly executed could consume an entire work day.

KP was grueling work, but shit burning was just outright disgusting.

Occasionally members of the band were selected for sandbag-filling detail. Sandbags were used in the construction of the squad size personnel shelters at each end of the barracks, as well as in the construction of the revetments encircling the various DISCOM buildings. The bags were made of some type of woven synthetic material[12] that would eventually fray from the sunlight and intense heat or be ripped open by shrapnel hits. Whatever the cause, when they leaked they had to be replaced with new bags. Participating in the detail was hot dusty work but was usually enlivened with much joking, many breaks taken in the shade, and gallons of yucky-tasting Kool-Aid. Due to the strenuous nature of the work and the predisposition of the baggers, supervision was typically lax.

At Đồng Tâm there was very little stateside or occupation-army–type busy work of the kind I had encountered at the 90th Replacement Battalion. Bandsmen had plenty of free time to do personal things. Like I said earlier, I read, snoozed, went to the PX or Charlie the Gook's place, checked out the

Division bugler duty was not a musical assignment. It entailed operating a reel to reel tape recorder/player located on the Đồng Tâm bandstand. The *bugler* would set up the proper call and play it at the appropriate hour. The call was piped across the base over a public address system. In this view a bandsman from the trumpet section is in the process of sounding a bugle call (author's collection).

Navy boats in the harbor, watched the aircraft landing and taking off from the fixed-wing airfield, and generally staved off boredom and depression as best I could. The VC never bothered us much during daylight hours, except for an occasional sniper who, from a firing position in a clump of palms, sent a few rounds over the berm. During the day Đồng Tâm was a relatively safe haven and troops walked around the base without flak vest, helmet, or rifle. Having your rifle didn't matter much, for, as I've already noted, troops on Đồng Tâm weren't authorized to have ammunition unless specifically ordered to have it. I suspect this was because of the morale problem the Green Machine vehemently denied having.

Morale within the rank and file of draftees and volunteer enlisted men had become a growing concern for the Army since the VC had launched their Tết '68 offensive the previous year. The increasing unpopularity of the war on the home front had discouraged young men from enlisting in the military, especially in the Army. The predominately volunteer USARV of the war's earlier years was being replaced by an increasingly greater number of conscripts. The average draftee was slightly older and more educated than his volunteer counterpart, which should have been a positive factor for the Army. From the standpoint of morale, however, conscripts proved to be more of a liability. In simplified terms, USARV was replacing motivated troops at an increasing rate with troops who simply didn't want to be in Vietnam, or in the Army for that matter.[13] The Army's growing need for combat troops was confounded by its one-year Vietnam tour of duty policy. Not only did USARV have to replace troops rotating out of Vietnam yearly, but up until 1969 the escalation of the war had required substantial increases in the quantity of troops being deployed to USARV.

The Tết '68 offensive had worsened matters. After four years of combat the viability of continuing the Vietnam War had begun to weigh heavily on the hearts and minds of many U.S. citizens, including those considered to be mainstream Americans who, like everyone else, hadn't a clue as to what was going on in Southeast Asia. It appeared that neither had the government. In a classic display of command ineptitude, General William C. Westmoreland— Commander of MACV (Military Assistance Command Vietnam) confidently announced in 1967 that the light could be seen at the end of the Vietnam tunnel of war. This soon proved to be a very bad metaphor, because the magnitude of Tết '68 (the VC attacked every major city and military installation in South Vietnam) convinced many conservative Americans the light he actually saw wasn't the opening at the end of the tunnel but, rather, the headlamp of an oncoming train. Although Tết '68 proved to be one of the most lopsided military victories in the annals of warfare (we won), it is also recorded as one of the greatest political disasters of all times (they won).

For whatever the reason, by the time I arrived in-country neither the war in Vietnam nor the one being waged on the home front was going well. At home youthful protesting had soured into draft card burning anarchy ("Hell, no! We won't go!"), and in Vietnam many of the troops were displaying attitude problems. That anonymous soldier at Biên Hòa airfield who, on my first day in-country, had advised me to be wary of Vietnamese kids bearing shoeshine boxes had been my first indication of discontentment within the ranks. That particular trooper had been out of uniform in public, an act punishable anywhere else in the Army. Additional indications were the widespread use of the degrading FTA acronym stenciled on military vehicles, jungle fatigues accessorized with love beads and peace symbols, the excessive use of alcohol, and the numerous reports of fragging incidents.

By 1969 the U.S. Army in Vietnam was visibly ailing from the effects of inadequate command, waning support on the home front, and ill-defined tactical and strategic military objectives. As the war continued year after year with no end in sight, the attitude of many of the troops comprising USARV degraded into *just putting in time until DEROS*, doing their utmost to stay alive.

On February 27 I received orders promoting me to the rank of SP-5, which, as the enlisted man's quip goes, is a "sergeant who can read and write." As with most things in the Army, the promotion came as a surprise. The promotion was essentially gratis. I hadn't spent the required time in pay grade E-4 to warrant promotion to E-5, but it was the policy of USARV to routinely offer promotion to temporary ranks as an inducement to re-up (reenlist) or promote morale by offering troops more cash than they would otherwise have received outside of a combat zone and sometimes both. It was also an expedient to fill leadership and command positions that were rapidly depleted by combat and the rotation policy. SP-5 had become such a common rank in Vietnam it no longer exempted one from the company duty roster, including KP and shit burning. It also made one eligible for sergeant of the guard, a combat function involving perimeter guard duty. Still, it was nice having a few extra bucks on payday and the slight status of an inverted rocker above my specialist eagles.

In the midst of all the terror, lunacy, and prejudice toward the Vietnamese, an unlikely friendship blossomed between bandsman SP-5 Frank Knightly and Mi Ling, a local girl. One day the division's ARVN intelligence liaison officer brought his sister with him to DISCOM to hear the band rehearse. Both he and she were highly educated and articulate, definitely upper-class Vietnamese. She was also beautiful in a delicate, attention-getting, cherry-blossom way. She gravitated to Frank. Their acquaintance lasted for quite a while, but I suspect if romance was involved it was one-sided. Frank was an honorable fellow who had a girlfriend back home. He probably just enjoyed her feminine company. I know the rest of the band did!

Other bandsmen got involved on one level or another with local girls, but to the best of my knowledge none of the relationships ever lasted to CONUS (Continental United States). A couple of bandsmen received Dear John letters from their wives and girlfriends. This was devastating to their morale as well as their well-being. Recipients of this kind of news from home had to be watched lest they do something rash or foolish.

Near the end of the month I *officially* became the unofficial band clerk and assistant supply sergeant (the latter a title, not a rank). Mister Johns said I could set myself up any way I liked in the supply room, a portion of which was also his billet. During the process I came across an intriguing note tacked to the wall in one of the far recesses of the room. It read, "We must have one love, one great love in our lives since it gives us an alibi for all the moments we are filled with motiveless despair." Wow. It blew my mind away; I realized another literate had been imprisoned in 'Nam. I later discovered the quote was by Albert Camus and came from his work in *Notebooks*.

My old Ansco 35mm rangefinder camera had become a causality of war when I had leaped off the shower water tank and rapped my knuckles on the butt of an M-16 during the VC attack of February 23. In the maneuver I had dropped my tripod with the camera attached. The old Ansco was beyond repair. My new pal Larry came to the rescue by offering me his Yashica Linx 14 rangefinder 35mm camera for a few MPC. He wanted to upgrade to a more expensive through-the-lens focusing 35mm camera. We both got what we wanted.

Near the end of the month I received a registered letter my parents forwarded from the Virginia State Police. After much home front speculation by my sister and her husband concerning the probability I had received a traffic summons or something along those lines when I had driven up from Fort Stewart to New Jersey, my parents had become duly upset about the possible contents of the unopened letter. I hadn't a clue as to why the Virginia State Police needed to contact me. I slit open the letter, read what it said, and shook my head in disbelief. It was notification that a stolen 1967 gray bottom/black top Chevrolet Corvette Stingray convertible, identification #194677S102521, bearing 1968 NJ license plate #LWO-920 had been recovered in Spotsylvania County, Virginia. They had been advised by the New Jersey Division of Motor Vehicles that it was registered to me and they now wanted me to make arrangements to pick the car up at the garage where it was stored. It actually had been my car. I had, however, immediately prior to my entering military service in 1967, sold it back to the Chevrolet dealer from which I had purchased it. I surmised the car had been stolen off the dealer's lot before the paperwork had been processed and the license plates removed. It had taken the police two years to find it. To make absolutely certain it wasn't my car, I asked my dad to check if my *blue* bottom/black top Chevrolet Corvette Stingray convertible was still parked in their garage.

It was!

I wrote the Virginia State Police a letter advising them the car was not mine and never heard another thing about it.

5

Republic of Vietnam, March 1969

Stated in terms of combat, March at the DISCOM compound crept in like a lamb and went out roaring like a lion, maybe a pack of lions. During the first few days of the month, DISCOM had caught a slight break when the VC redirected their mortar and rocket wrath toward the rotary-wing airfield on the north side of Đồng Tâm. Although things still went boom in the night, the booming was farther away and offered even the most skittish short-timer a larger window for uninterrupted slumber. While HHC & Band, DISCOM basked in the relative serenity of *distant* explosive sleepy time, the compound of 191st AHC was being blown to smithereens. Following an earlier bombardment directed at the airfield, tragedy struck in the waning hours of March 2 when a mortar round crashed through the metal roof of the 191st AHC Flight Operations Office, instantly killing Major John Anthony Petric, LT Dennis Sanders Coker, LT Carl Leonard Radtke, SP-5 Robert Lynn Heinmiller, SP-4 Carl Scott Douglas, and SP-4 George Ronald Lovellette.

Although it was now possible to enjoy slightly longer spans of uninterrupted rest, which I sorely needed, the initial euphoria of having been promoted one pay grade to SP-5 had worn off and my morale was again sulking down in the bowels of despair. In my letters home I openly shared my feelings with my loved ones. The VC and their incessant mortaring had me convinced I was going to die. I hated Vietnam and the Army and despised my fellow countrymen for having subjected me to a potentially terminal experience. Then, quite out of left field, Mister Johns informed me he had submitted my name to Battalion HQ to receive the Army Accommodation Medal. He said it was for the great job I was doing in the band.

The inmates were running the asylum, ho, ho!

In fairness to the soldiers of other wars, receiving medals in the 'Nam was just about SOP (Standard Operating Procedure). All you had to do to get one was your job without displaying a bad attitude to your superiors (you could have a bad attitude, you just couldn't reveal it). For enlisted men in good standing with their superiors the Army Accommodation Medal was a given. Bronze and Silver Stars had to be earned. For junior officers medals up to and including the Bronze Star were gratis, and for senior grade officers the Silver Star was the cutoff for freebies. Battalion and brigade commanders were routinely awarded Silver Stars at the end of their tours. The Congressional Medal of Honor was the really tough one to earn inasmuch as it was usually awarded posthumously and *you actually had to earn it.*

Along with March came even sultrier weather than February. During the day it topped 115 degrees and at night it dropped into the high 80s. My resistance was down from lack of sleep and I caught a cold. Playing a musical wind instrument with a head cold is nigh unto impossible in civilian life, but this was the Army, so I played as best I could. The cold just added to the total misery of my situation, as well as served as fuel for my overall cynicism.

After a few nights of attacking the rotary-wing airfield, the VC took a short breather in harassing Đồng Tâm with their mortars, rockets, and perimeter probes, which resulted in less standby alerts to keep us hunkered down and at the ready to defend the base. During this period the band's musical commitments away from Đồng Tâm increased dramatically. Because of

During the opening days of March 1969 the VC aimed their mortars at the Reliable Rotary Wing Airfield. Their targets were the helicopters and aviation facilities situated along the length of Đồng Tâm's north perimeter (author's collection).

the proximity of the supply room office to Mister Johns' billet at the rear of the bandstand, I became privy to information concerning what the band would be doing, where it would be doing it, and for whom it would be performing. Having more responsibility and knowledge of the immediate future helped with my morale. It also helped that Mister Johns was an affable commander. I felt he genuinely appreciated having me assist him with the administrative details of being bandmaster; after all I was a trained and experienced 71H30 personnel management specialist. I could type using all ten fingers, understood Army administrative protocol, and knew how to navigate through Army regulation manuals. I was, in essence, what every commander desired— a personal secretary—plus I could participate musically in the band. A friendship derived of close association that at times circumvented military decorum blossomed between Mister Johns and me.

Still, I wanted out of the Army and Vietnam ASAP. I spent my spare time, which had been lessened by my new responsibilities, at the AG (Adjutant General) office scouring over army regulations seeking the authority to REFRAD (Released from Active Duty) earlier than scheduled. I found my salvation in AR 635–205, paragraph 9, "Early Separation to Attend School." The regulation didn't specify whether it applied to *undergraduate* or *graduate* school! Loophole or not, it was a potential way out of the Army and Vietnam, so I decided to pursue it. Although it would require boo-coo preparation— letters to colleges, an admission test to pass, piles of Army paperwork in triplicate, etc., etc., etc.—it offered me an attainable goal: salvation from the morass of Army life and the dangers of Vietnam. Despite my best intentions to remain cynical, I began feeling good about my situation and happily hummed a spiffy tune from BCT days, although in a modified version: *I don't want to be an Airborne Ranger; I don't want to be in Vietnam....*

One day during the euphoria of my newfound happiness, Mister Johns said the DISCOM HQ company commander, CPT Jeffrey A. Hurt, wanted to see me. Mister Johns had no idea what he wanted. This was a highly unusual request inasmuch as the band had little contact with the HQ Company captain other than work detail levies. Now that I had found the means of shortening my military career and things were looking up for me, I approached the HQ hooch with some trepidation. Upon entering I couldn't help but notice the company clerk pecking away at a typewriter using two fingers and plenty of curses. He wore corporal's-rank pins on his collar points, which was unusual.[1] I spent about two hours with the captain in the company of the XO (Executive Officer) and HQ Company first sergeant essentially drinking the captain's Scotch and playing chess in his bunker billet, which was conveniently attached to the rear of the HQ office. Although the captain never told me what he wanted of me, word soon reached Mister Johns that my being reassigned to the position of HQ Company clerk would be a very good move for both the band and me. To sweeten the pot I'd been offered a billet in the captain's spacious bunker along with the company XO and first sergeant.

The band couldn't afford to lose a musician since we were already short-handed, and Mister Johns didn't want to give up his new clerk. I'd like to think it was more about the friendly rapport we'd struck working together, but I'm certain it was the clerk reason why Mister Johns refused the captain. I really didn't want to go over to DISCOM anyway, and I let Mister Johns know as much. A few weeks later the captain requested my presence again, this time in private, whereupon he asked me to do him a favor and research regulations concerning a hardship DEROS as it applied to marital problems! It was obvious the captain also wanted out of 'Nam.

* * *

Getting back to the band's musical schedule, the first day of the month began with three engagements. On the morning of March 1 a trumpeter was dispatched to play Taps at two memorial services, one for the 15th Engineer Battalion[2] and the other for the 9th Military Police.[3] Later, on the same day, the band reported to division HQ for an awards ceremony in honor of the division's departing CSM (Command Sergeant Major), Robert Gurney, who was being replaced by CSM Alfred Chesterton. A division CSM was the highest-ranking *enlisted* man in the division. A gala farewell party for the uppity-ups followed the ceremony. Tragedy was unfolding all around us and our commanders were celebrating in the fashion of Emperor Nero fiddling while Rome was burning, leastways that was my impression at the time.

Regarding memorial services, during the month of March the band would ultimately dispatch buglers to play at memorial services for the afore-mentioned seven fallen soldiers of the 191st AHC at Đồng Tâm (March 4), as well as services for fallen soldiers of the 6/77th Artillery at Cần Thơ Army Airfield (March 5), the 3/39th Infantry at Dipherio[4] (March 11), and the 2/39th Infantry at FSB Dirk[5] (March 23). For so many young men the light at the end of the tunnel had been extinguished forever.

One morning after roll call during a period of free time SSG William Jenson asked me to give him a hand collecting dirt on a jaunt outside the berm. He needed dirt to plant tomatoes in a wooden ammo box. I asked what was wrong with the dirt on Đồng Tâm.[6] He said that it was poison; nothing would grow in it. I fetched my entrenching tool, and after advising Mister Johns, who merely shrugged in response to our plans, walked to the main

5. Republic of Vietnam, March 1969

gate. Although we didn't have passes authorizing us to leave Đồng Tâm, SSG Jenson's request amused the MPs (Military Police) guarding the gate enough to let us cross over TL-25 and take a few shovelfuls out of the overgrown north bank of the Sông Mỹ Tho.

March had been a busy month for the band, which presented an occasional logistical problem for Mister Johns, who at times had to furnish musicians to play at conflicting performances held in locations sometimes miles apart. Transportation had to be arranged days in advance of performances and when the designated time arrived, a helicopter or fixed-wing aircraft could be delayed or diverted for other military purposes. This didn't happen too often, but when it did it always seemed to occur at the designated *pickup* time. Needless to say, the band became very familiar with hanging around PZs awaiting transportation. The Army axiom hurry up and wait was the unofficial order of the day. It didn't mean nothing,[7] though; the band had become adept at finding shady spots for snoozing.

My extracurricular clerical function offered me better insight into the nature of the band's mission, which, as I've already said, was primarily to

Although Đồng Tâm was in an agricultural area, no vegetation thrived in its Agent Orange–poisoned soil. In order for plants to grow, as bandsman William Jenson discovered, you had to import soil from outside the camp. *Ah, Bill, they are tomato plants in the ammo box, aren't they?* (author's collection).

"Operation Big Switch-Phase I" was held far southwest of Đồng Tâm in the city of Cần Thơ. The Division's administratively attached 6/77th Artillery Battalion turned over one battery of their towed 105mm howitzers to the 213th ARVN Artillery Battalion. Phase II occurred the following month and gave ARVN the remainder of the battalion's artillery assets (author's collection)

promote morale through ritual. Bands had been part of the American military since the Revolutionary War when fife and drummers accompanied soldiers into battle. In the days before radio communication, when wars were fought in mass formations, the beat of drums and the call of bugles directed troops by broadcasting their commanders' orders. As technology changed the tactics of battle, so the role of military bands changed. No longer needed on the battlefield for communications, their purpose became more closely associated with esprit de corps, which led to music becoming more a traditional component of the military than a tactical one. When troops being reviewed passed their commanders, they did it to the quick-stepping rhythm of a lively march, and the parade of soldiers began only after the drum major's baton came down!

The 9th Infantry Division Band participated in two distinct types of musical engagements: ceremonial and entertainment. Ceremonial functions covered memorial services, retreats, awards, departures, changes of command, graduations, reveilles, re-ups, base turnovers, honor guards, and unit arrivals, while entertainment included parties, the general's mess, and concerts. A concert could be as informal as playing for a few villagers in a remote hamlet or as formal as a full-blown recital onstage at a military base camp or in a Vietnamese city. Since trumpet players also doubled as buglers, performing solo at memorial, retreat, and reveille ceremonies, their musical schedule was busier than the rest of the band (and slightly more hazardous).

A small contingent of bandsmen handpicked for their talent at improvisation made up the dance combo and routinely performed at senior-grade officer parties, unit parties, and at the general's mess. Other than at rehearsals the full band rarely performed together. The size of the band assembled for a gig depended upon the mode of transportation available at the time and the nature of the performance. Because one Chinook helicopter, the largest rotary-wing personnel transport to see service in Vietnam, could accommodate about 23 musicians with weapons and instruments, it didn't make sense to utilize a second helicopter if 23 musicians were sufficient for the performance.

On gigs at locations outside of Đồng Tâm the band provided its own security. Depending upon the safety of the destination, one or two bandsmen were selected to function as guards to keep a watchful eye out for suspicious behavior. Since musicians were so few in Vietnam,[8] it was doubtful that the Green Machine would knowingly send us into harm's way.

Or so we thought!

When the band traveled by truck I always appointed myself extra security guard. I'd stand forward in the truck bed with my elbows resting on the cab's canvas roof, my M-16 locked, loaded, on safe, and in plain view, my gaze intently scanning the roadsides. My pal Larry, when not behind the wheel driving, always found his way into the truck cab and rode shotgun with the barrel of his M-79 grenade launcher poking out the open window. None of the other members in the band seemed to have any particular concerns about security, despite the reality that convoys were routinely ambushed. A couple of unescorted trucks roaring through the boonies loaded with musical instruments and neatly dressed soldiers had to offer easy pickings for the VC.

During the month, I acquired an application from Đồng Tâm's Education Center to take the Graduate Business Admissions Exam. I'd learned that the test was periodically administered in Saigon. Mister Johns assured me he'd make arrangements for a three-day leave and transportation to get me to Saigon and back. When I dropped the completed application into the mail slot at the Đồng Tâm post office a wave of happiness washed over me; I'd taken the first actual step to get out of 'Nam.

The VC's implementation of Tết '69 had resulted in more fatalities than usual, which kept the trumpet section busy dispatching buglers to different units both on and off Đồng Tâm. Transportation was typically arranged by the unit holding the memorial service. If the service were held in the field it usually meant a hotshot treetop ride for the bugler in a Huey Slick[9] or gunship.

On March 10 a large contingent of the band was dispatched by helicopter to Cần Thơ for phase one of a ceremony the Green Machine had dubbed Operation Big Switch. The 6/77th Artillery was *incrementally* being rotated out of Vietnam and was initially turning over one battery of their towed 105mm howitzers to the ARVN 213th Artillery Battalion. The band became involved because the 6/77th was administratively attached to the 9th Infantry Division the same way the band was administratively attached to DISCOM. Our CH-47 Chinook[10] set down at Cần Thơ Army Airfield and the band was picked up and delivered to the ceremony aboard 6/77th Artillery deuce-and-a-half trucks. On the drive we passed an aircraft boneyard, dozens of large tents with their sides rolled up, and a poignant reminder of war—a large pond with the tail boom of a helicopter protruding from its surface.

As it turned out, the flight had been more interesting than the ceremony. We mostly stood in formation in blistering heat waiting for dummy rounds to be symbolically fired in tribute and for ARVN to get the former 6/77th artillery pieces hooked up to their tow vehicles and assembled in the right order to pass by the reviewing stand. It was dusty, hot, and dirty. When we finally got to play we could hardly be heard over the drone of the engines. The Green Machine had placed the band on the far side of the parade ground, opposite the reviewing stand, with the long progression of towed artillery and associated vehicles passing in between. It was standard Army pass-in-review parade formation, acceptable for marching troops but not for noisy motor-drawn howitzers. Operation Big Switch consumed the entire day. The mess hall at Đồng Tâm had to be kept open beyond regular serving hours in order to feed us, a displeasure our normally grumpy cooks undoubtedly took out on the KPs.

Phase I of Operation Big Switch had been my first opportunity to observe ARVN troops close up. Their small physiques were boyishly slim and wiry. I did not know their army's age of conscription, so they may have actually been boys. The tight-fitting cut of their uniforms greatly added to my impression of youthful adolescence. Fatigue shirts were tailored and worn tucked into trousers with pegged legs. Brightly colored kerchiefs hung loosely around necks, a la Boy Scout style. The tailored fatigues may have been their Sunday going-to-meeting best. They certainly contrasted with the loose-fitting jungle fatigues worn by U.S. troops.

Although hostile activity directed at Đồng Tâm had slowed after the VCs' successful February 23 attack, they still continued to lob in a few mortars

5. Republic of Vietnam, March 1969

now and then and conduct an occasional probe along the perimeter. But the intensity had definitely subsided. The Green Machine, however, chose to sporadically keep us on hyper alert with incessant warnings of impending attacks. An entire VC battalion was rumored to be operating in the division's AO. The numerous roving security patrols guarding Đồng Tâm's four perimeters, however, reported encountering only small clusters of VC.[11]

A surprise letter arrived in the March 11 mail call. It was from Mister Stanley Crawley. Mister Crawley was the father of my boyhood friend Stuart. Stuart was the fellow who had asked me to send his regards to the bandmaster of the 80th Army Band at Fort Stewart, which had resulted in my becoming a bugler. The senior Crawley was a towering man of few words. He worked on the loading dock at the P. Ballantine & Sons brewery in Newark, New Jersey, and projected the look of someone who used his physical strength to earn his pay outdoors and in all kinds of weather. As a child I'd been afraid of him. His physique and tough-guy posture demanded respect, at least from a kid. His letter came out of the blue. Throughout the 15 years I had lived across the street from him and often had played with his son, I doubt he had ever said more than a dozen words to me. In his letter he informed me that during World War II he had been with the 9th Infantry Division and had taken a bullet through his foot fighting the Germans and Italians in North Africa. What impressed me most was the tone of his letter. My assignment to his old division and my experiencing combat as he had apparently elevated my status in his eyes from just another snot-nosed kid on the block to a fellow warrior. The unexpected bond of sentimentality forged from our having trodden similar paths obliterated the years I had feared him as a child. We were now brothers in arms and united in common spirit, the tough old guy and me. The realization gave my morale a quick boost for a few seconds.

On March 13 the timing of the band's musical commitments demanded that the band be split into two ensembles. Part of the band, under the command of Mister Johns, traveled to FSB (Fire Support Base) Moore to perform at a 1st Brigade change of command ceremony while SFC Townley remained on Đồng Tâm to conduct what remained of the band at an awards ceremony for some now-forgotten unit. I went with the FSB Moore group. The base was northwest of Đồng Tâm, along National Route QL-4, several klicks east of a large town the French had named Cai Lây. Its original Vietnamese name was Khiêm Ích, but it should have been Khiêm Yućk. We flew to the engagement in three Huey Slick troop transports. The flight was exhilarating. I sat next to one of the door gunners and had a spectacular view of the countryside through the aircraft's open side door. The Slicks set down inside FSB Moore's outer perimeter wire just outside the berm near the main gate. The base was huge and, except for a few tents and small wooden buildings, entirely filled with sandbag-bunkered structures. Firing positions and artillery pits abounded. Many of the perimeter bunkers had the added protection of wire cyclone fencing installed to detonate RPGs (Rocket Propelled Grenades) before they struck the bunker itself. Whereas Đồng Tâm promoted a faux civilized appearance, FSB Moore had the no-nonsense look of an all-out combat installation.

FSB Moore was home to the 6/31st Infantry and the 2/4th Artillery Battalions, as well as being the HQ base of the 1st "Recondo" Brigade. The change of command ceremony was to welcome the new brigade commander, Colonel John G. Hayes. Hayes was replacing COL John P. Geraci, who had been in command since October 1968 and had returned to CONUS on a hardship REFRAD to minister to a seriously ill wife. The division's chief of staff, COL Ira A. Hunt, had taken temporary command of the brigade while awaiting the arrival of COL Hayes.

After the ceremony was over Mister Johns received word that our pickup helicopters had been diverted to another mission and would be arriving later in the day. I took advantage of the delay to walk around the base and snap

FSB Moore was situated off of National Route QL-4, several klicks east of the city of Cai Lây, near the hamlet of My Thuan. It was home base for the 6/31st Infantry Battalion. On this day armored personnel carriers of the 2/47th Mechanized Infantry Battalion are on the property preparing to support a 6/31st field operation (author's collection).

5. Republic of Vietnam, March 1969

At times enemy action got heavy at FSB Moore. Defensive protection included cyclone fencing placed in front of perimeter bunkers in order to detonate rocket propelled grenades and rockets before they struck the sandbagged structure of the bunker itself (author's collection).

photographs of its fortifications, buildings, and artillery emplacements. While I was preoccupied with my camera, a loud explosion on a road across from the base sent a civilian bus careening into an oncoming vehicle, both ending up in a drainage ditch. I, of course, snapped a quick frame. Several Vietnamese farmers working in a field alongside the road glanced up, then returned to their labors. I assumed the bus had hit a land mine. No one around me seemed concerned, so I shrugged my shoulders and resumed exploring. Just as the sun was hinting at setting, I heard the helicopters approaching. We returned to Đồng Tâm as darkness fell.

During the next several days the band was preoccupied with the usual repetitive, mundane gigs, which kept us on Đồng Tâm. We performed at daily and weekly Reliable Academy jobs, played an NCO graduation, did a retreat ceremony, entertained at the general's mess party, and attended awards ceremonies. On March 16 Mother Nature added a new element to our mundane assignments; the sky clouded over and released a soaking deluge of rain. It was the first precipitation since my arriving in-country over two months ago and was merely a portent of things to come.

Following the change of command ceremony at FSB Moore, the band had some free time before the return of the helicopters. I was sightseeing when a sharp nearby blast got my attention. Outside Moore's perimeter, not far from where I stood, a civilian bus had collided with a second vehicle after having set off a booby trap planted in the dirt roadway (author's collection).

The next day, March 17, the band performed at a change-of-command ceremony held on Đồng Tâm for the 1/11th Artillery Battalion. Lieutenant Colonel Peter F. Witteried had assumed command of the battalion from one of his former artillery school classmates, LTC William L. Hauser. On the same day the band also attended an Honor Guard practice session at Division HQ.[12]

The Honor Guard ceremony came off the next day, March 18, and was followed by a practice awards ceremony for another now-forgotten unit and a memorial service for 9th Infantry Division Artillery. A couple of days earlier one of their aerial artillery observers, CPT Drew Gaylord of Headquarters and Headquarters Battery, was lost when the fixed-wing 0–1 Bird Dog observation aircraft he was flying crashed while approaching Đồng Tâm for landing. He'd been flying a late-night "eagle watch mission"[13] spotting enemy mortar fire and had lost track of his remaining fuel. His approach, consequently, fell short of the runway. His Bird Dog aircraft was observed by one of Đồng Tâm's perimeter guard bunkers to hit a tree and flip over. It was Captain Gaylord's third tour in Vietnam.

March 19 brought more of the same-same, the usual Reliable Academy gig, practice for a retreat ceremony at division HQ, and an awards ceremony for another forgotten unit. The next day was also uneventful, at least as far

5. Republic of Vietnam, March 1969

as I had been concerned, but the afternoon mail did bring a letter my parents had forwarded from USAG Fort Stewart. It contained my copy of the orders assigning me a secondary MOS of 02B30 trumpeter. The orders had been cut around the time I had departed Fort Stewart. While I pondered why it had taken almost half a year for the orders to catch up to me, the dance band was rockin' 'n' rollin' at an early evening performance at the EM Service Club. Later that night, just before lights out, warning of an impending large-scale attack circulated throughout DISCOM, and Đồng Tâm went on full alert. I placed my combat gear in an easily accessible pile at the foot of my bunk, dug out the magazine of ammo I kept hidden, and slipped on my jungle fatigues and boots. I'd remain fully clothed just in case I had to zip over to the armory for more ammunition. As it turned out, despite the dire predictions only a few random mortars exploded inside the north perimeter. Charlie might have been playing the disinformation game with the Green Machine or they were, perhaps, just out to destroy some helicopters.

In anticipation of the upcoming monsoon season the band was given the task of building a shelter for DISCOM's civilian laborers. They had grown accustomed to awaiting transportation under the EM shower's elevated water supply tank. It was a cool shady spot in the dry season and offered shelter from the rain in the wet season. None of us assigned to the work detail had any carpentry experience, but we were given the assistance of a Vietnamese contract laborer who did. We called him "Papa-san." Although he was probably no older than 40, he looked ancient, with deeply wrinkled brown skin, a scraggly silvered Fu Man Chu-style mustache and chin whiskers, a few lonely front teeth blackened from chewing beetle nuts, and a wiry, thin, not-quite-emaciated physique. He always wore a cloth wrapped around his head, a loose-fitting white tunic, and black silk pajamas he inevitably hiked up into shorts. He was a good fellow, possibly a VC at night, who took particular concern in watching over my carpentry efforts. He spoke no English, but when I proceeded to nail or cut a piece of lumber incorrectly, he'd shake his head disapprovingly and chatter remonstrations in his sing-song, high-pitched native tongue. The longer we worked together, the more he supervised, until I finally lost my cool and, pointing my finger at his concave chest, spewed out the accusation "You VC." It was an unkind thing for me to say, because he didn't fully understand English or the nuances of our teasing, but he knew what Americans and his countrymen did to captured VC. He got very upset and vehemently repeated, "No VC, no VC." I calmed him down with a big smile and a limp, heat-softened Hershey bar. Henceforth, every time I cut or nailed something improperly he'd look over at me, point, and accuse, "You VC! You VC!" He was a quick study.

During construction of a shelter for DISCOM's Vietnamese laborers, one of them who knew carpentry, nicknamed "Papa-san," took pleasure in incessantly shaking his head and chattering disapproval over my lack of carpentry skills. The fellow always came to work dressed like a VC, so we *Americanized* him with a bush cap, tee shirt, and jungle fatigue trousers (courtesy Larry Wolf).

After the shelter was completed, many of the Vietnamese laborers continued waiting for the bus under the water tank. At quitting time you could usually see a bunch of them squatting underneath. The shelter we had provided remained essentially vacant. The culture of Vietnam was ancient, with a long history of pride in doing things the same way as their ancestors had. They didn't readily accept change.

On March 21 there was a festive mood permeating division HQ. The sands of time had turned another year for Brigadier General Frank L. Gunn, the division's deputy commander, and a gala party celebrating the event was to be held at the general's mess, which, of course, necessitated the presence of the dance combo. I have always found it incongruous that young men were dying and bleeding throughout the division's AO (Area of Operation) and the big brass uppity-ups always found time to celebrate something. I suspect it was a post–World War II holdover attitude from occupation days in Germany and Japan.

On March 25 the band flew by Caribou to the farthest southern reaches of IV CTZ (Combat Tactical Zone). Division had loaned the band to MACV Advisory Team 50. Team 50 was headquartered in the charming old French city of Cao Lãnh in a complex once occupied by a French artillery battery. The installation was named Crum Compound in honor of 44th Special Tactical Zone senior advisor MAJ Edwin Waldren Crum, who was killed while heroically attempting to drag one of his wounded soldiers to safety during a February 1968 attack by the VC.[14] The 44th Special Tactical Zone had been created to reduce the operating areas of the overburdened 7th, 9th, and 21st ARVN divisions. Each of these divisions had given the Tactical Zone the responsibility of keeping one of their provinces along the Cambodian border secure. The zone was defended by CIDG (Civilian Irregular Defense Group), RF/PF (Regional Forces/Popular Forces, also known by GIs as "Ruff Puffs"), and mercenaries, all under the command of an ARVN colonel, who was under the *guidance* of U.S. Army Special Forces, MACV, Advisory Team 50, and a U.S. senior advisor.

The band was flown to nearby Tân Tich Army Airfield, an undefended

After the civilian shelter had been completed our Vietnamese laborers rejected it. They continued waiting for transportation under the EM shower water tank. It was a refreshingly cool place and their mentality was ingrained with doing things the way they had always done them. They didn't readily accept change (author's collection).

asphalt strip laid out in dense tropical growth. A deuce-and-a-half from Team 50 awaited us. After we climbed aboard we were informed we were being diverted to one of Team 50's outposts for the purpose of bolstering its small garrison of regional troops. A ground attack was expected and we were the nearest available troops. The Special Forces outpost turned out to be little more than a muddy clearing in the jungle encircled by a low berm connecting rudimentary firing positions. An outer ring of concertina wire finished off the defenses.

When we arrived the outpost was virtually uninhabited. We were greeted by an American soldier attired in camouflage fatigues. His uniform blended in nicely with the surrounding foliage. He wore no rank pins or identification tags. Upon seeing our STRAC uniforms he inquired what kind of troops we were. Mister Johns responded with a curt "Bandsmen," whereupon I heard Larry's voice admonish from the rear of our group, *"Combat bandsmen!"*

Nothing much happened at the Special Forces outpost and after a sufficient number of the regular garrison reported for duty we climbed back aboard the truck and completed our journey to Crum Compound. In order to reach our destination we had to drive through downtown Cao Lãnh, which I can best describe as being Vietnamese with a continental French twist.

Crum Compound consisted of several buildings constructed of a variety of materials and scattered over a large field. We set up in a flowered courtyard of what had once been a two-story private residence that now served as the HQ for the 44th Special Tactical Zone. The building retained its architectural beauty, and even the ugliness of the barbed wire and stacked sandbags filling its gracefully curved archways couldn't diminish the overall charm of the place.

The awards ceremony went well and included a performance by an ARVN band from the 7th ARVN Division. We played "The Star-Spangled Banner" and they played their own anthem. Speeches translated into both languages were made glorifying how brave everyone was. General Creighton Abrams, General Westmoreland's four-star USARV replacement, was in attendance. The ceremony was followed by cold drinks and snacks in the courtyard. We mingled with the ARVN musicians using sign language and hand signals to communicate. The ARVNs must have been very happy, because when they presented each of us with a cute enameled-metal 7th ARVN Division pin they all had that inscrutable Asian smile plastered across their faces.

We flew back to Đồng Tâm without incident, other than a frightening bout of slightly out-of-control wing-wagging as the result of a Vietnamese Air Force flight of F-104 Phantom jet fighter-bombers cutting across our path too closely; forcing our aircraft to fly through their turbulent jet stream. Luckily the pilots were able to get the Caribou under control before we lost too much altitude and too much of our post-ceremony snacks.

I was becoming accustomed to the flaps-down, reverse-propeller-pitch landings at the Reliable Airfield. It was to our good fortune the Caribou was designed as a STOL (Short Takeoff and Landing) aircraft. A coating of sand paint on the PSP runway gave its tires more grip. I knew all about sand paint. During two summers in my undergraduate college days I'd worked for Davoe & Reynolds, a paint manufacturer in the Ironbound section of Newark, New Jersey. They manufactured marine paints and had a contract with the government to make sand paint. Preparing the stuff had been a bear. Until now I never knew how it was used. It was heavy work wrestling a huge steel vat on worn rollers over an uneven concrete floor from the pigment lab to the oil-paint-vehicle filling valves, then to where skids of sandbags were piled and finally to the mixer. Filling it into cans by hand was frustrating. The stuff plopped messily out of the vat gate into the tin gallon cans. Years after my struggles with processing sand paint at Davoe & Reynolds, it was now keeping

The city of Cao Lãnh was quite a few klicks west of Đồng Tâm and required a long Caribou flight. The band landed at a small military airstrip near the village of Tân Tich and was picked up by a waiting HQ Company deuce-and-a-half from the 44th Special Tactical Zone. We were driven northward on Communal Route 145, but not to Cao Lãnh. We were unexpectedly diverted to a Special Forces camp on the outskirts of the city to bolster their garrison in expectation of a ground attack! (author's collection).

the plane I was aboard from careening off the runway. I might have mixed the very paint we were landing on.

Band assignments were light on March 26 with only a practice session scheduled, and I looked forward to enjoying what little comforts Đồng Tâm offered. The entire day had been uneventful and mail didn't bring any word from home. I wasn't in the mood to write, so I decided to have a peaceful evening, maybe start on a new novel I had just gotten from the base library. At around 2100 hours (9:00 p.m. in real time) a few mortars landed outside of DISCOM, followed by Đồng Tâm's warning siren. SFC Townley spread the word we were under alert status.[15] Following standard alert procedure we got into our combat gear and took positions in the bunkers, which is to say we grabbed our helmets, rifles, boots, flak vests, and pillows and sacked out in the personnel shelters. A half-hour before midnight a barrage of rocket fire exploded across Đồng Tâm and the warning siren sounded a second time. All of the rockets had detonated outside of the DISCOM compound. Several bandsmen decided the enemy had done their thing for the night and the alert was over. They returned to their hooches. I remained in the shelter with the more skeptical awaiting the all-clear signal. It hadn't come by midnight and

Cao Lãnh may have lost its French colonial masters, but not its French heritage. Most evidently French were the elevated concrete guard towers, and the lacy, wooden Eiffel Bridge across the Rach Cao Lãnh at the southern entrance into the city (author's collection).

5. Republic of Vietnam, March 1969

The headquarters building of the 44th Special Tactical Zone was in a former French artillery battalion compound. Prior to the artillery battalion it must have been the home of a wealthy French colonist, for even the harshness of the rusty strands of barbed wire and stacks of faded sandbags couldn't detract from the architectural glamour of the place (author's collection).

I was still in the bunker sitting on a wooden bench, elbows on my thighs, resting my head in my hands, half asleep, when I was abruptly jerked into full consciousness by a loud explosion nearby. The night sky outside the gun port on the south face of the bunker was ablaze in a brilliant red glow. One of our percussionists, SP-4 Gregory Thruston—a huge, powerful, black man— peered through the port to get a better view. The southern sky was on fire! Suddenly there was an explosion the likes of which I had never experienced. The earth shook violently and I was thrown from the bench. The concussion of the blast threw Thruston back from the small opening, across the bunker, and into the rear wall. It felt like the ground had physically leaped a foot or two. The air inside was choking with dust. Sand from bags above us trickled onto our heads. My initial thought was the bunker had been hit by an RPG round, which meant the dinks must have gotten through the wire while I had been snoozing and were now overrunning Đồng Tâm.

I removed the illegal magazine from the heavy rubber band that kept my helmet cover in place and snapped it up into my M-16. I had 18 rounds plus an additional 3 loose cartridges stuck in the webbing of my flak vest.

Not enough to stop a ground attack, but if I was going to die I was going to take a few of them with me. Another earth-shattering explosion knocked me off my feet and sent my rifle flying out of my hands. A hailstorm of secondary explosions rumbled across the earth. It was difficult to stand erect. Then, following a third horrific explosion, the staccato popping of small-arms ammunition bursting began filling in the gaps between shattering explosions.

It wasn't a ground attack—the VC had hit the ammo dump!

Heavy artillery ordnance was exploding! I could hear chunks of shell fragments whizzing through the air between the discordant blasts. Buckets of sand rained down on us each time a large chunk of shrapnel slammed into the bunker. I took a chance and peered out the gun port toward the Reliable Academy area. It was dark. Suddenly, over the din I heard a distant metallic voice. It grew steadily louder, instructing us to stay under cover and expect an enemy ground assault. I continued peering into the darkness. A slow-moving, quarter-ton utility truck passed on the road before me with an MP spewing out the warnings over a megaphone. I watched in admiration, for he was either one very brave or very foolish trooper. I wondered how the Green Machine expected us to repel a ground assault without ammunition. We would have been better off if he had been throwing out cases of ammo instead of issuing warnings.[16]

After five hours of nonstop detonations the last of the ammunition at the dump finally cooked off and by first light troops were emerging from their hiding places. The VC never launched a ground attack. They had the same problem as we did—ducking the shrapnel that filled the air smashing or puncturing everything it hit. The DISCOM area was a mess. Variously sized chunks of jagged metal lay everywhere. Many of the buildings had been penetrated, sandbag revetments were leaking sand, and sheets of corrugated metal roofing were bent at crazy angles. Inside the band barracks the plywood wall partitions were all down, our bunk beds toppled, and the window-screen material ripped open. A red windup travel alarm clock I'd kept on a shelf near my pillow had taken a direct hit and now lay in pieces on the mattress. It had been a loaner from my girlfriend, who had purchased it while attending a semester at Wroxton College in England.

After everything finally settled down the Green Machine had nothing to say about what happened; the Army had an aversion to publicizing disaster. They probably felt that what we didn't know couldn't negatively affect our morale. They evidently assumed we had enough positive morale left to affect. That week the division newspaper, *The Old Reliable,* ran an article about the band with the happy title "March Is the Month for Music Makers" but nary a mention of the disaster at the ammo dump.

5. Republic of Vietnam, March 1969

Late in March the VC blew up 500 tons of artillery and small arms ammunition at the Đồng Tâm munitions storage depot, and they did it with a single lucky mortar round, which sailed through an open locker hatch! (author's collection).

The physical damage from the blast radiated 360 degrees from the ammunition storage depot, which ran along the western half of the Đồng Tâm's south perimeter. The facilities and troops closest to the blast caught the worst of it, in this case the U.S. Navy. Their compound was the closest (author's collection).

116 *Memoir of a Tour in Vietnam with the 9th Infantry Division, 1969*

After the last of the ammo at the depot cooked off, the entire DISCOM compound was littered with chunks of artillery and rocket shrapnel. The width of the wooden bench in this view is about 18 inches. The large chunks of burst artillery rounds were jagged and heavy and lay strewn across the parade ground, on the roofs of structures, inside of buildings where it had punched through walls, and deeply embedded in sandbag bunkers and building revetments (author's collection).

On March 27, the second day after the attack, the band participated in a practice session for a 15th Engineer Battalion award ceremony. Out of curiosity and with permission from Mister Johns, Larry took a roundabout route to the practice site, detouring through the Navy compound situated near Đồng Tâm's main gate. We skirted the eastern extremity of the ammo dump and observed shattered buildings, destroyed bunkers, bits of helicopters, and chunks of burst artillery rounds everywhere. It was obvious the Navy, whose compound was nearest the explosion, had borne the brunt of the attack.

It hadn't been until a week later, after I received a couple of clippings my parents had cut out of the local newspapers, that I began to understand the extent of the damage the VC had inflicted on Đồng Tâm. The attitude of the Green Machine had been *ho-hum, no big deal*, but the newspaper articles hinted at a different story. One article efficiently summed up both the attack and attitude of the Green Machine in one sentence: "The Headquarters bivouac of the U.S. 9th Infantry Division at Đồng Tâm, 35 miles southwest of Saigon, was torn up so severely by hostile fire that U.S. newsmen were barred from the scene."[17] Years later onetime battalion commander of the

5. Republic of Vietnam, March 1969

Division's 4/39th Infantry, COL David Haskill Hackworth, would compare the attack to what the Allies experienced on the Anzio beachhead. The highly decorated colonel had endured the attack firsthand, recuperating from a gunshot wound in the bunkers below Đồng Tâm's 3rd Surgical Hospital. Decades later he would relate how he had been glad to get out of Đồng Tâm because it was "like living downrange of a shooting gallery."[18] The division reported 60 causalities, including three fatalities. The actual causality count, as I later learned, was well over 100. As I said, the Green Machine liked to minimize bad news.

I wrote my parents about the attack and, after cursorily reporting some of the details of the damage and assuring them I was fine, proceeded to show more interest in the size and quantity of canned fruit they were mailing me via PAL (Pacific Air Lift). That's how ultimate weapons reacted back in the 'Nam. Death and destruction abounded everywhere, but canned peaches were hard to come by!

Rumors began circulating around Đồng Tâm that the division was going to be pulled out and redeployed to Schofield Barracks in Hawaii. Going home had been, and probably remains, the dream of every soldier in combat, and I viewed this rumor as just that, a dream. It didn't make sense for the Green Machine to pull out the last division it sent to Vietnam, especially since IV CTZ was still infested with VC. The Mekong Delta wasn't a happy place. Its inhabitants had confused loyalties. Much of the Delta's population was related to, affiliated with, or politically motivated toward the VC. We apparently weren't winning all that many hearts and minds.

Inasmuch as rumors can sometimes be true, I decided if I was going to enjoy a USARV-promised out-of-country R&R, I'd better let the DISCOM HQ company clerk know of my upcoming eligibility (at Fort Stewart a clerk would have kept track of this and would have let me know). I'd been in-country three months and would become eligible after four months. Because I was sick of slanted Asian eyes and yellow skin (their skin was actually more brownish than yellow), I chose Australia. The HQ company clerk made *uh-oh* noises and informed me Australia was the most popular R&R destination and allocations had to be filled months in advance. He said I should have requested Australia when I first arrived in-country, which would have been a neat trick since I had been more preoccupied with adjusting to my new environment and staying alive than with vacationing. He suggested Taipei since quotas going in that direction were always open. All I could think was more slant-eyed people. I stuck to my guns and requested Australia. The clerk gave me one of those long-drawn out, two-syllable OKs that end with the "K" being pronounced an octave higher.

The discouraging news about R&R, the more than likely false rumors about the division pulling out, the absence of mail from my girlfriend, and the aftereffect of the ammo dump explosion wilted my morale to the extent I didn't want to be in the band anymore. I was angry. I wanted to inflict hurt on the VC. I walked a couple of blocks to the sniper school and informed an instructor I recognized from playing retreat at their school that I wanted to be a sniper and kill VC. He said give him a minute and left the room. When he returned he told me I was too tall to be a sniper, they'd have too much trouble hiding me in the bushes. When I returned to DISCOM, Mister Johns explained why I really didn't want to be a sniper and why he really wouldn't approve my or anyone else's transfer out of the band. He reminded me that we were shorthanded several musicians as it was. It had been a reprimand, but one done in a most understanding way.

Actually the band's TO&E had suddenly become nearly fully staffed, and we now had almost 40 bandsmen, the only problem being that some of them weren't qualified musicians. One fellow, an airborne SSG with a rebellious streak who wore his rank badge and airborne wings pinned to the front of his baseball cap in contravention of Army regulations,[19] joined the percussion section to play triangle. *Ding, ding.* This wasn't an entirely necessary function, since the triangle was not key to the type of music we played and its sound could be reproduced on the glockenspiel. If you had enough bananas you could probably train a monkey to play the triangle. Disregarding the fact our new NCO percussionist's ability was rather limited, he did look STRAC in his tailored, starched, and pressed jungle fatigues. I assumed his advanced training in combat skills might be useful at some point, although he did mention his apprehension about being under fire with a bunch of bandsmen. On reflection, his observation may have been valid.

The ranks of the band and DISCOM were being systematically filled with career types, which surprised me. I thought at this late stage of the war (fifth year) all the older lifers who hadn't been to 'Nam had been smart enough to avoid coming. There was actually an ancient SFC lifer I liked who came to the DISCOM HQ Company. I don't remember his name or what his function was in the company, probably top kick (first sergeant). He was without doubt one crazy old combat coot. He'd fought in World War II and Korea. The black, subdued CIB (Combat Infantry Badge) sewn above his left breast pocket had two stars within its wreath.[20] Vietnam would be his last war and this was a good thing for him, as well as for everyone else in the Army. For some reason unbeknownst to me, he gravitated toward me and during his short tenure with DISCOM always called me out of the personnel shelters during an attack to join him in watching the fireworks, usually from the *top* of the shelter![21] One morning after breakfast he just wasn't there anymore. He might have rotated out of 'Nam, but I think the medics netted him and off he went back to CONUS.

I do recall another replacement first sergeant who came to the HQ Company. He was a tall, slightly overstuffed fellow whose race was neither black nor white. It was hard to tell because his skin coloration was an undeterminable balance of the two, but his facial features leaned toward Caucasian. He spoke with an accent that was impossible for me to place. Speculation among the band settled on Louisiana Cajun. When his head was not under his helmet he wore a DI cap, which, because of his exotic complexion and great bulk, made him look kin to Smokey Bear. He was not loved by the band. Our feelings may have been predicated upon the joy he took in overseeing our work details. Although his uniform displayed no CIB on his jungle fatigues, he obviously considered bandsmen beneath his warrior's standards.

One fine day several bandsmen were detailed to work on top of a new style of wooden, sand-filled, company-size personnel shelter the engineers were erecting to replace several older and battle-damaged sandbag shelters. The work entailed shoveling sand and dirt piled in the center of the inner roof down into the shelter's hollow wood walls. Our beloved first sergeant was cooling himself in the shade of the shelter below the workers. One of the fellows accidentally dribbled a little of the gritty stuff off the edge of his shovel. It went over the side of the wall and dropped onto the wide brim of Smokey's hat. The HQ Company's top kick quickly removed the hat, examined it, looked upward, and then all around him. When he looked upward, the boys on top of the shelter ducked. This farce was repeated several times until the first sergeant scratched his head, looked around one final time, and then moved away from the bunker. I guess he never figured out what was happening.

In regard to the new shelter, when the engineers first started its construction they also began systematically demolishing the old sandbag bunkers. The new bunker was situated in a central location at the south end of the band barracks in the opposite direction from the old bunkers.[22] Early one evening three rounds of heavy ordnance landed smack-dab in the center of the DISCOM parade ground. The rushing sound made by the incoming projectiles was matched only by the magnitude and proximity of the explosions. The concussions catapulted me out of my upper bunk berth and onto roommate Albert's French horn case. The VC weren't supposed to have artillery in IV CTZ. In the confusion to survive the attack the barracks center aisle had become jammed with panicked troops, some running toward the nonexistent old bunkers and some toward the new company shelter. I had sustained a slight but painful injury when I landed on Albert's instrument case and was in the process of hobbling to the new shelter when I careened flat-faced into a wall of sand and dirt. The engineers had piled the fill material needed to complete the new DISCOM shelter right between the band barracks' rear exit and the shelter's nearest entrance![23] After regaining my sensibilities, I scampered over the dirt mound along with others who had also unexpectedly hit the pile. When I reached the baffled opening of the shelter I discovered SP-4 Milton Lee flattened against the outside wall of the shelter, arms outstretched, madly clawing at the wooden wall. I grabbed him by the waist and shoved him through the entrance. Milt had lost it, which was unusual for him, for he was an otherwise solid trooper who could always be depended upon. It could happen to any one of us, for we all existed on the borderline of insanity, constantly facing death or injury. It didn't take much to cross over the line; an unexpected encounter with a mound of dirt could do it.

The artillery impacts, as the Green Machine explained to Mister Johns, had been nothing to worry about. Just a little friendly fire from the 1/84th Artillery Battalion (self-propelled 155mm and 8-inch cannon), who in their haste to set up a fire mission had elevated the firing angle of their tracked 155mm howitzers just a teensy bit too high. Had they had set it any higher, General Ewell would have been playing records at his next gala event.

The month of March concluded with several more band engagements, all performed on Đồng Tâm: a party for Division Artillery on the February 27, a re-up ceremony at division HQ and a change of command ceremony for the 93rd Engineer Battalion on February 28, an awards ceremony for the 15th Engineer Battalion on the 29th, and the usual daily gigs at the Reliable Academy.

I still had over 200 days to serve in Vietnam.

It seemed like an eternity.

6

Republic of Vietnam, April 1969

Contrary to the lyrics of the old song, April didn't bring showers, leastways not in the Mekong Delta. What it did bring was a new commanding general. The band's first few days of April were occupied with various performances connected with outgoing Major General Julian J. Ewell's departure.[1] Although General Ewell's affairs kept the entire band busy, we were able to cut loose a bugler from the festivities to play Taps at a memorial service at FSB Moore held by the 15th Engineer Battalion.[2]

The actual departure ceremony, which was little more than an overblown change of command ceremony, occurred at division HQ on April 2 when Major General Harris W. Hollis officially took command of the 9th Infantry Division from Major General Ewell. General Ewell had commanded the division for the past 13 months and was now being reassigned to the lofty post of commanding general of II Field Force

On the night of April 5 I drew my first perimeter guard duty. It was Easter weekend. The VC had left us in peace for the last couple of days and, as usual, everyone was apprehensive about the next bout of attacks. Because Sunday was a day off for most troops on Đồng Tâm, Saturday evening had become club night for troops desiring drinks or stateside-type entertainment. The entertainment was usually provided by the USO (United Servicemen's Organization). The EM Club wasn't one of my favorite places to spend a Saturday evening, although I did go once to leer along with the other guys at a scantily clad all-girl Australian band. On this guard mount, because of my E-5 rank, I was made sergeant of the guard. My primary duty for the evening was communication. I was to remain in the TOC (Tactical Operations Center) bunker[3] and supervise communications between four perimeter bunkers, the officer of the guard, and G-3 (Operations). The perimeter bunkers were positioned about 100 yards apart. If any activity occurred in our area of responsibility I was to notify G-3 and get their permission before authorizing the guards to open fire. Bình Duc village was within our field of fire and any movement detected in the village could be as innocent as a villager taking a dump or a midnight stroll. The activity could also be friendly roving patrols, although this was doubtful since security patrols were usually farther out searching for VC mortar crews.

Guard duty began with my being picked up at DISCOM in a deuce-and-a-half. I was the last guard to be retrieved, and we drove directly to the east perimeter. The guards aboard the truck already looked tired, and their appearance was a bit scruffy by band standards. The officer of the guard, a very young second lieutenant, acted edgy. I surmised the lieutenant was an OCS (Officer's Candidate School) graduate with a high school education. He kept fidgeting on the bench seat and staring at Mister Johns' loaner .45 automatic cinched around my waist. His weapon was a standard-issue M-16. The guards were systematically dropped off at their respective mounts, four per bunker, and the lieutenant and I continued on to the TOC bunker, which was a short distance behind the perimeter.

The TOC bunker was rudimentary even by Army standards, a metal CONEX shipping container cocooned in sandbags and containing a folding

I rarely visited the Đồng Tâm EM Club, but once I learned the "Australian All-Girl Band" was featured, I just *had* to check out the round-eyed ladies (author's collection).

chair, a small table, and two telephones. I informed the lieutenant this was my first sergeant of the guard duty, whereupon he explained that the black telephone connected simultaneously to all four bunkers, and the red one was a private line to G-3. All one had to do was pick up the receiver and connection would be made. No dialing necessary. My job was to routinely speak to the guards to ascertain they were still awake or, worse, alive[4] and to secure permission from G-3 before any of them opened fire. The lieutenant's job was to float between the bunkers and keep everybody awake and alert.

It all seemed very rudimentary, or so I thought.

The night began well. The troops in the bunkers rotated sleeping on four-hour shifts—two guards in the rack and two on duty. Everything seemed peaceful. The unfriendlies missed their usual weekend 2200 hours mortaring, as well as the one they enjoyed launching at 0200 hours. We may have dodged the bullet, or in this case the bombs. I'd been concerned Easter weekend would attract enemy action and had psychologically prepared for the worst. At around 0300 hours I was having difficulty keeping awake, I kept nodding off. I had no one in the command post to relieve me after a four-hour shift. I realized I'd missed the 0300 hours commo check with the bunkers. I was only a few minutes late, so it was no big deal.

I picked up the black bunker telephone handset. The guards were slow in answering, but then the hour was late—well, actually early morning. I casually asked the first voice that came on the line how everything was going. He answered, "Cool," which I interpreted as OK. I then asked to speak with the lieutenant, thinking maybe he should drop in on the command center once in a while to check on me. The voice at the other end asked, "Who?" I responded with, "The lieutenant, you know, the fellow with the little black bar on his collar."

"Ain't seen him all night," another voice chirped and then another, "There ain't no bar out here."

Uh-oh, it then dawned on me that I hadn't heard from the lieutenant all night either.

"Well, when he shows up have him call me." I didn't know what else to say. Something was amiss. He said he'd be floating between the bunkers. Had I somehow misunderstood him?

A few minutes later everything hit the fan, figuratively speaking. The call indicator light on the open telephone line to the bunkers lit and before I could get the handset up to my ear I heard the excited words, "We've got movement! We've got movement in the wire!"

It was early morning and I knew from personal experience that, after staring out into darkness for hours on end, shadows sometimes appeared to be what they are not. I was about to explain the usefulness of peripheral vision for identifying things in the dark when I heard the pop and hiss of a launched flare. I bolted to the opening of the command post praying the flare wasn't green. It wasn't; it was yellow—one of ours. While I stood watching the flare drift over the berm, another flare popped and brightened the perimeter. The telephone call-waiting light began blinking again. I picked up the receiver.

"Movement in the wire, movement in the wire, we've got movement in the wire, permission to open fire!"

Another voice, "Ain't nothin out there, asshole."

And another, "Let's smoke 'em."

I thought I heard repressed laughter in the background. None of the bunkers had identified themselves so I hadn't a clue as to whom I was speaking. I thought they might be jerking me around, what with my being a bandsman and all that kind of crap. Maybe they were just funning me, but I could hardly take the chance infiltrators were advancing on our position. I picked up the red telephone receiver to notify G-3. I identified myself, which guard mount I was with, and relayed the request to open fire.

The person at the other end of the line said, "There ain't nothin' out there."

The bunker telephone lit again, "Permission to open fire, permission to open fire, permission to open fire!" I could hear the urgency in the speaker's voice; I didn't know what to do, so I told everybody to pop more flares and identify *specific* targets. Outside I heard the distant popping sounds of flares being launched along the line of bunkers. We were agitating the entire perimeter.

"Permission to turn the machine gun! Permission to turn the machine gun! There's movement behind us!"

That request got my attention, *big time*. I sternly ordered all bunkers not to turn their machine guns. Hell, *I was positioned behind them!* These guys must have been smoking pot or something. I didn't know what to do. I cursed the absent lieutenant and his ancestors and ordered more flares. *Pop, pop, pop!* Outside the TOC bunker it looked as bright as daylight. Flares were floating overhead *inside the perimeter!* The entire length of the east berm resembled Times Square on New Year's Eve. A burst of machine-gun fire ripped through the night! I screamed, "Stand down! Stand down!" into the bunker telephone receiver. Then, as if by magic, the gunfire raggedly tapered off as the flares dimmed in the sky. A calm voice came on the bunker line and advised me everything was cool.

The voice was the lieutenant's. He must have been in one of the bunkers all along, probably catching up on his sleep, when the machine-gun fire had awakened him. I wondered if the night's fiasco would be reported. I doubted it, but if it was it'd be logged in as enemy action, maybe even having resulted in an enemy kill or two. The 9th Infantry Division had a reputation for inflating body counts.

Things settled down quickly. Tranquility returned to the east perimeter as the last of the parachute flares drifted to earth in an eerie muted glow and the silence of darkness returned. I never found out what had caused all the fuss that night, nor was I was ever assigned sergeant of the guard duty again. In the big picture of survival *it didn't mean nothing*.

In regard to the young lieutenant, the educational level of Army officers serving in Vietnam ran the gamut from high school graduates with OCS training through college-degreed ROTC reserve officers all the way to West Point-commissioned regular Army officers. What you got as an officer varied with the luck of the draw. The person in charge of your life could be a 19-year-old with the same educational background as the Good Humor man who sold ice cream on your block back in The World or some career-oriented lifer type whose primary mission was personal advancement in the military. It was a frightening proposition, but a necessary one, since USARV protocol demanded officers serve only six months in a combat command—infantry, armor, or artillery—and six months in a combat support or administrative command. The intended purpose of the Green Machine was to expose as many officers as it could to different types of combat commands. It would have worked had there been an increasing pool of officers available; but negative sentiment toward the war on the home front had effectively eroded the ranks of those seeking commissions, and the Army was now forced to use high school graduates. At each and every end of the month payday, the Đồng Tâm payroll officer asked if any of us would like to be an officer. I always declined with a respectful but enthusiastic "No, sir!"

The morning after being relieved from guard duty I wasn't required to attend roll call, nor did I have to perform on any work details. I had the day off to catch up on my sleep. Musically I didn't miss a thing because it had been a light day for the band, the only commitment being the weekly graduation ceremony at the Reliable Academy.

The following day, April 7, the band's schedule was far more interesting. A bunch of us boarded a Chinook and flew to FSB Schroeder for a concert. FSB Schroeder was farther west than FSB Moore. It straddled a sweeping curve in Route QL-4 near the Rach Ông Ve highway bridge (on reflection it might have been the Rach Bày Tiên, as the two streams came together a short distance north of the bridge). The helicopter pads were positioned across the

On April 7 the band returned to FSB Moore to perform in concert. The area surrounding a makeshift stage was crawling with troops. The bandmaster said it was the biggest turnout he'd ever seen. The turnout, however, wasn't for us. The band was merely the opening act for a Korean rock band that featured scantily clad female go-go dancers (author's collection).

highway opposite the main part of the base, which occupied a parcel of former agricultural land cultivated by a network of unusually wide irrigation canals. The engineers who constructed the base had left the canals in place for drainage. Much like FSB Moore, the barracks and other structures were mostly sandbag bunkers mixed in with a smattering of wooden buildings and tents. The base bordered on the southeastern fringe of the Plain of Reeds, a vast tract of dense, razor-sharp, six-foot-tall grass that offered unlimited concealment for the VC. I suspect enemy action at FSB Schroeder got intense at times.

FSB Schroeder served as the HQ of the 2/39th "Recondo" Infantry Battalion. I'm not certain which artillery unit supported them, because I can't recall seeing any artillery on the base. It might have been the 2/4th Artillery and their guns temporarily moved to another location in support of an operation being conducted outside of what would have otherwise been the effective range of artillery at FSB Schroeder.

FSB Schroeder had been formerly named FSB Dirk. It had received its new name during the previous month to honor the battalion's fallen commander, LTC Robert B. Schroeder. He had been KIA on February 13 during an aerial reconnaissance. In his enthusiasm to satisfy his brigade commander's wish to interrogate a VC prisoner, he, upon seeing a small group of armed Vietnamese, ordered the pilot of the LOH[5] (Light Observation Helicopter) he was aboard to set down. Schroeder dismounted from the aircraft and singlehandedly pursued the enemy. He was killed in the process.

The concert was held in a large tent named the First Recondo Religious Center. The band played a mix of contemporary music and old favorites. The new battalion commander, LTC Robert A. Sullivan, attended the concert along with some of his staff. The turnout was light inasmuch as there was never a lot of troop interest in the sanitized tunes we played, but the colonel and his aides seemed to have enjoyed our performance; leastwise they said they did and in appreciation invited the entire band to join them in the officers' mess tent for refreshments.

There was a much smaller ARVN patrol base several hundred yards southwest of Schroeder. Its garrison had the responsibility of maintaining the security of the Rach Ông Ve Bridge (or was it the Rach Bày Tiên—hmmm—?) as well as a second highway bridge over the nearby Rach Ông Hung. Every bridge crossing on a major thoroughfare in IV CTZ was defended by ARVN troops. Sometimes their fortifications consisted of heavily barbed-wired and sandbagged firing positions at both ends of the bridge and sometimes the rusty hulk of a tank the French had left behind when they vamoosed back in 1954. Bridges were choice targets for VC sappers. Blow up a bridge and vehicular commerce is frustrated. Destroyed bridges didn't affect the military as much as the civilian population. The Army could have a Bailey bridge in place within hours or fall back on its airmobile assets to move troops and supplies.

On April 9 the band returned to FSB Moore to play a concert. The Green Machine was accelerating the number of band performances in an effort to bolster morale. The esprit de corps of the division was on the wane. On the home front Tết '68 had effectively undermined the credibility of the U.S. government and military. The youth of America were flirting with anarchy. Support among middle-class Americans for continuing the Vietnam War was at a turning point. The nation was divided between the hawks and the doves, with the middle-ground position narrowing. Added to this was the complication and agitation of black equality, the women's liberation movement, the make love not war hippie movement, and a motion picture industry that was just beginning to capitalize on America's discontentment with the war by producing big-budget films cashing in on the growing negativity toward the war. As more and more conscripted replacements filled the ranks of the division, the attitudes they brought from their indoctrination on the home front began negatively affecting overall morale within the division.

The prevailing attitude of the troops at DISCOM pretty much matched my own attitude: *stay alive until DEROS*. The war's lack of progress, coupled with the military's failure to establish measurable objectives, had infused soldiers with the aura of hopelessness. The widespread corruption of the South Vietnamese government, not to mention that of our own military, added to that feeling. For those of us wandering around Indian Country it was hard enough to tell the friendlies from the bad guys, let alone fathom the moral credibility of the war.

I have always felt the war was wrong, that President Harry S. Truman had erred in not honoring President Franklin D. Roosevelt's original promise to the People of Vietnam[6] that the United States would support their efforts to cast off their colonial French masters to govern themselves. President Truman's administration blatantly supported the reinstitution of French colonialism in Vietnam and in doing so had planted the seeds for one of America's longest, and perhaps most culturally devastating, war. When Dwight D. Eisenhower became president he foolishly continued sending aid to the French in the form of weapons and military advisors.[7]

After the French withdrew in disgrace from Vietnam, America took over conducting the war, at first with equipment, munitions, air support, and a handful of military advisors charged with the mission of training and assisting the South Vietnamese military. The election of President John F. Kennedy brought his New Frontier platform and renewed hope for America, but not in Vietnam. His administration oversaw the establishment of the Green Beret, a special force of soldiers highly trained in counterinsurgency, and MACV, the organization that would oversee the deployment of regular ground forces.[8] In essence the United States had been laying the groundwork for conventional warfare in Vietnam.

The next president, Lyndon B. Johnson, ran with the concept. Under his administration the war escalated from a few thousand advisors to a ground force of over half a million combatants. After five years of fighting and thousands of deaths on both sides nothing had been accomplished, other than in the minds of our political leaders and the military. The light-at-the-end-of-the-tunnel speech by General Westmoreland in 1967 had been the proverbial straw that broke the home-front camel's back. Amid massive public home-front discontentment with the war, the military, and the government, the band was supposed to inspire morale in the division by keeping the spirit and traditions of the Army alive. What I witnessed wasn't worth saving. I was having enough trouble with my own morale, let alone inspiring that of others.

Unlike for draftees, for lifers the war represented just another assignment in the evolution of their careers, unless of course some necessary piece of their anatomy got blown off. Then it also became an end for them. For lifers, Vietnam service offered a potential career boost in the form of accelerated promotions, medals, inclusion in the brotherhood of warriors, and oodles of war stories to be told over and over. Being in combat could either help or hinder a career. Most of the lifers I encountered had brownnoser attitudes, which was viewed by conscripts as a kind of hypocrisy. It added to the inevitable breakdown of morale and discipline within the ranks. To illustrate this point, a favorite epigram among draftees when knowingly treading upon the rules was *What are they going to do, send me to 'Nam?* Career soldiers had to consider their futures in the Army, while draftees just had to stay alive for 365 days.

Speaking of being sent to 'Nam, one night during a particularly vicious mortar attack I shared a drainage ditch with a trooper whose face I didn't recognize. We were stuck in the ditch for quite a while and the conversation eventually got around to our mutually inquiring if the other was an RA or US? This fellow was neither; his service number began with NG! Now, for those not familiar with the prefix NG, it stands for National Guard. For most of the Vietnam War the Army National Guard and Army Reserve did not universally participate in the war effort—that is, unless one of them screwed up.[9] In the case of my ditch mate, he had skipped enough meetings to suffer the punishment of activation and deployment to Vietnam!

Screwing up and being sent to 'Nam wasn't an uncommon occurrence, either. Several musicians in the band had also run afoul of the law back in The World and as a consequence had been given the option by the court of enlisting in the Army or going to jail. It was hardly morale-boosting to be risking one's life knowing one's patriotic service to his country was another man's punishment. Having had observed the Green Machine in combat for approximately four months, I was certain lunatics were handling matters at the top. There was absolutely no doubt in my military mind that the Army originally created by geniuses had morphed into something far less in Vietnam.

Well, moving on. The April 7 concert at FSB Moore initially looked like it was going to be a standing-room-only affair for the band. There were troops reclining everywhere—on top of bunkers, on vehicles, on artillery pieces, literally anywhere they could secure an unobstructed view of their very own division band in concert. That's what it looked like at the start of our performance. Our stage was a flatbed trailer. After we finished playing, the applause we received was ragged but greater than usual. Even before the clapping ended, however, we were shooed off the improvised stage and replaced by a Korean rock 'n' roll band accompanied by several scantily clad go-go dancers. As the girls climbed up onto the stage the roar of the crowd became deafening! The 9th Infantry Division Band had been merely the opening act.

April 11 brought me some respite from the drudgery of Đồng Tâm. I left on a three-day pass to take the Graduate School Entrance Exam in Saigon. By this time even the mortar and rocket attacks the VC enjoyed launching against Đồng Tâm had lost their adrenaline-pumping affect. Bombs falling out of the sky had become so commonplace it now meant something only

I *assumed* I'd get a helicopter lift to Saigon to take the Graduate Records Exam, but that didn't happen. On the day of my departure there were no helicopters available, so the bandmaster gave me the bandwagon, a driver, a guard, and the loan of his .45 automatic sidearm, which he sternly advised to keep hidden on my person at all times. I also took my M-16 and flak vest—just in case the environment along the route got hostile (courtesy Larry Wolf).

While driving along the 40-mile route to Saigon we passed some interesting scenery, including an ARVN artillery battery of 105mm towed howitzers setting up for a fire mission in an empty farm field (author's collection).

when they hit nearby. I had sent my application and $15 fee to Seton Hall University to take the Graduate School Entrance Exam. They advised me the test would be given on April 12 at the Vietnamese-American Association office in Saigon. I thought the Army would transport me to Saigon in a helicopter, but the available air assets in IV CTZ had dried up due to increased combat operations in the area. Mister Johns kindly offered me the use of the bandwagon along with a driver and guard. All of the band's commitments during the three days we'd be away were at the Reliable Academy, except for a dance combo gig for our new division commanding general's first mess party. The DISCOM transportation pool's three-quarter ton weapons carrier was adequate to handle the band's transportation needs while we were gone— that is, if the mechanics could get it started.

So on the morning of April 11 the three of us jumped in the bandwagon and off we went. None of us, including the driver, knew how to get to Saigon, let alone the Vietnamese-American Association office, but we had a map and advice on where to stay. There was a hotel in Saigon operated by a former GI who had married a Vietnamese woman. He would help us out with directions in town. Đồng Tâm was situated about 40 miles south of Saigon, and on the map it looked like a fairly straightforward trip.

We rolled out of the DISCOM compound, drove along the base road skirting the lineup of Navy riverboats berthed in the harbor, picked our way through the area damaged by the ammo dump explosion, passed the former USO Bob Hope Show stage, and zipped out the main gate. We were on our own! I inserted a magazine into my M-16, pulled back the bolt to chamber a round, put it on safe, and said a silent prayer to St. Christopher for him to watch over us. As I was praying, we passed the ANH Steambath Massage Parlor, an allegedly nefarious PX concession operated by civilians. I'd never been inside, but it was my understanding that the attractive young Vietnamese girls employed within its walls assisted in more than just a cleansing of the body. It was rumored to have been tolerated by the division as a necessary evil needed to maintain morale.

Provincial Route TL-25 ran along the north bank of the Sông Mỹ Tho. The surrounding scenery was tropical Asian and very lush, which in military terms meant way too much concealment. I took my usual sentry's perch above the truck's cab. For extra measure I removed a few magazines from my pockets and threw them on the canvas top beside me. I was wearing full combat gear, which in the band meant helmet, flak vest, bandolier of extra ammunition, rifle, personal first aid kit, and gasmask. I also had a few M-67 fragmentation grenades Larry had secured for me from his buddies at the Reliable Academy armory. The hand grenades had been an afterthought, and I wasn't all that comfortable with having them. Their kill radius exceeded the distance an average person could throw one, which meant it had the potential of being just as deadly to the thrower as it was to the target. I hoped I looked vigilant enough to discourage any VC sniper hiding in the bushes along the roadside.

The buildings on the riverbank were an odd mixture of architecturally pleasing French and hardscrabble Vietnamese. The stark contrast between shacks and residences graphically illustrated the reason for Vietnamese discontentment with colonialism. The Delta was a land of those who had much and those who had very little, the latter being the majority of the population and of Asian birth. Through the policies of our government, which represented "We the People"—the sanctimonious self-appointed defenders of world freedom and social equality, not only supported this deplorable situation but wantonly killed those who were fighting for the freedom to govern themselves and end the inequalities.

I, too, was prepared to kill them, not because I believed in what our government was doing but because I was a soldier and honor bound by my sense of duty and loyalty to my country and fellow soldiers. Still, I harbored the enemy no ill will. The VC were soldiers, too, a bit irregular in their tactics and dress, but soldiers nonetheless. My attitude toward them may have been influenced by my father. Thirty-two years before my birth he had been a soldier in the Imperial German Army, our nation's enemy at the time. Dad had spent five years (1914–1918) in the trenches of the Champagne fighting the French. He had been a forward observer with a heavy artillery regiment. His job had been to crawl as close to enemy lines as possible while stringing out telephone wire behind him. Once in position he would direct the cannon fire to target. For his troubles he'd been shot, gassed, and bludgeoned. It was hard for me to envision him as ever having been the enemy. He was a kind, intelligent person who was proud to be an American citizen. Besides, he was my dad.

My father's military background had undoubtedly tempered my feelings toward the VC. They were, as we were, soldiers executing some politician's will, which in the final analysis is precisely what all good soldiers do. For me, killing Charlie wasn't a personal thing. We ultimate weapons had been trained to kill without remorse and not think too much about things concerning politics and the morality of war.

Several klicks east of Đồng Tâm we turned northward onto Local Route 256. The terrain was mostly checkerboard rice paddy land, occasionally interrupted by dense stands of jungle growth. From the perspective of patrolling, these stands or tree lines were not good things; it was where Charlie hid himself in ambush. Every now and then we'd pass a field with what appeared to be a bulldozed pile of mud displaying a Republic of Vietnam national flag flapping from a pole at its center. Based on the overall size of the mound and the flag, I assumed they were patrol bases for smaller ARVN units. As we continued northward we also passed quite a few ancestral burial plots. Although peasants lived in ramshackle dwellings (by U.S. standards), their ancestors spent eternity in substantial concrete or stone enclosures. The typical burial site was aboveground and included a stone tomb surrounded by a low stone wall. They were distinctive and very decorative. We also passed well-constructed miniature roadside temples. I don't know what their purpose was in the religious scheme of things, but I always kept them under close scrutiny, just in case the religion was VC.

When we reached the intersection with Route QL-4 we turned eastward. We were now on the main artery into Saigon. A short distance down the road, at an intersection with Provincial Route LTL-6A, QL-4 veered sharply northward. We unfortunately didn't veer with it. The driver missed the turn and only after the road turned southward did he notice a sign indicating we were on our way to the city of Mỹ Tho, which was in the opposite direction. Following a brief conference we made a U-turn and backtracked to the intersection. I could see why we had missed the turn. The QL-4 turn sign was lying on the ground all shot up, and, in all fairness to our driver, the layout of the intersection had favored LTL-6A. Once again headed in the correct direction, we eventually came to the village of Tân Hiêp, where Local Route 256, the continuation of the same dirt road we had taken earlier, intersected with QL-4. Although it would have been faster for us to have kept on Route 256 up to this location, we wanted to stay on as many paved roads as possible. Paved roads were harder for the VC to booby trap and were patrolled in greater frequency by the MPs.

Traffic along QL-4 consisted of a steady flow of ARVN and U.S. military vehicles, interspersed with a few civilian automobiles, trucks, busses, and a plethora of Lambretta motor scooters. They came in two varieties: the single seat scooter and a larger minibus version that could seat half a dozen people in an open compartment. The Lambretta made a distinctive popping sound when the driver backed off the throttle. I kept my eyes on each one as they popped by us lest a hand grenade be thrown our way. Vigilance was one of the keys to survival in the Mekong, and a prudent trooper assumed every Vietnamese civilian he encountered was a possible VC—make that a *probable* VC.

As the day wore on we eventually reached Tân An, the largest city along our route to Saigon and also the HQ FSPB (Fire Support Patrol Base) of the Division's 3rd Brigade. On our approach to Tân An's city limits, we saw the density of buildings lining Route QL-4 became greater and of more substantial construction than the peasant hooches we'd been passing all morning. Many were commercial buildings of some sort. All needed cosmetic attention. At the west end of Tân An, Highway QL-4 crossed over the Sông Vám Có Tây on a high steel overhead-truss bridge. QL-4 was the only road in the city that crossed the river and traffic was bumper to bumper. Caught in the jam, we moved forward a few feet then paused, moved forward, paused, etc., etc., etc.

Once beyond the bottleneck of the bridge, traffic thinned out, and we resumed our journey at normal highway speeds. At Bên Lức we crossed over the Sông Vám Có Đông. South of the bridge in the middle of the river was a large U.S. Navy ship, the USS *Harnett County*. It was one of those World War II-vintage LSTs (Landing Ship Tank) designed to nose onto a beach, open its huge bow doors, and dispense a cargo of tanks, trucks, and troops. It now served as a temporary mother ship, providing berthing and billeting accommodations for PBR boats (Patrol Boat River) and crews of River Division 591 who were awaiting completion of the new Naval Support Activity Saigon-Detachment Bên Lức facility.

6. Republic of Vietnam, April 1969

Ten months earlier we would have had to detour north of the Sông Vàm Cỏ Đông Bridge to a makeshift crossing. During the morning of June 30, 1968, enemy sappers dropped a 150-foot span of the bridge into the river with explosives. A temporary pontoon bridge had been erected north of the damaged crossing to keep traffic flowing. Although the area continually came under heavy VC fire, repairs to the QL-4 crossing were completed during the following month and the Sông Vàm Cỏ Đông Bridge reopened, this time with better security.

North of Bến Lức the scenery took on an aura of prosperity, leastwise more prosperous than what we'd seen so far. We passed an ARVN battery of 105mm howitzers set up in a vacant field. Their artillerymen were positioning aiming stakes. It must have been a temporary fire support base, because no defensive perimeter surrounded the position and each of the cannon was placed to fire in a different direction.

We eventually arrived in the southwest section of Saigon and were immediately faced with a problem—the end of Route QL-4. Our option consisted of several different roads, but we didn't know which one to take. We decided to aim for the Saigon River and what we hoped would be the center of the city. The route we chose passed the Phú Thọ Racetrack, a landmark that had attained some notoriety during Tết '68 when it had been commandeered by the VC for a command post and field hospital. It had been the scene of some of Tết '68's fiercest fighting when on February 10, 1968, the 199th Light Infantry Brigade took it back. The stands were pockmarked with bullet holes. We decided the densely populated area of the city we were passing through was Cholon, Saigon's Chinatown. Dusk was beginning to settle and we still weren't certain of our destination.

Fortunately for us we were intercepted at a traffic light by MPs patrolling in a spit-shined quarter-ton utility truck. They informed us it was illegal for us to carry weapons in the Saigon Capital Zone.[10] We explained that we had just arrived in town from Đồng Tâm, where there was a war going on and everyone carried weapons. We explained we were looking for the hotel run by a former GI. They told us to unload our weapons and keep them out of sight; we were perfectly safe in Saigon. They knew the location of the hotel we sought and gave us driving directions. They also instructed us to turn in our weapons at the hotel desk for safekeeping. Suddenly, small-arms fire cracked nearby and the MPs scurried off in the direction of the shots. I reloaded my M-16 and now fully understood why Mister Jones had loaned me his pistol along with solemn advice to keep it hidden on my person at all times while in Saigon. He apparently had been here.

Saigon was a large city with big fancy city buildings. The streets were paved, curbed, and lined by sidewalks. We passed many beautiful parks and gardens, department stores, townhouses, and, best of all, girls attired in miniskirts and high-heeled shoes! I'd become so accustomed to unadorned females draped in pajama dress that the brightly colored outfits and the cosmopolitan appearance of the gals I now viewed reminded me of the way ladies dressed in urban America. These babes were not peasants; they were city girls—and very nice ones at that. Perhaps General Sherman had been wrong: war wasn't entirely hell.

We eventually found our hotel. It was a couple of blocks off of Tự Do Street, the main drag through Saigon's former French Quarter. We were in the heart of the city. Inside the lobby of the hotel an American stood behind the reception desk and warmly greeted us. A tiny, light-skinned Asian child contently played with her doll in one corner of the lobby. I assumed the little girl belonged to our host. After we checked in we mentioned our encounter with the MPs to him. He uttered a few derisive comments about Saigon MPs and told us to keep our weapons locked and loaded on safe in our rooms. Apparently Saigon wasn't as secure as the MPs had led us to believe. It wasn't a situation of all-out warfare like the kind being waged in the Delta, but the VC liked to kidnap or execute a citizen or soldier every now and then. They kept the South Vietnamese National Police, affectionately known as White Mice, and the Army MPs busy zipping around town chasing after them. Just as our host was advising us we'd get used to it, a distant explosion rattled the windows. None of us, including the child, flinched and he commented, "See what I mean?" He handed us a city map and suggested I use the Army bus service to the Vietnamese-American Association. The Green Machine apparently ran a scheduled bus route throughout the city in order to transport the legion of U.S. military office personnel working in town.

The next morning I parted company with my buddies and wandered over to the bus stop, which was on Tự Do Street a couple of blocks away from the hotel. On the walk I passed soldiers carrying brief cases instead of rifles. Their shoes were spit shined and their fatigues crisply starched, all very STRAC. Back at Đồng Tâm I had heard about "Saigon warriors," and it was refreshing to do a little prejudicial pecking of my own. In 'Nam there were different degrees of REMF (Rear Echelon Mother Fucker), as the infantry types like to label combat support troops they believed did their fighting with pen and paper in the safety of the phantom rear. I was never quite certain where the "rear" was since all of South Vietnam was nasty unfriendly in different degrees. But with pretty ladies in miniskirts plying the streets and no weapons permitted, Saigon seemed as close to being a "rear" as anywhere I'd experienced in Vietnam. I think REMF was a misnomer, though, it should have been BEMF (Bureaucratic Echelon Mother Fucker), referring to those who held your fate in their hands while living in relative safety and comfort. It wasn't about MOS; it was about exposure to risk and overall living conditions. Eleven Bravo types had difficulty understanding the concept. In their estimation if you weren't infantry, armor, or artillery—you were REMF, which defied logic because it didn't take into account airmen who were shot out of the sky, truck drivers who were ambushed driving convoys through Indian Country, the military policemen who guarded them, and, of course, the pussy-ass bandsmen who sweated it out at Đồng Tâm waiting for bombs to fall on their heads or be sniped at or booby-trapped in some godforsaken village while playing merry music to a people who hated our intrusion into their lives. Fellow trumpeter PFC Lawrence Corigliano eloquently summed it up when he once said in sympathy with the plight of ground pounders: "At least we get to shower every day." Maybe a daily shower qualified one as a REMF.

While waiting at the Army bus stop the Old Europe ambience of Saigon struck me. I had heard it was once known as the Paris of the Orient. Although much of the magnificence of its French-inspired architecture was now desecrated by sandbagged entranceways and barbed-wire firing positions manned by tough-looking guards with machine guns, it still remained a beautiful city. For reassurance I tapped the butt of the .45 automatic hidden in the waistband underneath my fatigue jacket. I had some empathy for these Saigon Warriors, who had to walk around town unarmed under the false pretense they were safe. Just thinking about it gave me the creeps.

The Army bus arrived and, *lo and behold,* it was a back-in-the-US-of-A–style vehicle with air-conditioning, comfy seats, and glass in the windows! There were even advertisements in the placard holders running the length of the bus above the center aisle (mostly yucky re-up ads). I snuggled down in my seat and enjoyed the ride.

The Vietnamese-American Association was housed in an ancient, musty office building with well-worn wooden floors that creaked when you walked across them. The room in which the test was being administered reminded me of the classrooms back at Florence Avenue Grammar School in Irvington, New Jersey, the vintage 1930s-style public school where I had attended kindergarten through third grade. The wooden flooring at Florence Avenue School had also been well-worn and creaky.

There were only a few applicants taking the test. The administering official vigilantly watched over us from a perch at the rear of the room—no cheating allowed. The test was difficult. My brain had been numbed by over a year of participating in the Army lifestyle, an environment that didn't view individual thought or intellectualism as desirable traits and where doing precisely what one was told was lauded with achievement awards and meritorious decorations. Well, I did the best I could on the test, and when I put down my pencil it was with the resignation of one who assumes it hadn't been good enough. I'd just have to run out my tour in 'Nam. I doubted even my professor friend back at Seton Hall, Dr. Jack Stumas, could help me now.

It was still early afternoon when the Army bus service delivered me back to Tự Do Street. At the hotel I joined my buddies for lunch. Our congenial host, who also functioned as our waiter, recommended a few hotspots in town if we wanted to get laid. I hadn't thought of this possibility and didn't welcome the opportunity, but it excited my two pals. We were warned that the gals who proliferated in Saigon's numerous bars worked for the management, their job being to encourage soldier boys to buy them drinks at outlandish prices. Our drinks would be alcoholic, but the girls' drinks would be only colored water GIs called "Saigon tea." After several rounds of drinks were consumed we would be asked by the gal who had singled us out to join her upstairs to make "boom-boom." Our host said, moral objections aside, it was all very legal. The bar girls were essentially pretty peasant girls who had been cleaned up, perfumed, and covered over with makeup and western-style dress to make the troops feel more at home in the saddle. The bar girls were family-oriented creatures who gave the money they prostituted themselves for to their families. They earned far more screwing GIs than they could ever earn farming with mamma and papa-san on someone else's land. Bar girls and prostitution were among the ways U.S. policy furthered economic opportunity for the downtrodden peasants of South Vietnam.

Armed with this knowledge, we embarked upon an adventure of Saigon barhopping. When the shadows cast by the barstools grew a bit longer with the late-growing hour, we stopped for dinner at a small restaurant that offered seating for only a small handful of customers. Our affable hotel host had made reservations for us. We negotiated the maze of city streets riding in people-powered rickshaws. The restaurant was in the living room of a private resident and was operated by an elderly French couple. He was the waiter and she the chef. The only option on the evening menu was oil and vinegar dressing with Roquefort cheese on the salad or oil and vinegar without Roquefort. The dinner was superb! After paying our tab, we decided to return to the bars. It was now dark and I felt uneasy about wandering around town, but I had the comfort of the .45, which in truth didn't feel all that comfortable tightly cinched against my stomach by the waistband of my trousers. The textured pistol grip chaffing against my moist skin was giving me a rash and the barrel was pointing downward at, well, you know what.

6. Republic of Vietnam, April 1969

We quickly found a noisy bar full of GIs and pretty girls. As we entered through the doorway we were immediately targeted by three cuties. I tried to wave off the one who had singled me out, but she was determined to fleece me out of several "drinks" and, perhaps, some reasonably priced recreational time in the sack. After my friends disappeared upstairs, my companion attempted to coax me upstairs, too, by pointing to the ceiling and emphatically repeating over and over, "Boom-boom, boom-boom." It was all very romantic. I kept emphatically repeating, "No boom-boom, no boom-boom." We did this for over half an hour until she resignedly sat back in her chair, huffed, and folded her arms across her waist. She had invested boo-coo time in me only to have been denied her livelihood. I felt guilty about that and slid several bills across the table, which I think may have exceeded her fee. She grabbed the money, jumped up out of her chair and spat out, "You dinky dou," which in Vietnamese parlance meant *crazy*. Without intending to do so, I probably had offended her sense of professional pride. Maybe she was right; maybe I was crazy. I'd been in the Army long enough to qualify. Crazy or not, I'd had

After four months of living and working in the impoverished Mekong Delta, Saigon offered a bit of a cultural shock. It was a classically beautiful city with stores, office buildings, sidewalks, curbs, and girls attired in miniskirts and high heels! I could now better appreciate how Dorothy felt upon viewing Oz for the first time—Saigon certainly wasn't the Delta (author's collection).

While driving through Saigon I had my first glimpse of an authentic "Saigon warrior," who, as rumor had it, was an Army bureaucrat who did his fighting with a briefcase. I spotted one walking along the sidewalk and there wasn't a weapon in sight (author's collection).

The Army operated civilian-style scheduled bus routes throughout Saigon. The buses I rode were air-conditioned, had real glass in the windows, and displayed interior advertising signs along the top edges of the car body, just like the buses back at home (author's collection).

6. Republic of Vietnam, April 1969

On the return drive from Saigon we encountered a traffic backup along Communal Route 256 north of Chợ Búng hamlet. Snipers hidden among the palms were disrupting the flow of traffic at a clearing by taking potshots at passing vehicles. Suddenly a Huey Slick roared down from the sky blasting the tree line with its machine guns. After everything settled down we continued on our journey to Đồng Tâm (author's collection).

enough of the Saigon nightlife and returned by myself to the hotel. My buddies upstairs could fend for themselves.

Fortunately my fellow travelers got safely back to the hotel, and the next morning we headed back to Đồng Tâm. The bandwagon was, thankfully, still parked where we'd left it. The heavy chain threaded through the spokes of its steering wheel and around the clutch pedal may have had something to do with it, but upon reflection, I doubt any self-respecting Vietnamese thief would have ever considered it worth stealing. It looked all-too decrepit in its faded olive drab, its metal hide pockmarked with shrapnel punctures, paint scrapes, and rust spots. It was not a pretty vehicle like the polished military vehicles I saw plying up and down the streets of Saigon.

Other than the lurking danger of bar girls the trip had been uneventful. No VC had jumped out between Saigon's buildings to ruin our day and so far there were no signs of enemy activity along QL-4. We were anxious to get back to Đồng Tâm, so when our truck approached the village of Tân Hiệp we threw caution to the wind and turned onto the more direct, unpaved,

Route 256. The sky was threateningly overcast. Just north of the village of Chợ Búng we encountered what initially appeared to be a roadblock backed up in a string of stopped Vietnamese vehicles ahead of us. As we decelerated we noticed several civilians cowering behind the vehicles. We slowed to a stop, grabbed our M-16s, and dismounted from the truck. As we approached the vehicles we were met by much unintelligible chattering and finger pointing toward a distant tree line on the far side of a sprawling rice paddy. The morning light was dimmed by heavy cloud cover, and we couldn't see what the problem was until several gun flashes brightened in the bushes. *Snipers!* We took cover with the Vietnamese and began nervously chattering and pointing toward the tree line ourselves!

Although the snipers were within the effective range of our rifles, they were too far away for us to get a bead on them without telescopic sights. Luckily for us the reverse was also true. Their rounds were hitting nearby, but nothing too close. Then, without warning, a Huey Slick rolled out of the sky blasting the tree line with its M-60 machine guns. I'd been so preoccupied with how we'd get past the snipers I hadn't heard its approach. After the sniper fire died down, the chopper hovered above our position with one of its door gunners peering down at us. We waved up to him. He smiled broadly beneath large tinted goggles and with his right hand he formed the V peace sign. The helicopter then darted off like a friendly passing dragon in the sky. They must have spotted the white recognition star on top of the bandwagon's engine compartment and deduced we were in trouble.

We arrived back at Đồng Tâm in time for chow. It was Sunday afternoon cookout day, another Green Machine idea to bolster morale. Actually it was a pretty good idea. We got to barbecue our own steaks the way we wanted them cooked and fraternize on a semiformal basis with the officers. Occasionally, lobster tails were available.

In the context of officers, one evening during a mortar attack the DICOM HQ Company XO (second in command) caught a tiny splinter of shrapnel metal in his arm and was treated at the 3rd Surgical Hospital. They stuck a bandage on the wound, gave him a sling with a Purple Heart pinned to it, and told him to take it easy for a few days. The inopportune wounding, unfortunately, wreaked havoc with DISCOM HHC Commander CPT Jeffrey A. Hurt's mental state. One morning I encountered him intently pacing off steps between the mess hall and his office-bunker-billet. I respectfully asked him what he was doing and he said he was counting how many steps he'd have to run to get back to the safety of his bunker![11]

On the topic of officers and bunkers, just about every senior-grade officer I encountered at Đồng Tâm slept in the security of a fortified billet. Our own

6. Republic of Vietnam, April 1969

battalion commander, the aforementioned COL Arthur P. Hanket, added the dimension of comfort to security. His billet was a private, air-conditioned mobile home encased in a sandbag revetment. To stop aerial projectiles from entering through the mobile home's thin sheet-metal roof, an elevated wooden platform supporting several layers of sandbags had been erected over the entire structure.

* * *

On April 14 the band sent a bugler over to the 6/31st Infantry Battalion HQ on the other side of Đồng Tâm to play Taps at a memorial service. The 6/31st was having a bad month. An unprecedented eight memorial ceremonies would be held in April just to pay homage to their fallen.

The month, however, wasn't too bad for the top brass. In April the dance band performed at three of the new division general's mess parties and on April 23 at a party for our very own COL Hanket. I never quite understood the frivolities demanded by those in the higher division echelons. While the troops were enduring the hardships associated with survival in an adverse psychological and physical environment, constantly exposed to death and injury, they awarded each other *courtesy* decorations, entertained themselves with parties attended by female subordinates and guests (nurses, nurses' aids, volunteer candy stripers, donut dollies, Vietnamese nationals, USO entertainers, and the like), and enjoyed an occasional connubial visit from their wives. For them the war was more of an inconvenience than a struggle for survival. The higher the pecking order the more luxuries and sandbags.

Field-grade officers (second lieutenant through captain)[12] didn't have it quite as comfortable. Because they were required to serve six months in direct combat (armor, infantry, or artillery) and another six months in combat support their luxuries were limited to what they could get away with. The enlisted ranks spent the entire year in their assigned MOS, whether combat or combat support. As I mentioned earlier, the concept behind the six-month rotation policy was to expose a greater percentage of officers to combat operations to better enable them to command troops. The policy backfired. As the war escalated and more troops arrived in-country, the demand for field officers exceeded the rate at which the Army could furnish them. Each and every payday, which faithfully occurred at the end of the month, the pay officer continued recommending purchasing U.S. Bonds, re-upping for another tour in 'Nam, and attending OCS.

As I also mentioned before, by 1969 the officer situation had become so desperate the Green Machine was accepting high school graduates as candidates for officer training. The real fallacy undermining the concept was that by the time an officer became proficient at commanding troops in combat he was rotated out of his unit. To the average ground pounder humping the bush, this policy appeared highly discriminatory and did much to undermine morale.

On the topic of morale, in addition to the one-week out-of-country R&R, soldiers were entitled to two weekend in-country R&Rs. In-country R&Rs were offered at Vũng Tàu and Cam Ranh Bay. Each location offered fabulous beaches, fabulous Vietnamese ladies, fabulous food, and fabulous entertainment. I never had the opportunity to enjoy an in-country R&R, but I did get to Vũng Tàu once or twice on band gigs. The rumor was the beaches were covered with volcanic black sand. I got to see only the airfield, and *it* was covered with nonvolcanic black asphalt.

On April 15 the band played an awards ceremony at DISCOM without me. I was one of the award recipients. The Army Commendation Medal

A concert brought the band to the HQ 2/39th Infantry Battalion at FSB Schroeder. The base bordered on the southeastern fringe of the Plain of Reeds, west of Cai Lây, and occupied both sides of a gentle curve in National Route QL-4. It had formerly been named FSB Dirk (author's collection).

6. Republic of Vietnam, April 1969

The concert at FSB Schroeder was held in the First "Recondo" Chapel, which was nothing more than a large Army tent distinguished by a cross affixed to the top of its front ridgepole upright (author's collection).

Mister Johns had recommended me for had been approved by the Green Machine. My pal, the DISCOM HQ company commander, CPT Hurt, pinned it on my uniform but, thankfully, stopped short of kissing each of my cheeks in the fashion of the French military.

During the next ten days the band remained on Đồng Tâm playing the usual Reliable Academy gigs, memorial ceremonies, parties for the chosen few, award ceremonies, and something new—a troop arrival gig for the 1/11th Artillery Battalion. The boys were rotating into Đồng Tâm. *Lucky them.*

Near the end of the month, on April 26, the band played two separate jobs in Cần Thơ. The first, which occurred in the morning, was for the 6/77th Artillery. It was phase two of Operation Big Switch. The one battery previously turned over to the 213th ARVN artillery on March 10 had been a success and now they were turning over the remainder of their assets in preparation for being withdrawn from Vietnam. For the band it was essentially a repeat performance, although a bit muggier weather-wise and of longer duration

Sunday at DISCOM was cookout day. Everyone belonging to the HQ Company got to barbeque their own hamburgers and steaks—that is, everyone who wasn't on the duty roster, or in the case of the band, off performing at a gig. I got to attend only a few of these outings, which suited me fine. They were an obvious attempt by the Green Machine to instill morale in the troops. I'd have preferred bunkered sleeping accommodations like the ones the officers enjoyed (author's collection).

(this time the 6/77th had more equipment to turn over). The lifers repeated everything they had said at the Phase I ceremony, but now they lengthened the festivities with self-adulation about how well they had organized the mechanics of the turnover. The band, however, still couldn't be heard over the vehicles as they roared past the reviewing stand, but it really didn't matter. Official Army records would indicate one marching band had been in attendance. All was as it should have been, as the official record would indicate when it was prepared in quadruplicate and filed away forever.

Upon the conclusion of Operation Big Switch the band was driven to the 52nd Signal Group in a deuce-and-a-half they had sent for us, and we played at their change of command ceremony. Cần Thơ was a fairly large city as well as the provincial capital of Phông Định Province. Although it was located within the 9th Infantry Division's AO, no division units, other than the administratively attached and now departing 6/77th Artillery, were stationed there. The HQ of IV CTZ plus a variety of specialized Army support

6. Republic of Vietnam, April 1969

The brass bigwigs of the Division lived and operated on a level that distanced them from the hardships faced by the common soldiers of Vietnam. They bolstered their morale with private parties, visits from wives, ego-boosting ceremonies, and the like. While the infantry humped the bush and the band traveled through Indian Country unprepared and unequipped for disaster, the senior grade staff of the 9th Infantry Division partied. Their attitudes might have stemmed from post–World War II occupation Army mentality (author's collection).

and administrative units were scattered in and around Cần Thơ. The U.S. Navy had a large support facility a few klicks up river from the city. Since we were the southernmost band in Vietnam, we often performed outside the division's AO and even occasionally performed for units that were not directly affiliated with the 9th Infantry Division.

Being the true artists that we were, I suspect we'd have played for just about anyone who'd listen to us!

7

Republic of Vietnam, May 1969

The month of May began musically with a change of command ceremony for 3rd Brigade. The ceremony was held at 3rd Brigade HQ in Tân An, the city with the largest population cluster in Long An Province. COL Levin B. Broughton, the brigade's departing commander, had become seriously ill after commanding the 3rd Brigade for approximately two months and was being relieved by COL Dale J. Crittenberger, who would later tragically lose his life in a helicopter accident.[1] Although I wasn't aware of it at the time, approximately half of all helicopter losses in Vietnam were the direct result of accident or malfunction. The band often flew to musical engagements on helicopters, but I never thought much about crashing. When aloft I was always aware of the possibility of being shot down; had I known of the high incidence of malfunction and accidental crashes I might have added that worry to my fret list. Anyway, the Caribou transport plane we flew landed safely at Tân An Army Airfield, which lay slightly west of the city's center.

Tân An Airfield was constructed by Company C, 15th Engineer Battalion, and Company D, 86th Engineer Battalion, to support an earlier 3rd Brigade operation named "Enterprise." The airfield initially opened in March 1967 and utilized a straight portion of Route 223, a dirt road connecting several villages along the eastern edge of the Plain of Reeds with Tân An. By the end of 1967 the improvements made at the airfield had resulted in a 2,500-foot-long, paved fixed-wing runway; a helicopter strip with 28 pads; an air ambulance dust-off pad; and a Chinook landing pad. When the airfield went into full operation its combat support facilities included a 40-bed hospital operated by Company C, 9th Medical Battalion; a weather detachment; a rearming and refueling facility; an air traffic control tower; a battery of tracked 40mm "Dusters"[2] of the 5/2 Artillery; and searchlights of HQ Battery, 29th Artillery. The change of command ceremony was being held for 3rd Brigade HQ at their FSPB east of the center of Tân An. A couple of deuce-and-a-half trucks from the HQ Company awaited us when we landed.

Although I'd driven through Tân An a few weeks earlier on my road trip to Saigon, the route we'd taken had been different and nothing looked familiar. In what I assumed was the center of the city our little convoy rounded a small grassy square reminiscent of a New England common back in The World, and we turned onto the road that led to 3rd Brigade HQ. The ceremony must have been more boring than usual, because I have absolutely no recall of it. For those interested in knowing about change of command ceremonies, a typical ceremony involved snagging a complement of unfortunate troops, dress them up in their cleanest Sunday fatigues, then making them stand in parade formation under the blistering sun before a reviewing stand full of senior-grade lifers making speeches about the swell job the departing commander had done for the brigade and America's cause in Vietnam and how very fortunate they are to be getting a new commander with such wonderful credentials. The band had to stand in the heat alongside the troops and kick off the ceremony with a stirring rendition of "The Star Spangled Banner," which was followed by a chaplain's benediction blessing our holy cause and machine guns, then listening to droll speeches, and finally—at the closing— playing a rousing quick-time march over and over as many times as needed until the last sweat-saturated trooper had passed the reviewing stand. Sometimes if the physical layout or size of the ceremony site didn't permit a formal pass in review, the band would simply play a tune or two while the troops just stood in place sweating. For most of us in the band, change of command ceremonies were all too repetitive and, frankly, boring as hell. I used to mentally tune out into la-la-land and think about other things, like a cold drink and a cool shower. One time while in daydream mode I missed the opening bars of a John Phillip Sousa march! It was easily understood why alcohol flowed so freely in the military; it helped ease the doldrums of one's situation.

The band returned to Tân An on May 7, for, of all things, a *practice* change of command ceremony for the 2/4th Artillery. Precisely who needed the practice is questionable, but it certainly wasn't the band. Since the last visit to Tân An six days earlier, band gigs included playing at an awards ceremony for our own DISCOM troops on May 3 and a couple of days later, on May 5, at a combined awards/change of command ceremony for the 162nd AHC in Vĩnh Long.

The actual change of command ceremony for the 2/4th Artillery Battalion occurred the morning of May 8. LTC Floyd C. Adams, Jr., had taken command of the battalion from LTC Robert Dirmeyer. Back at Đồng Tâm,

VC activity was heating up both on and off base. We had to leave a trumpeter behind at Đồng Tâm to play a memorial service for the 3/39th Infantry Battalion. After the band retuned from Tân An the dance combo performed at a general's mess party. That night the VC resumed their nightly 10-2-4 Doctor Pepper schedule of firing mortars into Đồng Tâm. After a short respite, the business of waging war Delta-style had returned to normal.

During the previous several weeks the weather had been becoming noticeably muggier, and on May 9 the skies finally let loose in a torrent of rain. The stuff came down so violently it instantly flooded the barracks. I had to use whatever I could find to elevate my footlocker above the floor to prevent its contents from becoming sodden. Sandbags were removed from the tops of revetments and piled in front of the outside doorways to divert the tide of water gushing in. Those billeted on the upper level of the barracks had the last laugh over us denizens of the now aquatically deep ground-level floor. The mortars rounds the VC lobbed into Đồng Tâm might very well get the ones now perched higher first, but those troops would greet their maker in dry PJs. On the subject of pajamas, just about everybody slept in their standard-issue olive-drab undershorts—the loose-fitting kind with a long, open, vertical slit in front that occasionally twisted around your—ah—private parts in a most excruciating way.

Along with monsoon season came blisteringly hot temperatures when the sun was shining and dramatic 20-25 degree temperature drops when it rained. One minute it'd be 115 degrees in the shade, then before you could say "incoming" it was 90 degrees and pouring! The rain felt like 55-gallon drums of water being dumped on your head, and it typically started without warning. The Green Machine thoughtfully provided rain gear in the form of a hooded, rubberized-cloth poncho. You slipped the thing over your head, secured it at the neck with a tie string, and in short order became overheated and sodden from sweat. The rubberized finish prevented proper ventilation. When the rain stopped and the poncho was removed, you were just as wet as you would have been had you been rained on. Most of us chose to forego the poncho and let the rain do the soaking. Our tropical fatigues were quick-drying nylon, except for the armpits and crotches, which took longer to dry and more often than not left a scratchy, crusty, white salt line. We caught head colds, too. The instant drop in temperature gave us the chills, and this coupled with the lack of proper rest due to constant nighttime enemy mortaring lowered our resistance to infection. Sneezing, wheezing, and stuffiness made making music very uncomfortable, especially for those who played wind instruments.

The rain also intensified the insect problem. The bugs propagated in the

7. Republic of Vietnam, May 1969

humidity. As great a threat as the VC were, the bugs became the nightmare. Many were big crawly creatures that even after you'd flattened them with a solid smack of a jungle-boot heel they'd pop up and scamper off. I waged a campaign of total war by swatting them, stomping them, and brushing them aside, but they were still winning. Finally, in desperation and overt contravention of Geneva Convention Rules, which the Army *unfaithfully* observed in Vietnam, I resorted to chemical warfare. I purchased a product at the PX called Bug-Be-Gone and sprayed every flying and crawling thing that came within striking distance of me. Some got through, but I was able to turn the tide of discomfort to the plus side, leastways during my off-duty hours. Spraying the air around you with bug juice wasn't authorized during band performances.

While I was being drenched by monsoon rains and eaten alive by bugs, I waited with bated breath for news of my acceptance into graduate school. I hadn't yet heard my test results from having taken the Graduate School Entrance Exam and wasn't even certain who would be contacted: me, my parents, or Seton Hall University. My old professor friend, Dr. Jerry Stumas, repeatedly told me not to worry, he'd see to it I got accepted. He was the dean of the business school and his recommendation went a long way with admissions. If I did get accepted I'd have to request early separation from the Army. Only God knew how long that would take in a combat zone. I might REFRAD before the paperwork was processed.

One morning after band practice Mister Johns figuratively dropped a bombshell and announced we'd be getting a new bandmaster in a couple of days. He had completed his one-year tour of duty in Vietnam and was now being reassigned to a three-year posting in Germany. His wife was a German national and he was looking forward to being reunited with her. Germany was going to be his last assignment in the Army; afterwards he would retire and perhaps remain in Germany with her. I'd miss him, but I wasn't sad to see him leave. Change was a part of Army life and I'd grown accustomed to it. Our beloved mascot, Bummer, had already departed with Cary Mathews, as did trumpeter Jesus Esquivez and a couple of other bandsmen I'd known for so brief a period of time I can't even remember their names or what instruments they played.

On another day, while I was entertaining the still-healing (from his shrapnel wound) HQ Company XO with a game of chess, the CO asked me to escort a transient officer to the BOQ (Bachelor Officer Quarters) billet, which was on the second floor of one of DISCOM's four barracks. I helped the lieutenant with his luggage, and we started chatting about Army life. The conversation got around to how unpleasant it was to be a lowly lieutenant and how great it must be to be an SP-5. The lieutenant obviously knew little about KP, shit burning, or standing perimeter guard with crazy people. I didn't enlighten him, though; I let him keep his fantasies.

On May 9 the band again sent a trumpeter over to 3/39th Infantry Battalion HQ for another of their memorial services. The following day most of the band played at a change of command ceremony for the 1/84th Artillery Battalion. LTC Robert L. Schroeder (not to be confused with the earlier-mentioned LTC Robert "B." Schroeder) was taking over command of the battalion from LTC Edward L. Queeney.

The 3/39th Infantry Battalion's misfortune continued. On May 12 two more memorial services were held in remembrance of their fallen. All four ceremonies were on Đồng Tâm.

Monsoon season hadn't dampened the VCs' desire to blow us up. Their aerial attacks continued with as much ferocity as in the dry season. A quick succession of near misses, some frighteningly close, convinced me to spend more time in DISCOM's recently completed company-sized personnel shelter. As I have mentioned before, the bunker was a huge affair made of wood and backfilled with sand and dirt. Like its older sandbag counterpart it had baffled openings, but unlike the sandbag bunkers there were no firing ports other than a few tiny square openings for ventilation. It was, however, spacious and with plenty of headroom. Wooden bench-seats lined the interior circumference and permitted troopers, if the shelter wasn't too crowded, to sack out for the night, which is precisely what some short-timers chose to do.

A short-timer was highly perceptive and survival sensitive and, therefore, a very dangerous soldier. The genre may have been unique to Vietnam. Short-timers could sometimes be spotted by a little swagger stick[3] some of them carried to warn others of their status. If you recall, one of the first projects I undertook upon arriving at DISCOM was to prepare a countdown calendar. The other name for a countdown calendar was a *short-timer's* calendar. Every troop setting foot in the Republic of Vietnam knew precisely when his one-year tour of duty would expire and he would be eligible to return to The World. That was the purpose of the short-timer's calendar, to keep track of the *when* on a daily basis. Each morning another date on the calendar was ritualistically ticked off. The number of one's remaining days in Vietnam was a popular topic of conversation, as common a parlance as asking where you were from back in The World.

DEROS was the Holy Grail of a 'Nam trooper's existence. After surviving bullets, bombs, snakes, insects, weather, illness, and lifers for 12 months, as the sacrosanct day neared EVERYTHING and EVERYONE within a short-timer's immediate environment became expendable in regards to their survival. Short-timers were highly nervous troopers. One did not get in their way or do anything to disturb the guarded euphoria they felt. The light was growing brighter at the end of their tunnels, and the goal of getting out of 'Nam was in plain view.

I kept my distance from short-timers. *One day and a wakeup* was their total reality. I both envied and feared them, not because I was afraid of them but because they could not be depended upon. With the end so close at hand it was understandable that a short-timer wasn't going to risk his life for yours. I left them in peace, which was the unofficial policy of the band—no duties off Đồng Tâm one week prior to DEROS (unless, of course, the needs of the Army conflicted). A short-timer could, therefore, run out his remaining days in-country in the safety of the personnel shelters.

The 365-day rotation policy of USARV was psychologically a morale-busting protocol the "New Action Army"[4] had instituted specifically for Vietnam service. From a military perspective it was also a foolish protocol, the kind of policy a lunatic would devise. By the time troops gained enough experience in combat to understand their enemy and have the confidence to be effective soldiers, their tours were half over. The problem was compounded with the officers, who rotated out of combat every *six* months. For a variety of reasons the average unit from squad to company size was typically undermanned; the 12-month rotation meant somebody was always coming or going, which made even inexperienced troops vital to every mission. New guys had little time to learn the ropes and often paid for it in pain or with their lives. Second Lieutenant Donald Leta, a classmate and brother Triphibian Guardsman from my ROTC days at Seton Hall University, lasted a little over a month after arriving in 'Nam early in 1968. He was KIA on February 13, 1968, while on patrol.

The band hung around Đồng Tâm for the next three days, the only musical commitments being bugler assignments at the Reliable Academy and two memorial services, again for the beleaguered 3/39th Infantry Battalion. Up until March 1969 the 3/39th Infantry Battalion had been part of the 3rd "Go Devils" Brigade. After March they were part of the 1st "Recondo" Brigade.

Many battalion memorial services were held on Đồng Tâm because each of the division's battalions had satellite HQ and billet accommodations on base. The exceptions were the three infantry battalions comprising the 2nd "River Raiders" Brigade. They were billeted aboard four Navy vessels that had been rebuilt from LSTs into floating barracks ships and designated as APBs (Amphibious Propelled Barracks). The roster of these barracks ships included the APB-35 USS *Benewah*, which also hosted the HQ element of the 2nd Brigade APB-36 USS *Colleton*, APB-39 USS *Mercer*, and APB-40 USS

Nueces. The *Mercer* served as the flagship of Navy River Assault Squadron 9-Task Force 117, the overall unit commanding the jointly operated Army-Navy Mobile Riverine Force. During my time in-country the *Benewah*, the *Mercer*, and another LST were anchored in the middle of the Sông Mỹ Tho, directly across from Đồng Tâm.

The 2nd Brigade's nickname, "River Raiders," came from the brigade's first joint operation with the Navy, codenamed "River Raider I" and begun on February 16, 1967. It had been the test bed for the Mobile Riverine Force concept. The Navy elements of the force were unofficially known as the "brown water navy," so named for the muddy water environment of their inland mission.

My initial impression of the brown water navy had been color: row after row of olive-drab vessels all flying the brilliant ensign of our country. The repeated flashes of red, white, and blue contrasted strikingly against the green of the jungle, the pale blue of the sky, and the mud brown of the Sông Mỹ Tho. It was quite a sight, an audacious visual statement that boldly proclaimed: THIS VESSEL IS THE UNITED STATES OF AMERICA! Even a political skeptic (had one been privileged with the view) certainly would have felt a twinge akin to nationalistic pride—but perhaps not. You had to experience the vacuous loneliness of coping with sustained fear to comprehend the emotion. Back in The World many of our fellow citizens were burning and desecrating our flag. Here we were dying for it!

* * *

Getting back to the band, I was rarely assigned bugler duties, primarily because I didn't know most of the calls. My TDY bugler's function with the 80th Army Band back at Fort Stewart had entailed playing only one call, Taps, which, while being about as poignant a melody as any, is an easy tune to learn. I never had to learn any other calls and, therefore, didn't. One afternoon Mister Johns asked me to blow Assembly for a DISCOM ceremony. I had a vague idea how Assembly sounded from having heard it once or twice, so I played it as I thought it should be played. Other than Mister Johns and a couple of my fellow trumpeters, no one else in DISCOM had a clue how the tune went, so I got away with it, but later that day Mister Johns told me I'd better work on my bugle calls!

At times I even had trouble with a few of the calls I did know. Retreat is a long, stirringly involved bugle call. I had to play it at the Reliable Academy in front of assembled troops. I started it out right but got distracted part of the way through and had to ad lib a bit. I can still visualize the piercing glare the Reliable Academy commander threw my way from under the brim of his helmet. He apparently knew the call better than I did!

Once I was loaned to an ARVN outpost to play *their* version of Taps. Mister Johns wrote out the tune on a piece of paper and handed it to me, saying no one else in the band knew how to play it so I'd do as well as anyone. A Huey gunship picked me up at the Reliable Airfield a few blocks away and off I went. The ceremony was at a tiny ARVN guard post alongside FSB Schroeder. I played the call as best I could and, thankfully, none of the ARVNs mentioned a thing about my performance. The fact that none of them, including their officers, could speak English may have had something to do with their silence. My pick-up flight didn't arrive as scheduled and when I realized it wasn't going to come I found a comfy corner in one of the ARVN bunkers to snuggle in for the night. I was concerned for my well-being, but with FSB Schroeder only a stone's throw away, how bad could things get? I found out later that evening when I was awakened by gunfire.

The ARVNs were blasting the countryside from their perimeter defenses. Flares were popping everywhere. The scene was surreal. The guns of FSB Schroeder, however, remained silent, although I did notice some of the flares were popping from their perimeter. I grabbed my M-16 and took a position on the berm. Lying on my back to expose as little of my body as I could and using my thumb to pull the trigger I fired off one magazine rock 'n' roll style over my head. The spent cartridges bounced off my helmet and chest. I was having trouble reloading in my awkward firing position when I felt my foot being shaken. I looked through the tips of my upright jungle boots into the face of an ARVN. He was shaking his head from side to side. I could barely make out his features in the dim flare light, but he wore that inscrutable grin. I assumed he meant cease fire, inasmuch as the rate of gunfire from others at the base had grown ragged, with just a few random shots sounding. I threw him the thumbs-up sign, which might have meant something else in Vietnamese. The ground attack, if it had really been an enemy attack and not a water buffalo in the perimeter wire, was over. A Huey gunship came for me first thing in the morning. After my harrowing experience alone *in the land of the nine dragons*,[5] Mister Johns let me have the rest of the day off to recuperate. I needed it.

* * *

The new bandmaster, CWO-2 Jack C. Kottermann, materialized in time to accompany the band on two May 14 performances at Cần Thơ. An awards ceremony for IV Corps HQ was held in the morning at their facility and in the afternoon a concert at a site named Eakin Compound. Eakin Compound looked more fun than combat with its brightly painted buildings, a pool, and a snack bar. Mister Johns handled the awards ceremony and Mister Kottermann the concert. Mister Kottermann scored a few happy points with the band when he let us have the four-hour interval between gigs to do whatever we wanted. Most of us walked into town and checked out the bar girls on the strip. After the concert we got back to Đồng Tâm in time for supper.

When performing in concert the band typically played nonmilitary tunes from Broadway shows, movie themes, old standby favorites, and watered-down contemporary music. Musical arrangements were mostly prepared by trombonists Charles F. Bradley and Patrick Townley, the latter, if you remember, also the band's first sergeant. Some arrangements might have been prepared by Mister Johns and other musicians in the band, but as far as I know the trombone section had the corner on arranging concert tunes. All marching music for military functions was mostly played *as scored* by the respective composers. Who could improve on Master of the March John P. Sousa's work?

On May 15 the band was airlifted under the command of Bandmaster Jack C. Kottermann in three Huey Slicks southeast to a 3/47th Infantry Battalion change of command ceremony in VC-infested Kien Hoa Province. The ceremony was held in a dense coconut grove off of Route TL-25 at a compound named Tiger II. Route TL-25 paralleled the Sông Bến Tre as far east as the Chet Sây Cũ ferry (over the Kinh Chet Sây Cũ). The ferry replaced a highway bridge the ARVNs had demolished in order to deny enemy forces access into the city of Bến Tre during Tết '68. The helicopters set down in a clearing on the Bến Tre side of the ferry and we rode to Tiger II aboard 3/47th Infantry Battalion trucks. There mustn't have been any helicopter pads or LZ (Landing Zone) sites at Tiger II, but if there were they weren't available to the band.

Tiger II was more of an encampment than a patrol base, set within 2nd Brigade's land base complex collectively known by the even more exotic-sounding Tiger's Lair. There were no tigers at Tiger's Lair; leastways there weren't any that I saw. The name was derived from the 3/47th Infantry's nickname, "Tiger Battalion." Their new battalion commander, LTC Bruce Williams, was taking over for LTC Ishmael Pack, who not only had been the commander of the 3/47th Infantry since November 1968 but had also been acting commander of 2nd Brigade between January and February 1969, temporarily replacing the assigned commander, COL George E. Bland, who had been WIA (Wounded in Action). The ceremony went off well, but we had to wait at the clearing most of the afternoon for the helicopters to pick us up. The heat had been insufferable. Most of us dozed off. That evening the dance band contingent had to freshen up before entertaining the new commanding general and guests at another of his mess parties.

On May 15 the division officially turned over its armored cavalry asset—

A, B, and C troops of the 3/5th "Black Knight" Armored Cavalry—to the 1st Brigade, 5th Infantry Division (Mechanized). The Black Knights had been detached from the 9th Infantry Division and operating under command of the 5th Infantry Division up north along the DMZ (Demilitarized Zone— the demarcation line between North and South Vietnam) since February 1968. Armored vehicles such as the M48, Patton, medium tank were too heavy to operate successfully over the muddy roads and marshy lowlands of the Mekong Delta. Tanks were needed up north, where the ground was firmer, to assist in combating the more conventional tactics and weapons of the NVA. The 500-mile separation between Đồng Tâm and Camp Evans, the Black Knights base camp, had caused sufficient logistical support problems for the 9th Infantry Division to dictate permanent attachment to the 5th Infantry Division. The Black Knight helicopters of D Troop would, however, continue to operate out of Đồng Tâm in support of 9th Infantry Division operations.

Mister Johns turned command of the band over to Mister Kottermann without ceremony or fanfare. In a very nice gesture of command, on May 16 the new bandmaster permitted several of us to accompany Mister Johns to his departure point under the pretense of being guards. The pickup zone was at a little-used military airstrip several klicks northeast of Đồng Tâm. We loaded the bandwagon with two cases of beer, four cases of soda pop, several large bags of potato chips, C-rations packs, a garbage can full of ice, and, of course, Mister Johns. Larry did the driving. The airfield was situated on Route QL-4 at the crossroads of a connecting road that ran between Route 256 and the city of Mỹ Tho. The airstrip was west of the village of Bến Tranh. We took Route 256 north to the connecting road intersection and then cut over to the airstrip. The airstrip was just that, a single strip of tarmac laid in a large cultivated field. In the distance, several adult peasants working alongside a few children busily scratched at the surface of the earth. Larry parked the bandwagon near the end of the runway. If the peasants had taken notice of our arrival they certainly didn't show it.

It was blisteringly hot in the open field, so we set up in the shade of the deuce-and-a-half. We ate potato chips, drank beer, and reminisced about the jobs we had played and our fellow musicians who had already gone home. We were speculating about how our former canine mascot, Bummer, would react to snow on Cary Mathews' family farm when a couple of Vietnamese kids joined our party. They were curious about what we were doing. We gave them C-ration chocolate, some chips, and a few sodas, and after hanging around for a while they trudged off to rejoin their companions working in the field.

Mister Johns kindly told us we were the best band he'd ever had the honor of commanding. We were a good bunch, but I doubt we had been his best band. Warrant officers also commanded numbered Army bands comprised of professional musicians; we were just a bunch of regular troops snagged from the ranks of other military occupational specialties because we could also play musical instruments. Mister Johns' joy about getting out of 'Nam in one piece and his emotions associated with leaving fellows he had shared so many harrowing adventures with must have gotten to him. We all got a little misty-eyed when his Caribou touched down and taxied to a stop at the end of the runway not far from us. Its rear loading ramp descended and the crew chief, armed with an M-16, waved for Mister Johns to come aboard. Mister Johns said his final farewell and wished us all good luck. At the ramp he turned and waved. We all stood at attention and threw him our best lifer salutes. He responded by stiffening his body and formally returning our salute. He then disappeared into the belly of the aircraft. We waved farewell one last time as the aircraft lifted off.

After the Caribou was out of sight we decided to hang around the airfield a while longer. No sense returning to the drudgery of Đồng Tâm just yet. We still had plenty of drink and snacks. We continued in our merriment until a sharp blast interrupted the festivities. One of the kids had tripped a booby trap or maybe stepped on a mine. It sounded like a hand grenade exploding. The adults gathered around what was left of the boy. We remained transfixed where we were, spectators to a tragedy. The reality of death in the Delta knocked the merriment out of us. What had happened to the Vietnamese kid could have happened to any one of us. We drove back to Đồng Tâm. The party was over.

* * *

While we had been celebrating Mister Johns' safe departure from Vietnam the band sent a bugler over to FSB Schroeder to play Taps at a memorial service for the 2/4th Artillery Battalion. On the same day, the band received ten shiny new trumpets, which I handed out to those who wanted them. I kept my old beat-up horn. It had a nice sound, and I didn't have to worry about banging it around as it had been issued to me in already banged-up condition.

Mister Johns had commandeered part of the supply room for his billet area and the remaining space hadn't been utilized in the most efficient manner. Mister Kottermann chose to sleep in the band barracks and asked that I rearrange the supply room. He had a nice way of issuing orders, sounding more like polite requests. Redoing the supply room kept me busy between HQ Company work details and typing Mister Cottingham's many reports.

7. Republic of Vietnam, May 1969

The band had another concert scheduled for May 17, this one a win-their-hearts-and-minds performance at a public park in downtown Mỹ Tho, a picturesque riverside city that literally buzzed with civilian activity. The dress of the city folk was more varied than that of the peasants living in the boonies, ranging from western style to traditional Vietnamese with a splash of color. Traveling along the paved streets of the city I observed a bevy of adolescent girls in all-white outfits consisting of the familiar pajamas but worn underneath a slit tunic called an *áo dài*. A first, I foolishly thought the white might symbolize their virginity, but I later learned it was the traditional outfit of schoolgirls. The band had journeyed from Đồng Tâm on two deuce-and-a-half trucks and a smaller weapons carrier. Our short convoy came via Route TL-25, the dirt road that skirted the north bank of the Sông Mỹ Tho. Once in town the driver of the lead truck had difficulty finding the concert site. He stopped at a street corner when SFC Townley spotted a European-looking pedestrian standing on the sidewalk and asked directions. The pedestrian was an aged French gentleman who spoke just enough English to understand our predicament. He pointed in the direction of the park, which was only a block away.

Had we turned one street earlier we would have run into the National Police roadblock cordoning off the road in front of the concert site. We doubled back and turned onto the correct street. The police waved us through their barrier. Mister Kottermann was riding in the cab of the weapons carrier behind us. He threw the officers a courtesy salute as he passed by them. They, of course, responded to his salutation with inscrutable smiles plastered on nodding heads. I'd have thrown them a different kind of salute. The National Police were known to unnecessarily rough up GIs they detained, even if it was for minor infractions not resulting in arrests.

The concert stage was a charming structure enclosed in a large white latticed gazebo set in a bed of lush, manicured, tropical plantings. The bandstand offered some relief from the sun but not the humidity. Our faded tropical fatigues were already showing dark spots where our sweat had accumulated. The atmosphere was festive, and the concert drew a much larger crowd than expected, much larger than the two assigned band guards could keep vigilance over. I hoped the National Police were on their toes; there were certainly enough of them present and they were highly visible in their white uniforms. Because of the friendly nature of the mission and the allegedly secure locale, we'd been ordered not to bring our weapons on stage. They were stowed aboard the trucks with our instrument cases and cameras under guard of our three loaner HQ Company drivers.

The concert went well, lasting a little over one hour. Our performance was followed by an ARVN band that, surprisingly, played western-style music similar to the type of music we had just played. Vietnamese city folk were far more sophisticated than their rural counterparts. The imprint left by French colonialism was evident in most of the large villages and cities I'd been in and reflected in the architecture of the buildings, in the layout of the streets and parks, and in the cultural atmosphere, which was far more cosmopolitan than in the boondocks. One almost expected to see Maurice Chevalier and Catherine Deneuve chatting over café au lait at a street-side outdoor café. Over 100 years of colonialism couldn't be eradicated overnight. Despite the ousting of the French, the rubber plantations of the Michelin Rubber Company remained the major employer in South Vietnam, other than the government and its huge army.

Following the Mỹ Tho concert the band had no performances scheduled for the next four days other than daily bugler gigs at the Reliable Academy and morning band practice on alternate days. My name wasn't on the company or band duty roster, so I had plenty of free time and soon became bored. That was the nature of service in 'Nam—boredom spiced with a pinch of terror every now and then. When not on duty a troop could write letters to loved ones and friends back in The World, send them recordings made on a 3-inch reel-to-reel tape recorder, hang out at the snack bar or EM Club pool, read, go to the chapel and pray, taunt VC prisoners locked up in the MP stockade, shop at the PX or Charlie the Gook's retail emporium, or just snooze. Although catching up on one's rest was one of my favorites, I was in a shopping mood. I made several visits to the PX, during which I purchased two 35mm cameras—a Pentax TTL (thru-the-lens focusing) to upgrade the Yashica rangefinder camera I'd gotten from Larry and the other to be sent to a stateside friend—a 35mm slide projector, a small photo album with "Vietnam" imprinted on the cover, a portable typewriter, a pair of high-power binoculars, a few Kodak prepaid film-processing mailers, and a plastic model airplane assembly kit of a P-40 War Hawk fighter, the plane Chennault's Raiders flew against the Japs when Vietnam was still known as French Indochina. The PX had plastic glue but no paints, so I purchased a few indelible color markers in earth tones so I could apply upper-body camouflage to the model.

After blowing a goodly chunk of April's pay at the PX, I wandered over to Charlie the Gook's place and purchased a silk robe for my girlfriend back in The World, an ivory Buddha statuette for my parents, a decorative wall plaque of an Asian scene made of inlaid ivory on a black-lacquered wooden board for my sister, and some other stuff I can no longer remember. I was now content, albeit broke, so I read and snoozed away my remaining time off.

On May 19 VC mortars struck Company A, 709th Maintenance Battalion, instantly killing SP-5 Charles D. Buchanan and SP-4 Richard Carbone. Early in the morning of May 22 SFC Townley ordered us to *saddle up* with flak vests, battle harness, ammunition, weapons, and instruments. We were flying on a Chinook up north to Tân Tru in Long An Province. I use the more formal term "ordered" instead of "asked" because change was beginning to manifest itself in the band. Very slowly, almost imperceptibly, stateside military discipline was creeping in. It had started under Mister Johns' command with a few more-than-routine DISCOM-inspired inspections: crisply starched and pressed uniforms on gigs, thoroughly cleaned combat gear and rifles, and tips and heels of jungle boots polished more carefully than previously. It then progressed into the realm of off-duty appearance: no graffiti on uniforms, no love beads or peace pendants; no unauthorized insignia; no more wearing of the favored tropical bush cap; closely trimmed haircuts at all times, etc. Compared to most other troops in the 9th Infantry Division who were not directly associated with division HQ or the MPs, the appearance of bandsmen during performances had always been uniform and military. We *looked* like highly motivated soldiers, maybe even lifers. We now were expected to look and behave like lifers all of the time! Off duty I wore my father's Imperial German Army Iron Cross as a pendant around my neck for good luck. Some dickhead NCO lifer from the HQ Company confiscated it thinking it was a surfer medallion. I later got it back from Mister Kottermann, who understood its significance. He advised me to leave it in my footlocker with my other personal stuff. I couldn't do that; it was my lucky charm. So I kept it in my pocket and used it as a key ring. Perhaps I had become a bit too superstitious.

All of the troops, equipment, and facilities on Đồng Tâm were systematically being spiffed up to occupation-Army standards. I even witnessed one infantry unit on stand down at Đồng Tâm doing PT in their billet area. In view of the heat, this was NUTS. The muscles of the average ground pounder were as tight as the skins on our snare drums from humping 70-plus pounds of gear across the mucky boonies. Even the support troops at Đồng Tâm had a slightly lean and mean look from living in a sweltering tropical environment. As much as I thought about it, I couldn't understand why troops operating in a physically taxing terrain needed PT. The only rationale I could come up with was *lifers*: regardless of their rank they didn't have to be rational, they just had to follow orders. The changes undoubtedly originated on a higher level, a level very distant from the realities and debilitating heat of Vietnam.

The Green Machine must have forgotten there was a war going on.

* * *

Our Chinook got us to Tân Tru safely and we set down in an open field sandwiched between a dirt base road and a village. A long row of sand-filled, 55-gallon steel drums draped with spiral concertina barbed wire separated the base from the village. There was no earthen perimeter berm. Although the HQ FSPB of the 2/60th Infantry Battalion was more commonly referred to as Tân Tru, its official designation was Camp Scott. The name was given in honor of 2/60th Infantry Battalion officer LT James Howard Scott, who had been killed in action on February 5, 1967. The base was a short distance from the north bank of the Sông Vám Ćo Tây, the river that passed through Tân An.

Camp Scott was over a mile southwest of Tân Tru and was physically in the village of Ap Tân Thanh. The base was situated immediately south of a sharp bend in Route 225 and was bordered by two side roads that intersected in a "T" with Route 225. Camp Scott was more commonly referred to as Tân Tru because that was what the Vietnamese called the area. As soon as the last bandsman stepped off the Chinook and was clear of its rotors, the big machine lifted off. We walked along the base road into the heart of the base. Along the way we were greeted by a very young-looking lieutenant who escorted us to the ceremony site, which was nearby. We were thankful it hadn't started raining.

The change of command ceremony commemorated LTC Gregory T. Dillon's turning his command of the 2/60th Infantry Battalion over to LTC Fred K. Mahaffey. LTC Dillon's rotation out of the battalion followed a normal six-month combat tour. Over the course of 1,388 days in-country, the 2/60th Infantry Battalion had suffered 380 fatalities, the greatest number of any single unit in the division (by way of comparison, HHC and Band DISCOM suffered only seven fatalities, but then DISCOM was only a stone's throw from the division's surgical hospital, making medical attention almost instantaneous).

The next day part of the band performed at a morning practice change of command ceremony at Đồng Tâm for the 9th S&T Battalion (Supply and Transportation). Other than the daily bugler gig at the Reliable Academy, which I had not been assigned to play, there weren't any other commitments for bandsmen. I stayed in my hooch and wrote to my parents and girlfriend.

Mail call brought a letter from an old childhood pal, Newton Eineman. He had recently completed a four-year enlistment in the Navy that included sea duty off the coast of Vietnam, which technically made him a Vietnam veteran. I use the term "technically" not to lessen or deny his status as a Vietnam veteran but only to point out that living among the enemy was a bit more intense than seeing them from five miles off the shoreline in a heavily armored battle cruiser. Having put that forth, I found it was uplifting to hear from Newton until I read how morally wrong he felt the war was and how he had joined a growing national organization called Vietnam Veterans for Peace. From what Newton wrote they were activists with the ultimate goal of ending the war, which, ironically, was precisely the same goal as that of the 9th Infantry Division, only they pressured the government while we pressured the enemy. I must have taken his involvement with Veterans for Peace the wrong way, because to this day, even after his passing, I'm still miffed by what he wrote in his letter. I guess he never realized how preoccupied I was with staying alive and maybe I didn't need the intellectual distraction of considering my responsibility in the morality of the war. When daily survival is paramount to one's continued existence the nature of right or wrong becomes absolutely meaningless.

Newton's letter extinguished what fading embers remained of my morale. It was the first I'd heard of Vietnam Veterans for Peace and, frankly, I found it difficult to accept the reality that *any Vietnam veteran would turn against his brethren while they were still engaged in battle.* I once read Vietnam had been a series of ten one-year wars rather than one ten-year war. Maybe some veterans had loyalty only to soldiers of their own in-country year. Like I said, at the time I didn't care about the morality of the war or whether it was right or wrong. The way I bottom-lined my situation was that a violent and capable enemy was doing his utmost to kill me. Back in The World the antiwar activists, in their cause of political warfare, were unknowingly aiding the enemy—*my enemy.* With every antiwar rally or event, the enemy's resolve grew stronger and our morale weaker. It was tough being an Army bandsman charged with instilling esprit de corps in an emotionally beaten-up army. It was even tougher being a soldier in an army fighting without the support of his peers, friends, and neighbors on the home front. I had less than 100 days left to serve in 'Nam, less if the Army granted my early out. I just had to keep my sanity and body whole a bit longer.

On May 24 the band got to explore one of the Navy's APB ships anchored in the middle of the Sông Mỹ Tho. The 3/60th Infantry Battalion's commander, LTC Peter B. Peterson, was being relieved by some officer whose name I forgot to record. The ceremony was held aboard the 2nd Brigade HQ ship, the USS *Benewah.* After the ceremony was over we had some time left to roam around the big vessel. The new 3/60th commander invited us to stay aboard for lunch. I was surprised to find everything decorated in olive drab— everything except the blue fatigues of the Navy crew. We ate our lunches in the air-conditioned comfort of the ship's mess, enjoying food tastier than the stuff they served at Đồng Tâm. The Navy had a panache the Army lacked.

Maybe sailors, being mostly volunteers (a few were draftees who had definitely lucked out with two-year tours in the Navy), had better attitudes. It showed in the pride they took in keeping their vessel STRAC. They certainly had better chow.

The brown water sailors of the Mobile Riverine Force who occasionally transported the band to performances wore the same jungle fatigues as the Army and, unlike their blue-clad brothers, possessed similar attitudes as soldiers did concerning their Vietnam experience. Their attitudes may have been influenced by their close association with the Army and their close proximity to the enemy. They lived on Đồng Tâm or nearby on ships and took the same poundings we did. When the VC had blown up the ammo dump in March, the fatalities had all been sailors.

There was none, or very little, of the interservice animosity between the brown water navy sailors and the soldiers of the Mobile Riverine Force. They looked like us and shared our attitudes. The first time I'd ridden aboard a Tango boat[6] I couldn't determine who the commander of the vessel was since none of the crew wore any insignia, let alone rank pins. Upon my inquiry as to the identity of the captain, I'd been told not to worry about it. *It don't mean nothing.* The sailors of the brown water navy were protective of the well-being of the soldiers they transported. Army helicopter crews were the same. Neither of them delivered troops into harm's way and then left them stranded on the ground, regardless of the risk to themselves or their craft. I don't know the psychology behind it. Perhaps it was official protocol, but I think it had more to do with the sense of responsibility and honor that arises between participants engaged in a common cause. *In the bush we watched out for each other.*

It wasn't quite as friendly on Đồng Tâm. Our division HQ base camp hosted a large population of soldiers with diverse ethnic and educational backgrounds who were members of different units. One of the Green Machine's fundamental precepts of building esprit de corps was unit identity. Many of the soldiers who fought under the overall command of the 9th Infantry Division were part of distinct and individual combat and combat support battalions that had forged their histories in battle under the banner of different divisions. When asked what unit he were with, the average trooper in the division would typically respond with his battalion designation, i.e., 4/47th Infantry, 2/4th Artillery, 162nd AHC, etc., and not the 9th Infantry Division. We were all a part of the same team but from the different components making up that team. Each trooper, however, typically viewed his unit as the *very best* because that's what his commander told him. To exemplify this, DISCOM troops and bandsmen were 9th Infantry Division cadre all the way. To give DISCOM troops some sense of unit identification, a lapel pin consisting of a stylized fleur-de-lis encapsulated within a sun with heavy, elongated rays set over a horizontal three-quarter moon was devised and issued to DISCOM troops.

Following the ceremony aboard the *Benewah* and the Tango boat ride back to DISCOM, the band crammed aboard the bandwagon and drove across Đồng Tâm to division HQ to participate in a ceremony bidding COL Conners farewell. They then scurried over to the HQ of the 9th S&T to play a change of command ceremony for the arriving COL Ernest A. Vuley, Jr., who was replacing departing COL Edward K. Yellman. May 24 had been a busy day.

The month continued as an active music season. On May 26 a portion of the band was loaded aboard a deuce-and-a-half truck and transported approximately 35 klicks (about 22 miles) to FSB Schroeder to perform a second concert, the first having been so well received. We had to leave a bugler behind at Đồng Tâm to play at a morning practice retreat ceremony at Division HQ (the actual ceremony occurred later the same day in the afternoon). Once again we set up in the First Recondo Religious Center, which, to refresh your memory, was, in spite of its impressive-sounding name, a standard-issue, company-size canvas tent erected over a wooden platform. Folding

Tân An was in III CTZ far north of Đồng Tâm in Long An Province. The military airfield originally had been part of Communal Route 223. In this view the landing strip is slightly above center and can be discerned as the wider portion of the roadway (author's collection).

Within a klick of the airfield we passed a grain storage facility that was highly reminiscent of the Butler grain bins found just about anywhere in Midwestern USA (author's collection).

Among the statistics of the Vietnam War was the sad fact that approximately half of the 5,100 plus helicopters lost during the war were due to accident or malfunction. Had I known this I'd have added helicopter travel to my worry list (author's collection).

metal chairs served as pews. To signify its religious purpose, a simple Christian cross was affixed to the tent's ridgepole above the entrance. Although there was a smattering of wooden structures, the majority of the enclosed structures at Schroeder were either sandbag bunkers or tents. The corrugated metal roof of a nearby wooden building had evidently taken a mortar hit and its entry puncture was being patched over by a solitary engineer.

The layout of FSB Schroeder was different from that of Đồng Tâm or FSB Moore. Its facilities straddled Route QL-4, with helicopter pads on the south side of the highway and the main part of the base on the opposite side in a large field crisscrossed by wide, deep irrigation canals instead of the more typical shallow, narrow ditches. There was no surrounding earthen berm, nor were there security gates on the highway. Civilians and undetected VC could pass as they pleased.

After the concert the band remained at FSB Schroeder for lunch, which was served in a large tent. If there was a standard-style mess hall at Schroeder, the building that housed it wasn't at all obvious or visible. They might have received meals prepared by the mess hall at FSB Moore and delivered in insu-

Rows of olive-drab Navy river craft lined the docks at Đồng Tâm Harbor, each brazenly flying our nation's star-spangled red, white, and blue flag in an unwritten statement that audaciously announced to the enemy: THIS VESSEL IS THE UNITED STATES OF AMERICA. It was shameful Americans back in The World were desecrating our flag while in Vietnam we were dying for it (author's collection).

The only time I fired my weapon in anger occurred after I played a memorial service gig at a small ARVN outpost just outside the perimeter of FSB Schroeder. The Green Machine couldn't spare a helicopter to retrieve me, so I spent the night at the outpost. In the wee hours of morning all hell broke loose. In this view the outpost is in the center of the photograph immediately beyond the cab of the 2/39th Infantry Battalion water truck (author's collection).

lated marmite food containers, the same way troops in the field were fed hot and cold meals. The band got back to Đồng Tâm late in the day. The dance band combo had to hustle to prepare for an officers' party at General Hollis's mess.

The following day, May 28, turned out to be an interesting one for the band. In addition to the usual gig at the Reliable Academy, there were two separate memorial services for the 3/39th Infantry Battalion—one at FSB Moore and one at Đồng Tâm—and a concert at Tân An. I was assigned bugler for the Đồng Tâm job and didn't make the concert.

On May 29, in order to fulfill musical assignments, the band had to be split into two smaller groups, with one band being required to make a long Caribou flight to Vũng Tàu to perform at a change of command ceremony for the 214th CAB and the other remaining on Đồng Tâm to play an award ceremony for D Troop, 3/5th Cavalry. I got lucky and drew the Vũng Tàu gig.

7. Republic of Vietnam, May 1969

As nasty ugly as Vietnam's tropical terrain was from a ground pounder's perspective, the coastal city of Vũng Tàu was an exception. Once called Cape Saint Jacques by the French, the town was situated on the east coast of the Vũng Tàu peninsula in the province of Phước Tuy. The peninsula jutted into the South China Sea and stood at the mouth of the main shipping channel into Saigon Harbor. Two mountains, Núi Lớn (Big Mountain) and Núi Nhỏ (Small Mountain), rose from its southern tip, dominating the otherwise flat peninsula. The unusual black-sand beaches, the relative safety of the area, and plentiful tourist accommodations at Vũng Tàu made it an ideal in-country R&R location for troops on three-day passes.

Phước Tuy Province was in III Corps CTZ, outside the limits of the 9th Infantry Division's AO, and situated quite a few klicks east of Đồng Tâm. The 214th CAB was attached to the Division's 9th Aviation Battalion and the cer-

In addition to the barracks ships, the Mobile Riverine Force (2nd Brigade) also maintained a complex of land bases several kicks east of Bến Tre collectively known as "Tigers' Lair." During May 1969 the band performed a change of command ceremony at one of these installations. It was situated in a dense coconut grove and called "Tiger II" (author's collection).

Mỹ Tho was the capital of Định Tường Province. It was essentially off limits to 9th Infantry Division troops. Its security relied heavily on the National Police (in this view the fellow who's dressed like a Good Humor man). The band performed a "win their hearts and minds" concert at a lovely city park in downtown Mỹ Tho (author's collection).

emony was for one of their assets that operated out of Vũng Tàu Army Airfield—the 147th ASHC (Assault Support Helicopter Company). Known as the "Hill Climbers," the 147th flew Chinook helicopters and provided medium-lift utility. Traveling to Vũng Tàu entailed a long, fairly uncomfortable Caribou flight. When we finally touched down at the army airfield we were a bit early for the ceremony and were given some time off for sightseeing. I wandered around the airfield snapping photographs. In addition to the Chinooks of the 147th ASHC I saw fixed-wing OV-1 "Mohawk" aircraft belonging to the 73rd SAC (Surveillance Airplane Company-Army) and Caribou aircraft of the 535th and 536th TAS (Tactical Airlift Squadron-United States Air Force).

Off in the distance the jutting peaks of Núi Nhỏ and Núi Lớn loomed like twin sentinels guarding the channel gateway into Saigon. A substantial radar installation (Army) capped the peak of the larger mountain (Núi Lớn). Although the band never left the airfield while at Vũng Tàu, it was my understanding it was as safe a place as anywhere in Vietnam. Many years

Ho, ho, ho, the lunatics were running the asylum. Very little surprised me in Vietnam as much as witnessing seasoned infantry troops in formation doing calisthenics. These fellows were already lean, mean, and combat toughened. They needed a rest, not PT. The lifers who ordered this exercise regimen demonstrates the questionable mentality of the senior officer corps in Vietnam (author's collection).

The final band gig for May entailed a nifty helicopter ride to Vũng Tàu to perform a concert for the 147th "Hillclimbers" Assault Support Helicopter Company. The French called Vũng Tàu "Cape Saint Jacques." The military airfield was situated near the tip of the Vũng Tàu peninsula, which jutted out into the South China Sea at the mouth of the main shipping channel into Saigon. Vũng Tàu was said to be a beautiful city, but the band didn't get to see it. We remained on the airfield, which wasn't all that pretty (author's collection).

later I read about the high price paid in causalities by the troops who had secured Vũng Tàu in 1968. Rear areas, if any truly existed in Vietnam, were a matter of dates. A rear location on one day could be hell the next and vice versa.

The remaining two days of the month involved playing an award ceremony at division HQ and a concert at the EM Service Club, plus a very revealing gig aboard the USS *Mercer* at anchorage in the Sông Mỹ Tho. I use the word "revealing" because the *Mercer* gig was a practice session for a farewell ceremony! The 3/60th Infantry Battalion was scheduled to depart from Vietnam on July 7. The many rumors concerning the division's withdrawal were beginning to take on a bit of substance.

Hallelujah!

All was not joy, though, leastways not with me. On the evening of May 31, in response to a comment written about a subtle change my girlfriend had perceived in my personality, I revealed my state of mind concerning Vietnam:

Late in May the band was driven through Indian Country from Đồng Tâm to FSB Schroeder to perform a concert. It was a mentally harrowing journey fraught with potential danger. Passing through Cai Lậy I spotted two suspicious-looking Vietnamese females squatting curbside with large open bags. They were intently observing our approach. I clicked off the safety of my rifle expecting an ambush. Thankfully nothing happened (author's collection).

7. Republic of Vietnam, May 1969

No sooner had we passed the squatting ladies when we encountered another Vietnamese standing alongside the road who also seemed too interested in us. Although I observed no weapons on his person, a small fragmentation grenade could easily be concealed in a trouser pocket. My eyes locked on his and as we passed I turned toward him with my weapon at the ready. Our gazes met and held until we were well out of his grenade-throwing range (author's collection).

Vietnam isn't a hell for me. I am only a musician. I fight with chords and phrases. Others have it worse. It is the irrational situation that makes me upset and bitter. It is a world with different values. One must retain little reminders of past stability.

I haven't changed, but I'll never again be as I was. I've seen things too grossly inhuman not to affect me. Old values will have to be adjusted and some discarded if I am to live with myself.

I had 78 days left to serve in Vietnam.

8

Republic of Vietnam, June 1969

I'd like to report my euphoria on learning the first component of the division was officially scheduled for withdrawal carried over into June, but that would be a gross misrepresentation of the truth. Đồng Tâm was not a place to revel in happiness for too long; something always occurred to dash your hopes. In my case it was the continued lack of news concerning my request for early separation from the Army. Neither my parents nor I had heard from either Seton Hall University or the testing service that had administered the Graduate Records Exam. The last word I'd received from my professor friend, Dr. Jerry Stumas, had been his reassurance for me not to worry; he'd get me in.

I, however, was worried. Getting accepted into Seton Hall's graduate program was only half the battle. The Army still had to approve my early out, and paperwork couldn't be initiated until after I received official notification from Seton Hall. It was a kind of Catch-22 and, believe me, I was hypersensitive to the catch.

Speaking of catches, the withdrawal of the 3/60th Infantry Battalion also had a catch associated with its departure. Soldiers of the 3/60th who had *more* than two months left to serve in-country were being reassigned to other units in the division, while soldiers from *other* outfits within the division with *less* than two months remaining in their tour became eligible for departure as part of the 3/60th. The procedure was highly involved, disruptive, and led to unforeseen complications, complications that would ultimately confuse *my* eligibility date to return home.

After the initial delight of learning the division was systematically being withdrawn faded, soldiers whose existence had been already centered upon the day they could return to The World became overtly cautious and hyperparanoid. Nobody wanted to die or be maimed with the end in sight. For all intents and purposes, by publicizing its withdrawal plans the Green Machine had elevated the DEROS status of every swinging dick in the division to that of a short-timer!

The band's schedule of performances for June began on the first day of the month with two separate change of command ceremonies, one aboard the USS *Benewah* and the other at Cần Thơ. The latter gig involved an overnight stay to facilitate the band's performing an early morning concert for the 164th CAG (Combat Aviation Group). It was held at the Stateside Lounge, which was in a private Vietnamese establishment called the Mekong Hotel. The hotel was the exclusive billet of the 164th CAG. Although the 164th wasn't a 9th Infantry Division asset, it was the parent organization of several aviation units attached to the division's 9th Aviation Battalion. I didn't make the trip to Cần Thơ. I remained on Đồng Tâm with the other half of the band assigned to the *Benewah* gig.

Not only was lifer-ism becoming increasingly more apparent in the spiffed-up appearance of the troops, bizarre "improvements" were also being made at the DISCOM compound. Between outbursts of rain the engineers

Someone influential in the Division's command hierarchy decided DISCOM needed concrete sidewalks between all of the compound's buildings. Although the rumors concerning the Division withdrawing from Vietnam had been substantiated, the sidewalks were installed anyway. DISCOM was beginning to resemble a stateside lifer-land (author's collection).

hurriedly poured concrete walkways to connect DISCOM buildings with each other, supposedly to keep combat boots cleaner and feet drier from the monsoon wetness that flooded the grounds daily. Wet loamy soil was no longer tracked into offices and barracks. Although enemy activity directed against Đồng Tâm had momentarily slowed, I viewed the project as a potential boon for VC mortar men. I didn't even want to imagine the destructive enhancement of exploded concrete bits zinging through the air along with the metal shrapnel. The unexpected slowdown in enemy attacks, however, was odd. The VC had probably known before we were told that the division was pulling out and they didn't want to change anybody's mind about our leaving. Their inactivity aided the Green Machine in maintaining the illusion the division had completed its mission.

Along with the physical improvements came a new HQ Company work detail: *gardening*. COL Hanket wanted his bunkered, air-conditioned mobile home beautified, so he ordered pretty flowering annuals to be planted along the concrete walkway leading up to his hooch. His hooch was as ugly as a warthog's butt, but the flowers did elicit some interesting comments from the troops. The flowers, unfortunately, didn't fare well; they soon wilted in the herbicide-saturated ground. COL Hanket should have put SSG Jenson, the tomato grower, in charge of the project. He understood the toxic effect of Đồng Tâm's soil on vegetation.

Speaking of vegetation, the band had the opportunity to vegetate over the next couple of days, having only division bugler Reliable Academy practice sessions on the bandstand and a change of command ceremony for the 9th Signal Battalion to deal with. The change of command ceremony was at Đồng Tâm. LTC Richard K. Bowers was turning his command over to LTC Clarence E. McKnight. On June 5 band activity away from Đồng Tâm resumed. The band flew to Cần Thơ to perform at a change of command ceremony for the 51st Maintenance Company (Light Equipment Direct Support). After the ceremony and break for lunch the Navy invited us to visit their U.S. Naval Support Activity Detachment at Bình Thủy. The Navy base was a few klicks northwest of Cần Thơ on the west bank of the Sông Bassac. We landed at Cần Thơ Army Airfield, and a Navy bus resembling a stateside school bus picked us up. *The bus was painted medium gray!* I instantly understood the elation William Wordsworth felt upon viewing a host of daffodils.[1] This was the first non-olive-drab military vehicle I had seen or ridden in since arriving in Vietnam. For an instant my heart filled with pleasure; I, too, could dance with the daffodils. You had to have been in 'Nam five months to appreciate the visual effect on one's sensibilities.

My elation continued as we passed through the Support Activity's main

8. Republic of Vietnam, June 1969

A personal treat came my way when the band visited the U.S. Naval Support Activity Detachment at Bình Thúy. Just about everything at the base was battleship gray. After five months of olive drab the sight was intellectually exhilarating. In addition to U.S. and Republic of Vietnam flags, the flagpole at the main gate also flew an "Admiral Aboard" pennant. The big Kahuna sailor was none other than the Commander Naval Forces Vietnam, Admiral Elmo R. Zumwalt, Jr. (author's collection).

entrance gate. Everywhere I looked I saw gray: gray cars, gray trucks, gray buildings, gray heavy equipment. Only a smattering of parked olive-drab Army, Marine, and ARVN vehicles present for the festivities darkened the overall splendor of Navy gray.

The Navy bus dropped us off near the detachment's officers club. The Navy was hosting what amounted to a military homecoming day and the band had been invited to join the celebration as guests of the Navy (probably to bolster the attendance, which I noticed was rather light). While the rest of the band finished securing their gear on the bus I wandered over to an interesting monument I'd spotted. It was a memorial set in a neatly manicured garden in front of the officers club. The memorial consisted of a large suspended sign displaying numerous tiny, engraved, brass plaques (there were 147 of them) topped by a painted marker bearing an inscription: TO THE BRAVE MEN OF TASK FORCE 116 WHO DIED FIGHTING TO PRESERVE A NATION.

While I was contemplating all of the names, I caught a glimpse of a tall fellow walking toward me along with three other men—two in olive-drab jungle fatigues, one wearing Class B khakis, and the other in civilian dress. The name and branch of service tags on the tall fellow's fatigues grabbed my attention. Both were gold on a blue background. I had never seen this combination and was curious. As the group neared I noticed three stars pinned to the lanky fellow's collar points. I immediately snapped a quick photograph with my ever-present camera and then jumped to rigid attention. As the group passed I threw my best conscript's salute. The tall one returned my salutation with an authoritative, "Good afternoon, Marine." I responded with a crisp, "Good afternoon, Admiral." His name tag revealed he was none other than Admiral Elmo R. Zumwalt, Jr., Commander, Naval Forces, Vietnam. He obviously hadn't expected a visit from the Army. The fellow in Class B khakis, a veteran Marine by measure of his graying hair and timeworn facial features, gave a scowling glance at the U.S. Army tag on my uniform as he passed ever so close on the admiral's heels, never thinking that I, a lowly conscript in the social order of things, could possibly ever give a damn about being a Marine.[2]

The Navy base seemed friendly enough, so Mister Kotterman gave me permission to stow my combat stuff in the bus and enjoy the revelry with the rest of the band. While some of the guys were perusing the pleasures of the support facility's PX and snack bar, Larry and I walked over to the airfield where the Navy had some of their equipment on display. The "Black Ponies" of VAL-4 (Light Attack Squadron-4) had just arrived in-country two weeks earlier and were showing off a few of their American Rockwell OV-10A "Bronco" fighter planes. The Black Ponies had the distinction of being the only fixed-wing propeller attack squadron in the U.S. Navy. Their mission in Vietnam was to provide air cover for Task Force 116's riverine operations. Opposite the VAL-4 Bronco aircraft rested a "Seawolves" Huey UH-1B gunship from Navy Detachment 7, HA(L) 3 (Helicopter Attack [Light] Squadron 3).[3] All of its armaments had been removed and were displayed on the ground in front of its nose cowling. There were rocket pods and rockets, two .50 caliber machine guns, two mini-guns, and assorted ammunition belts. Detachment 7 had been slated for reassignment to Tây Ninh and would be departing Bình Thùy within weeks. Behind the Seawolves' gunship, mounted on trailers in a hangar, were two variants of PBR gunboats used by the Bassac River Patrol Group.

From the standpoint of mass annihilation the weaponry the U.S. military employed against the VC in the Mekong Delta was horrifically impressive. Electronically fired mini-guns and Vulcan cannons were capable of mowing down huge swaths of humanity in a single burst. The .50 cal machine gun, firing a high-velocity bullet a half-inch in diameter, could punch through sheet steel or devastate human flesh. The weapon had originally been designed to knock out enemy aircraft and disable light equipment. Although its use against ground troops was outlawed by the Geneva Convention, in Vietnam this stipulation had been made void because the North Vietnamese communists didn't subscribe to the terms of the convention. U.S. forces enjoyed unchallenged air superiority in South Vietnam, could deploy troops rapidly via air mobility, and could rain massive firepower upon the enemy in the form of heavy artillery, napalm, rockets, and powerful aerial bombs that blew 100-foot diameter craters in the muck. Highly sophisticated electronic surveillance devices able to detect ground movement or human scent were employed, as was night-vision equipment. The enemy U.S. troops faced in the Delta weighed in at about 100 pounds soaking wet, wore flimsy silk pajamas, traveled barefoot or on rubber tire-treaded sandals, carried a simple cloth sack containing rice and ammunition, and was armed with a Chinese-manufactured AK-47 assault rifle. They fought without superior firepower, air cover, or rapid mobility. *It made you wonder why the war was in its fifth year.*

* * *

Upon returning to Đồng Tâm, SFC Townley and a handful of bandsmen assigned to him had to get their collective butts in gear and boogie across the street to the Reliable Academy to play a sniper school graduation ceremony. The next day, June 6, the band's musical commitments involved five gigs that had everyone's butts boogying. We were fragmented into several smaller musical components. On the schedule was the daily Reliable Academy assignment, a change of command practice for 9th Division Artillery, Honor Guard practice at division HQ, an evening Honor Guard and Retreat ceremony for division HQ, and one other gig, a concert in Mỹ Tho.[4] I was assigned to the Mỹ Tho gig along with part of the band. We were told to expect trouble inasmuch as the VC had attacked targets throughout Mỹ Tho during the night. We departed Đồng Tâm in the bandwagon dressed in full combat gear. I had stuffed my pockets with loaded magazines and the pockets were bulging. For good measure I also brought two full bandoliers of ammunition with me—just in case. I noticed Larry's pockets were bulging, too. In addition to his M-16 he also had his favorite M-79 grenade launcher.

The drive to Mỹ Tho was uneventful and when we arrived in the city it looked like nothing had happened. Life went on. The band's mission apparently was in support of the Army's win-their-hearts-and-minds objective. The gig entailed providing entertainment for a Vietnamese civic action project. The local government was sponsoring schoolchildren planting trees around the city.

The actual Division Artillery change of command ceremony came off at division HQ on the morning of June 7. COL Daniel Dale Stedhan assumed command from COL R.G. Gard, Jr., who was moving up the division ladder to the lofty position of Major General Hollis's chief of staff. COL Gard was replacing the outgoing COL Ira A. Hunt, who had recently departed the division without much fanfare on June 1 for an equally lofty posting in Washington, D.C.

On June 7 the band made its third trip of the month to Cần Thơ to play another change of command ceremony, this one for the 164th CAB, which had just been assigned a new commander. That evening, tragedy struck the DISCOM HQ Company when one of their troops accidentally fell into Đồng Tâm Harbor and drowned. He was from Vineland, New Jersey, but I didn't know him.

Although enemy activity directed at Đồng Tâm had perceptibly slowed during the last few days, it hadn't in the surrounding countryside. On June 8 a bugler was sent to FSB Moore to perform Taps at a memorial ceremony for the hard-pressed 3/39th Infantry Battalion. The next morning another bugler was flown to Tân Tru for the 3/34th Artillery Battalion.

* * *

The long-awaited letter of acceptance came from Seton Hall University on June 9. My friend Dr. Stumas had kept his word and seen to it that I got accepted, because my test scores couldn't have been all that good.[5] It was hard to concentrate on academia when survival was paramount in one's thoughts. After having awaited notification with so much apprehension, receipt of the letter of acceptance summoned no joy or mental relief within me as might have been expected. *It was as if the range of my emotional capabilities had been honed down to a narrowness of spirit, transforming what should have been happiness into indifference.* In accordance with Army Regulation AR 635–205, Paragraph 9, I immediately submitted a formal request for early separation to attend school.

* * *

On June 10 the band performed at an awards ceremony aboard one of the Navy APBs, on which ship or for what type of ceremony I don't remember (the band occasionally performed at Navy functions). After the ceremony the band hopped aboard a Chinook and flew to Tân An, where 3rd Brigade was celebrating what had been officially dubbed a "Flag Raising Ceremony." It was a one-of-a-kind affair that in substance, format, and boredom resembled a change of command ceremony. The format entailed the usual formation of sweaty troops assembled in the blistering heat before a reviewing stand, the substance the usual laudatory speeches made by bigwig brass about the great job they and the battalion were doing annihilating the enemy, and the boredom ... well, the boredom was just more of the same old meaningless stuff. There was, however, a musical twist. The band got to kick off the ceremony with two national anthems, ours and the Republic of Vietnam's. Ours was, of course, played first.

Several weeks later, in the July 2, 1969, issue of the *Old Reliable*, the newspaper revealed precisely what the flag-raising ceremony had been about. The article explained that when COL Dale J. Crittenberg had first taken command of 3rd Brigade in May he was "struck by the fact that the senior United States headquarters in Long An Province didn't have an American flag, nor did it have the customary Vietnamese flag."

During the past six months whenever the band had performed at 3rd Brigade HQ, I hadn't ever noticed there *wasn't* a flag. In IV CTZ, American flags were ubiquitous—on boats and ships, on tracked vehicles, buildings, even on my pal Larry Wolf, who kept a small parade flag on his person that he unfurled on occasion. Upon reflection I can't remember an American flag flying over DISCOM HQ. DISCOM was the equivalent of a full brigade with a "bird"[6] colonel in command. There might have been a flag, but if there was I can't recall ever taking notice of it. Well, anyway, COL Crittenberg was further quoted as having said it was "a great help to the morale of the American troops to have their flag flying over their camp." The colonel's take on what generated morale was certainly more positive and hopeful than mine; perhaps that's why he was a colonel and I a lowly SP-5. That day, June 10, the American flag and a Republic of Vietnam flag were dedicated along with a brass plaque inscribed, "June 1969—Dedicated by the Officers and Men of the 3rd Brigade, 9th Infantry Division, In Memory of the American Soldiers and Vietnamese People Who Have Died in Defense of Freedom in the Republic of Vietnam."

* * *

Now that the U.S. government had ordered withdrawal of troops from Vietnam the Army was redefining its objective of winning their hearts and minds to that of Vietnamization of the war. The bottom line was that we were leaving and they were staying (although 3rd Brigade would remain in Tân An longer than the rest of the division to assist in 25th Infantry Division operations).

On June 12 a memorial service was held at HHC & Band, DISCOM, for SGT John L. Kalivas, the aforementioned DISCOM HQ Company fatality. I missed playing at the ceremony, having been assigned KP duty instead. Despite my negative feelings about KP, the day hadn't been all that discouraging. I'd received word my R&R had been approved for July 7–July 14. I was going with the very last R&R group to Australia from Đồng Tâm. I decided I would celebrate my good fortune by rewarding myself with the purchase of a portable 3-inch, reel-to-reel tape recorder from the PX. I could then *voice* whatever glee I felt to my girlfriend or anyone else I knew who owned a tape recorder.

After being relieved from KP duty—at around 2130 hours (10:30 p.m.)—a very large mortar sailed into DISCOM and landed about 10 paces from where I was tucked in my bunk asleep. The blast blew a huge crater in the earth and the ensuing concussion toppled my bunk, with me in it, onto the floor. In the process I injured my wrists and sprained one of my big toes, which resulted in my typing Mister Kotterman's reports with the fingers of one hand and hobbling around DISCOM for a few days.

The proximity and ferocity of the explosion had effectively panicked my new roommate, Louis Kidd, an NFG SP-4 trombonist (my old roommate, Albert Denver, had been given a room all to himself). Kidd had hit the deck at full gallop, having dexterously catapulted off the upper berth as it toppled. I was able to grab hold of his ankle and pull him down onto the floor. I told him we had to wait and see if there were any other rounds coming in before we scurried off to the personnel shelter. I explained we at least had the protection of the sandbag revetment surrounding the barracks. We wouldn't want to be caught out in the open. We waited several seconds. No other rounds hit. It had been a close call. Like I said earlier, joy was a short-lived phenomenon on Đồng Tâm. All that had staved off our demise had been the sandbag revetment. The thin line separating life and death in the Delta could shift in an instant. It was something to think about. Was it arbitrary or divinely inspired? That's what I was beginning to think about more and more. Early next morning everyone had to check out the crater and gawk at it and each other before the engineers sent over a backhoe to fill it in.

June 13 brought more good news about my request for early separation to attend school. I received unofficial notification from Mister Kottermann that my request had been approved by two of three officers necessary for its approval. Everything was falling into place. Leastwise, it seemed that way at the time.

The next day, June 14, the band performed at a change of command ceremony for the 91st CS Battalion (Combined Service). It was the band's fourth trip to Cần Thơ during the month. The 91st CS Battalion wasn't an asset of the 9th Infantry Division. They, however, provided support services for all

8. Republic of Vietnam, June 1969

units operating in IV CTZ. Although I don't know what their function with the 9th Infantry Division was, I later learned two of their responsibilities were graves registration and food service.

After the band returned from Cần Thơ, I discovered Special Orders No. 165 lying on my bunk assigning me to the 90th Replacement Battalion for transfer to USATRF STA FORT DIX (United States Army Transfer Station Fort Dix) for separation from the army on October 20, 1969. It was dated about the time I had submitted my request for an early out. I spoke to SFC Townley about the orders and he advised me to just ignore them, for they'd probably be rescinded. I took SFC Townley's advice.

That evening a bunch of us were outside watching *Tales of the Green Beret*, the patriotic Vietnam War movie starring John Wayne. We were sitting on the bleachers guffawing at the wimpy phoniness of the mortar explosions when everything suddenly started sounding more realistic. *Boom! Boom!* Then Đồng Tâm's siren wailed. The authentic-sounding explosions weren't part of the movie; they *were* authentic!

On the morning of June 15 the band played an awards ceremony on Đồng Tâm for the 15th Engineer Battalion and later in the afternoon a change of command ceremony for the 6/31st Infantry Battalion. LTC Gerald Carlson was taking command of the 6/31st from LTC Ralph J. Peterson.

The next day, June 16, was a bit more exciting for the band. It began with a treetop-skimming ride on a brace of four Huey Slicks up north to Rach Kiên. The 5/60th Infantry Battalion's new commander, LTC Leo P. Sikorski, was replacing departing LTC Edward P. Cutlolo. As it transpired, LTC Sikorski's command would be short-lived; three months later, on September 17, he died in an air crash along with 3rd Brigade commander COL Dale J. Crittenberger. The rotor tips of the helicopter they were aboard accidentally struck the undersides of their AH-1G Cobra escort gunship (B Troop, 3rd Squadron, 17th Cavalry, 1st Aviation Brigade).[7]

The ride aboard the Slicks was exhilarating, to say the least. While pilots of the much larger Chinook helicopters tended to fly at higher altitudes and rely on their navigational skills, the hotshot Slick pilots favored flying above the treetops and navigated using roads and other physical landmarks. Each Slick could accommodate up to six or seven musicians and their instruments if the weather wasn't too oppressively hot (heat thinned the air and made lifting off difficult for fully loaded Slicks). Our flight landed north of the village, setting down on a muddy road connecting Highway TL-18 to Communal Route 225. We gathered our instrument cases and rifles and, carefully avoiding mud puddles to keep our boots as clean as possible, strolled into Rach Kiên. The village consisted of several ramshackle buildings of varying designs

It was difficult to discern where the village of Rach Kiên ended and the FSPB began. Both appeared to occupy the same ground. Like Camp Scott, Rach Kiên had no dirt perimeter berm. In this scene the concert site is at the left of town (author's collection).

that ran the gamut from homespun to French to downright Asian. A couple of 5/60th Infantry troops lolling around a parked utility truck pointed the way into camp. Much like FSPB Schroeder and FSPB Scott, there was no earthen perimeter berm. The layout of the base and village made it difficult to identify where one ended and the other began. Rach Kiên exuded an exotic Asian atmosphere that was enhanced by roaming Vietnamese civilians and chickens. Upon closer inspection it became apparent that the part of the village included in the base was within a ring of barbed-wire and two-tier guard bunkers. The ceremony was held in front of the battalion HQ building in an open courtyard that might have once served the community as a commons or perhaps a schoolyard. A selection of enemy weapons captured by 5/60th Infantry troops was arrayed on a table placed between twin flagpoles anchored in a substantial concrete base. Both the Stars and Stripes and the Republic of Vietnam flags were flying.

The ceremony went off as expected and after it was over the band was given the opportunity to explore the base and parts of the village. The speechifying had been mercifully short. Our helicopters were not due back for another hour and Bandmaster Kottermann gave his permission for us to wander around but cautioned us to keep away from a detachment of Vietnamese National Police and ARVN troops billeted in the village center. For whatever their reasons they held grudges against each other that occasionally erupted in gunfire. Mister Kottermann said if one of us became a causality he wouldn't know what category to use in his incident report—hostile or friendly? I think he was joking, but I kept a sharp eye out for Asian people wearing uniforms.

When the 5/60th Infantry Battalion first arrived in Vietnam it had been a mechanized asset of the 9th Infantry Division. At that time their base camp, known as Camp Robert Bethune in honor of their first fatality (Robert Edwin Bethune, KIA January 12, 1967), had been established at Bình Phước. In September 1968 the division swapped the 5/60th to the 1st Infantry Division for their 1/16th "Rangers" Infantry Battalion. The 1st Infantry Division's AO was northwest of Saigon in an area less inundated than the Mekong Delta. They needed more mechanized assets to battle main-force North Vietnamese regulars, while the 9th needed more ground pounders to chase VC through the mucky rice paddies of the Delta. The relocated 1/16th Infantry operated about one month under its old battalion designation and then, on October 21, 1968, was redesignated the 5/60th Infantry Battalion (the original 5/60th Infantry Battalion, now serving with the 1st Infantry Division, became the 1/16th Mechanized Infantry Battalion). The name switch was to reestablish the 5/60th Infantry Battalion as a 9th Infantry Division asset.

The band's schedule on June 17 was light except for a change of command ceremony held on Đồng Tâm for the 9th Signal Battalion. LTC Clarence E. McKnight was taking over for LTC Richard K. Bowers. LTC Bowers was on his way stateside to Fort Monmouth, New Jersey—*lucky devil.* After we returned to Đồng Tâm I had the rest of the day off.

On June 18 I learned my request for early separation from the Army no later than August 24, 1969, had completed its run through channels and had been approved. On the same day, the band had a concert at Đồng Tâm, an event for which I have no recall or record other than what Mister Kottermann had listed in the monthly band activity report to battalion HQ. I think he might have meant *practice* concert.[8] The band had two concerts scheduled for the month and the Đồng Tâm concert was, from the band's perspective, the biggie. The stress of terror and sleep deprivation coupled with the logistics of providing various scattered elements in the division with music certainly could have led to administrative errors. Most of us tried our best to get things right and under the circumstances that was all any reasonably disposed lifer could expect. Along with the now-forgotten concert or concert practice, the band sent a bugler across Đồng Tâm to play Taps at a 3/39th Infantry Battalion memorial service.

I had the next day, June 19, all to myself. Other than the unlucky musicians who had to play the scheduled Reliable Academy graduation gig, the entire band had the day off. For a few fleeting seconds I felt bad for the fellows assigned the academy gig; they had to remain seated the entire duration of the ceremony, listen to the same trite old speeches recited at each graduation, and perform the same old music. I found the repetitiveness of the music we played tended to hone off the edges of creativity, reducing making music to a boring mechanical task.

On the topic of the music the band played, some of the more popular march tunes played ad nausea were "Military Escort" by Harold Bennett, "Colonel Bogey March" by British Lieutenant F.J. Ricketts, "The Show Boy" by Will Huff, "American Patrol" by F.W. Meacham, "National Emblem" by Edwin Eugene Bagley, and John Phillip Sousa's "The U.S. Field Artillery" (otherwise known as "The Army Goes Rolling Along"), "The Thunderer," "El Capitan," "Stars and Stripes Forever," "Washington Post," "Semper Fidelis," and "High School Cadets." Occasionally, when we were playing the pass-in-review finale of ceremonies, a march had to be repeated three or four times to allow all of the troops sufficient time to clear the reviewing stand. We played some marches so often I no longer needed to follow the music sheets; I could play the notes by rote.

On June 20 the band boarded three Huey Slicks and traveled to the farthest reaches of Định Tường Province to perform a concert for the 4/39th Infantry Battalion at their new home at FSB Danger. It was the division's newest base, having been completed three months earlier in March 1969. Its design was unmistakably enclave contemporary and exemplified the fortress genre of military architecture, perhaps more so than any other of the division's combat bases. It was home to the battalion HQ of the 4/39th Infantry; their B Company; and a battery of six 105mm towed howitzers belonging to the 1/11th Artillery Battalion. The 4/39th Infantry Battalion kitchen and mortar platoons were stationed at nearby Ấp An Trí, the battalion's A Company in a defensive enclave called "Tombstone," C Company in a former schoolhouse compound dubbed "Claymore," and D Company alternating billets with B Company at Đồng Tâm and FSB Danger. Viewed from the air the four earthen perimeter berm walls of Danger formed a near-perfect square (or diamond, depending upon your preference). Our helicopters swooped low over the base and following a southwesterly heading and set down in a grassy field alongside several other helicopters on the outskirts of Ấp An Trí. Ấp An Trí was also known as Giáo Đức and was the HQ of Giáo Đức District.[9] After a

8. Republic of Vietnam, June 1969

short delay awaiting the arrival of ground transportation, the band boarded a couple of HQ Company, 4/39th Infantry deuce-and-a-half trucks and backtracked along Route QL-4 to FSB Danger. We were let off on the highway at the mouth of a dusty access road that led to Danger's main entrance. The fortifications inside FSB Danger projected a surreal moonscape aura of bulldozed earth accentuated by sandbag defensive bunkers jutting above each perimeter berm. An officer armed with a clipboard escorted us to the concert site.

I have a vague recollection of having earlier participated at a change of command ceremony for the 4/39th Infantry Battalion. The ceremony had occurred soon after I came to the band at a time when I was psychologically preoccupied with the tenuous nature of mortality—in this case, *my mortality*. What I recall most vividly, however, is Larry's heightened expectation at being exposed to the new battalion commander of the 4/39th, LTC David H. Hackworth. Hackworth was taking over command of the battalion from LTC Franklin A. Hart. Apparently Larry had been familiar with LTC Hackworth's illustrious career and status as one of America's most decorated soldiers. At the time there hadn't been an FSB Danger or, for that matter, a 4/39th HQ base camp. The ceremony had been held at a temporary 1/84th Artillery Battalion emplacement, which I believe had the bizarre name of FSB Dizzy.

When we played the June 20 concert at FSB Danger LTC Hackworth was no longer in command, having been relieved by MAJ James R. Taylor during the previous month. LTC Hackworth had received his seventh combat wound and by Army regulations and to the dissatisfaction of the good colonel, had to be removed from a direct combat posting. Under LTC Hackworth's command the 4/39th had dubbed itself "The Hardcore Battalion," and was known throughout the division for its dramatically named components: A was "Alert Company," B "Battle Company," C "Claymore Company," and D "Dagger Company." Rumor had it LTC Hackworth had rejected the division's choice of name for his battalion's new HQ base camp by insisting it be called "Danger" instead of division's choice of "Dickey." To bolster the morale of his troops, LTC Hackworth demanded that military courtesy be observed in camp and in the field. A verbal greeting was ordered to accompany each salute and went something like this: (soldier) *Hardcore Recondo, Sir!* (officer's response) *No fucking Slack!*

LTC Hackworth's illustrious reputation also included his being somewhat of a fair but hard-ass disciplinarian. Just in case any residual effect of his command lingered at Danger, I subconsciously kept buffing the tips of my jungle boots on the back of my fatigue trousers. Danger's dusty and muddy moonscape environment was hell on polished boot tips. I needn't have worried though, the 4/39th troops I encountered looked as scruffy as everybody else in the division. I even spotted an FTA carved above the MP guard shack entranceway at the main gate! *Hardcore with a bit of attitude!*

* * *

Along with summer solstice came two musical assignments—a morning change of command ceremony at Đồng Tâm for the 3/34th Artillery Battalion and an afternoon concert at FSB Schroeder. The following day, June 22, part of the band participated in a memorial service at Đồng Tâm Chapel while the rest of us prepared for an evening concert on our very own DISCOM bandstand. Mister Kottermann advised us to look and act sharp, as the division commander, Major General Hollis, was rumored to be in attendance. Everything on the bandstand had to be cleaned and organized, the bleachers turned to face the bandstand, instruments polished, chairs set up, etc., etc., etc.

In spite of a mountain of apprehension, all went well with the concert. It was a sell-out crowd consisting mostly of lifer types who wanted to be seen by the general. I taped the performance on my three-inch reel-to-reel. The playback was tinny and not at all balanced since I had placed the recorder at my feet, but the trumpet section sounded impressive. I'm not certain if the general came as rumored, but like I said, it was a good crowd. They even applauded when we finished! Culture was still acknowledged at Đồng Tâm. The musical arrangement prepared by SFC Townley and SP-5 Bradley was topnotch. If the general hadn't been in attendance, he'd missed a fine performance.

During the afternoon prior to the concert I'd been handed Special Orders No. 173 alerting me of my impending reassignment to the 90th Replacement Battalion, again for transfer to USATRF STA Fort Dix, but this time on August 17, 1969. I assumed these orders reflected my early separation request, which in itself was odd, because in the morning, upon my inquiry, I had been advised I wouldn't hear anything about my early out request until sometime in August! I was apparently being sent to Fort Dix for out-processing from the Army. This meant I had approximately two months left to serve in the 'Nam, which by any account was two months too many. The orders didn't make me feel like a short-timer, because in the Mekong Delta, where anything and everything could and did happen, two months was akin to a lifetime!

I had KP the next day, which was OK because the band had only a practice session scheduled. After lunch had been served and I was busily scrubbing pots and pans in the back room, SFC Townley interrupted my labors with "I told you so" and handed me Special Orders No. 174, dated June 23, revoking Special Orders No. 165 (the earlier one specifying an ETS date of October 20, 1969).

8. Republic of Vietnam, June 1969

* * *

On June 24 the band flew to Tân Tru to perform a concert for the 2/60th Infantry Battalion. Technically, after 16 hours of KP I could have passed on this trip, but I wanted to go. At the risk of sounding hypocritical (in view of my earlier diatribe concerning my distaste for cold weather), I found the oppressive heat and humidity insufferable. Although I hadn't enjoyed freezing my butt off in the almost arctic cold of Fort Leonard Wood, summertime in South Vietnam was equally unpleasant as winter in the Ozarks, only at the opposite end of the weather spectrum. In the midday sun the heat radiating from the tin roof of the barracks elevated interior temperatures to the level of a slow bake. At night the temperature dropped, but the humidity intensified, which encouraged the mosquitoes to maraud in abundance. The best place to cool off was aloft. Besides, a day away from Đồng Tâm took one's mind off the humdrum boredom of an occupation-army life, if that's what we were supposed to be doing—*occupying*. Getting back to Tan Tru, the band set up in a courtyard near the 2/60th Battalion HQ building that must have also served double duty as the center of social life. There were bleachers, a movie screen, and a basketball court. Across from us and in plain sight on the side of a bunker was the largest and prettiest re-up sign I'd seen in Vietnam to date. It was boldly decorated in patriotic red, white, and blue and had "RE-UP" painted on an inverted V—the "RE-" on a blue leg and the "UP" on a red leg. To balance everything off, the dash was included with the "RE" and an exclamation mark added to the "UP." **RE-UP**! Wow, it was a swell advertisement, except the V shouldn't have been inverted. A normally orientated V was used by the Army on posters to graphically symbolize victory in Vietnam, which led me to wonder what an upside down one signified.

I'm not certain I have the right day (June 25?), or even month, but something splendidly untypical of the Green Machine occurred one evening. Although darkness had settled over Đồng Tâm, it offered little relief from the bottled-up heat of the barracks. I decided to take a late shower to cool off, and while I was in the EM shower a firefight erupted along the east perimeter. Considering Đồng Tâm's four perimeters, the east perimeter had been the most susceptible to enemy attack. To the south the mighty Sông Mỹ Tho offered a substantial water barrier to thwart a ground attack, as did the Kinh Xáng to the west (sappers had been known to swim across the canal, but to discourage this type of assault, the perimeter guards sporadically tossed hand grenades into the water). The north perimeter had no water complications but offered wide-open fields of fire with little concealment or cover to mask an enemy advance.

The east perimeter was entirely another matter. The village of Bình Đuc complicated its defense. Bình Đuc was just off the perimeter in what the Green Machine had designated a "no fire zone." Although it was routinely patrolled, a determined enemy could and did use it to approach Đồng Tâm undetected. I'd been in the shower attempting to cool off when I heard the ruckus begin. At first it was the distant sounds of a small-arms exchange of gunfire, which was not at all unusual to hear at night. One of Đồng Tâm's roving security patrols had undoubtedly encountered VC up to no good. As I left the shower, flares began popping over the berm. Then the east perimeter defenses opened fire. I paused to watch the unfolding drama, feeling secure behind Đồng Tâm's protective dirt berm. I was soon joined by several other bandsmen. Machine-gun tracer rounds, both theirs and ours, cut through the darkness, sometimes striking immovable objects and ricocheting high in the sky. Flares ignited in yellow and green luminosity, creating a surreal spectacle of man's inhumanity toward himself, all presented against the backdrop of opaque political reasoning. Suddenly the lights in the buildings and along the base roads darkened. Đồng Tâm's electrical power was cut to deny the enemy potential targets for their rockets and mortars. While we were watching and listening to the fiery barrage of combat, the unmistakable *whump, whump, whump* sound of an approaching helicopter cut through the din of battle. Like an apparition inexplicitly appearing out of nothingness, the underside of a hovering Huey gunship materialized above us, the beam of its powerful underslung Xenon light sweeping from side to side, desperately scouring the area in search of something. Without collaboration, as a group we collectively surmised they must have wounded aboard and the blackout prevented the pilots, who were combat orientated and more than likely unfamiliar with the location of the 3rd Surgical Hospital landing pad, from spotting it. To get their attention we began frantically jumping up and down and pointing in the direction of the hospital. Suddenly, without warning, all the lights across Đồng Tâm flashed on, illuminating the entire base in brilliant artificial daylight. The helicopter instantly turned in the direction of the hospital and darted away. A few seconds later the lights went off, returning us to darkness, the spectacle of battle, and the unexpected realization that even the Green Machine was capable of compassion at times.

Speaking of compassion, even our erstwhile battalion commander, COL Arthur P. Hanket, could show a degree of compassion for his troops. The fellows at DISCOM who were responsible for securing and projecting the nightly movies got the idea it might be entertaining to have a private showing of pornographic films. This, as you might imagine, was a BIG NO-NO in the

Army, so it was done surreptitiously by soliciting funds to pay for the movies from those desiring to participate. I'm not certain where the X-rated films came from, but they arrived one evening and a showing was arranged behind closed doors in the band supply room. Attendance was good. The ancient black and white movies proved to be more humorous than lurid and a jokingly fun time was had by all, that is, until the room lights were turned on. At the rear of the room sat none other than COL Hanket! He slowly got up from his chair, looked around the room, and said in his best command voice, "If you don't see me, I don't see you."

The month of June was playing out as a concert season as far as band commitments were concerned. On June 26 the band boarded a brace of three Slicks and traveled to the village of Bình Phước to perform for the 2/47th (Mechanized) Infantry Battalion at their HQ base, Camp Panther, a name derived from the battalion's "Panthers" nickname. The helipads were situated outside the wire on the north perimeter off of a mushy raised road that traversed acres of inundated rice paddies ending in a complex of farm buildings. Camp Panther was immediately north of the junction of Route 207 (affectionately called "Thunder Road" by U.S. troops) and Route 206. Our flight set down on the road because the helicopter pads had been already occupied—one by a helicopter and the other by a tracked APC (Armored Personnel Carrier). The road was a churned-up mess of mud that oozed over our nicely polished boots when we jumped off the helicopters—not that muddy boots mattered much to me (other than my having to clean them). Walking on the road was like negotiating deep snow. We had to step high over churned-up ridges of mud and step deeply into ruts while performing a slippery balancing act using outstretched weapons and instrument cases to maintain equilibrium. Immediately outside of the fortification's gate was a large, partially covered, heavy metal sheet lying haphazardly across the road in junkyard fashion. I assumed its placement was to cover a particularly nasty spot. It served as an indication of what lay ahead. Beyond the gate were six sandbag-hardened firing pits with 105mm towed howitzers emplaced. They were noisily executing a fire mission—*BOOM-BOOM-BOOM.* In front of the HQ building of Battery B, 2/4th Artillery Battalion, stood a large, bright-red billboard bearing this greeting: WELCOME TO BEAUTIFUL DOWNTOWN BÌNH PHƯỚC.

Someone had a fertile sense of humor. From what I observed of Camp Panther there was *unequivocally* nothing beautiful about Bình Phước. It even made the surreal moonscape environment of FSB Danger seem inviting. As I progressed along the road the appearance of FSPB Panther failed to improve. Within the 2/47th Mechanized Infantry area, armored and soft-skinned vehicles of various descriptions were parked everywhere. Several vehicles had partially sunk into the mud and listed haphazardly. Tucked within all the military hardware, bunkers, and clutter stood an ancient Vietnamese burial monument. It was partially obliterated from view by stacks of wooden ammunition crates, the tops covered with panels of corrugated metal roofing material to keep the rain from soaking them.

The ceremony came off boringly typical and afterwards, immediately following the festivities, Mister Kottermann announced our pickup helicopters were running late and wouldn't arrive for another hour or so. With little else to do, except maybe find a dry place to wait out the delay by snoozing, Larry and I choose to wander around the camp and take photographs. We eventually gravitated back to the burial monument I had spotted on the way in. Its slight elevation offered a nice dry environment to hang out in. To stave off boredom we started kibitzing around inside the monument, staging goofy photographs. Band clarinetist SP-4 Gerald Lincoln soon joined us and in spite of his usually reserved decorum, took part in the frolicking by snapping a few photographs of Larry and me. I have little doubt that if we had we been observed by any of our Vietnamese allies our behavior would have been

The 5/60th Infantry Battalion had a small raised stage from which the band performed. On this gig I was appointed band guard and ordered to maintain a sharp watch for *un-friendly* friendlies (author's collection).

8. Republic of Vietnam, June 1969

One of the more outspoken battalion commanders of the 4/39th Infantry Division who viewed combat support troops as being less than worthy soldiers had a change of heart after spending several explosive nights on Đồng Tâm. He was happy to return to FSB Danger. *Gee, I wonder why?* On this day the band was at Danger to perform a concert. I felt snuggly safe in the midst of all those "Hardcore Recondo" troops (author's collection).

reported as an overt act of ancestor desecration. The helicopters eventually arrived and we returned to Đồng Tâm.

On June 27 a small contingent from the band performed at a Sniper School graduation held across the street at the Reliable Academy. I remained in the band supply room typing reports for Mister Kottermann. The rest of the band, with the exception of those on the DISCOM company duty roster, had the day off.

The next day about 12 of us crammed into two Slicks and flew to Rach Kiến for a concert at the 5/60th Infantry Battalion FSPB. On this trip the helicopters set down outside the east entrance into the camp on a recently graded Communal Route 225. This perimeter of FSPB Rach Kiến resembled a conventional military enclave, with strung concertina barbed wire, a guard bunker at the gate, and the typical, two-story wooden barracks beyond. The vast expanses of inundated rice paddy lands bordering each side of the road were occasionally interrupted by rustic hooches and raised burial monu-

The monsoon rains and tracked APCs of the 2/47th Mechanized Infantry Battalion rendered the roads at Camp Panther churned-up quagmires of deep, gooey muck. Heavy armored vehicles didn't fare well in the Mekong Delta (author's collection).

ments. As we disembarked from the helicopters several munchkin-size Vietnamese children gathered around us, apparently curious about our drums and oddly shaped instrument carrying cases. They undoubtedly had never observed soldiers armed with such bizarre-looking weaponry. I didn't have my trumpet with me on this trip because Mister Kottermann told me to take my rifle and extra ammunition instead. My function on this trip was to guard the band. I'm not certain why he felt the band needed a guard, since our performance was at a U.S. military installation, but I cheerfully complied with his wishes and vowed to keep a sharp lookout for any threat. (Mister Kottermann later informed me that soon after we had departed Rach Kién during our last visit, there had been an incident between the ARVN and National Police involving gunfire in the village.)

The band set up on a partially enclosed elevated stage erected behind the 5/60th Infantry Battalion HQ. The smooth, plywood rear wall of the stage had been painted white to serve double duty as movie projection screen. Several 5/60th troops were already seated awaiting our performance. I positioned myself to gain an unobstructed view of the entire concert area. It was reassuring to see several armed MPs about. I didn't know what threat I was guarding against but felt I was prepared to deal with whatever it was. The concert went off well, beginning with a stylized rendition of the obligatory "Star Spangled Banner," which was protocol at all military musical engagements, and then flowed into an uninterrupted melody of popular and hit tunes. Trombonist SP-5 Charles Bradley had prepared the arrangements and in recognition of his talent he had the honor of conducting the band in Mister Kottermann's stead. The conclusion of the concert elicited a ragged, unenthusiastic clap, clap, clap from the audience punctuated by a faint but clearly audible "Thanks for the clap" emanating from the stage (an obvious pun equating the pathetic response of the audience with a social disease well known to GIs invoking favors from local prostitutes). The voice sounded a lot like SGT Frank Knightly, who, due to a change in the band's TO&E, had been laterally promoted within the same pay grade from SP-5 to SGT. Frank was now an NCO. Take away his trumpet and he qualified by rank to lead an infantry squad into the bush! *Right!*

After the band packed up their instruments we trudged back to the Route 225 PZ to discover only one helicopter waiting. The other had been

The 2/4 Artillery Battalion's tongue-in-cheek welcoming sign at Camp Panther read, "WELCOME TO DOWNTOWN BINH PHUOC." There was unequivocally nothing beautiful about Bình Phuoc. During the rainy season Camp Panther was transformed into a giant mud hole and during the rest of the year a dusty, sweltering oven (author's collection).

diverted en route. I remained behind with SGT Knightly and several other bandsmen, while Mister Kottermann boarded the helicopter with the rest of the band. To pass the time, several of us chose to fool around with the same kids we'd seen earlier, when a 5/60th Infantry HQ Company deuce-and-a-half came barreling down the road. Apparently, upon the driver's viewing a handful of such good-looking troops, his attention must have been diverted from driving, because the truck went off the edge of the road and buried its five driver's-side wheels axle-deep in muck. What followed was a discordant spectacle of grinding gears, revving motor sounds, and spinning tires in a rocking effort to extract the vehicle. After it got free, we all cheered as the truck passed by us. It had been great entertainment! Our helicopter pickup arrived a few minutes later and off we went back to Đồng Tâm.

The band's musical schedule for the remainder of the month involved three gigs: a combined change of command and awards ceremony on June 29 for D Troop, 3/5th Cavalry held at Đồng Tâm's rotary-wing airfield, and on the following day a change of command ceremony for the Group HQ of the 307th Aviation Battalion at Cần Thơ Army Airfield and an NCO graduation ceremony at the Reliable Academy. The latter two ceremonies necessi-

Two 2/47th Mechanized Infantry Battalion APCs are having a difficult time extracting a third from a rice paddy. The mired truck had inadvertently slid off the road. The roar of engines and whirling of spinning caterpillar treads generated by the struggling vehicles has drawn the attention of a villager who has interrupted her chores to watch the performance (author's collection).

tated the band be split into two separate components, the larger of which flew by Caribou aircraft to Cần Thơ. The 307th Aviation Battalion, while not a direct asset of the 9th Infantry Division, flew in support of division operations providing aerial weapons and surveillance services.

The ceremony for D Troop, 3/5th Cavalry, added a new twist to what was otherwise a standard Army ceremony. Several of the officers wore blue 19th century horse cavalry uniforms accessorized with beige Stetsons, yellow scarves, and dangling sabers! Halloween costumes in June! I'm certain they took their unit's association with history and their dress quite seriously, but their playfulness gave me a chuckle. This was, after all, the United States Army. On the subject of wackiness and anachronistic costumes, another ceremony the band attended actually outdid D Troop, 3/5th Cavalry's colorful audaciousness. I don't remember where, when, or for whom the ceremony was held,[10] but their officers wore the same horse cavalry uniforms. But this unit also had a real horse! It blew my mind away, a living, breathing horse in the 'Nam. Like I said, I don't remember who these people were, but I do remember we had to play the Irish folk tune "Gary Owen" over and over.

It made them happy!

9

Republic of Vietnam, July 1969

It was now raining each and every day. The term *rain* was a misnomer for what the weather was actually doing. *Deluge, pouring buckets, raining cats and dogs, etc.* more accurately described what Mother Nature had unleashed upon IV CTZ. Being caught out in the open bereft of cover was like standing under a waterfall. The rain fell not in discernible drops but in a steady cascade of wetness that instantly overwhelmed Đồng Tâm's storm drainage ditches, roadways, and soldiers. It made level ground look more aquatic than earthlike; the floor inside the band barracks resembled the waterways of Venice. In abject desperation we removed several sandbags from the protective revetment surrounding the barracks and stacked them in doorways in a futile attempt to stem the tide of the runoff.

In spite of the inconveniences and discomforts associated with monsoon season, excitement for the division's impending withdrawal kept morale a notch or two higher than usual. Although I hadn't a clue as to how the withdrawal would affect my DEROS or REFRAD dates, I knew I was getting out of 'Nam by August 17 because that was the date specified on my latest orders. I actually didn't think of my departing in terms of a specific date but rather in terms of 48 days left to survive. Even after official acknowledgement had come, I still didn't revise the DEROS date on my short-timer's calendar for fear of jinxing myself. My instincts had been good as far as my personal situation was concerned, for unbeknownst to me at the time July would evolve into a month when the stinky stuff figuratively hit the allegorical fan that represented my life.

The monthly musical assignments kicked off on July 1 with a practice change of command ceremony for the 9th Medical Detachment. It was held at the 3rd Surgical Hospital compound a few blocks down the road from DISCOM. The practice came off without a hitch, and later in the day a bugler had to be dispatched to the 6/31st Infantry Battalion HQ on Đồng Tâm to play Taps at another of their memorial services.

9. Republic of Vietnam, July 1969

Along with the month of July came a 12 1/2 percent increase in pay and an administrative change in the Green Machine's method of cataloging its soldiers. The traditional service number assigned to soldiers when entering military service was replaced by social security account numbers. Both changes were effective on July 1. For a short time thereafter all special and general orders I received listed both numbers.

The next morning the band returned to the hospital grounds to perform the actual change of command ceremony. After the ceremony and lunch the band enjoyed a refreshingly cool Tango boat ride out to the USS *Benewah*, which was berthed in the middle of the Song Mỹ Tho, to participate in a 2nd Brigade, 3/60th Infantry awards ceremony. While most of the band was on hand for the *Benewah* gig, a member of the trumpet section had to be left behind on Đồng Tâm to play Taps for still another 6/31st Infantry Battalion memorial ceremony. The final band gig for the day was an afternoon awards ceremony for DISCOM held at our very own compound.

That evening I received a bit of a wakeup call before Taps and lights out. I was reading a novel while fiddling with my dog tag necklace when I felt something hard imbedded in the rubber grommet silencer encircling one of the tags.[1] Upon closer examination I picked out a miniscule shard of jagged steel. I checked my jungle fatigues and discovered a tiny pinhole in one of the shirts. The folded-over edge of the metal dog tag must have stopped the tiny piece of shrapnel from striking my chest! Contemplating what could have happened freaked me out, so I forced any speculation about what *could have* happened out of my thoughts.

On July 3 the Green Machine added to the overall confusion surrounding my personal status within the band and division by issuing Alert Orders for my pending DEROS of August 17, 1969. The orders concerned the shipment of my personal items to my HOR, itemizing what items were authorized to be packed in my footlocker and those that were not (no weapons, bullets, explosives, or Army property, etc.). I had tentative approval of my request for R&R in Australia but hadn't received official notification, which probably meant I wasn't going after all. Larry Wolf had just returned from R&R in Taipei (Taiwan) and was full of great stories about his visit.[2]

Later in the day the band was driven a few blocks from DISCOM to perform a concert at the 6/31st Infantry Battalion's billet area. Instead of attending the concert I was dispatched to Đồng Tâm's multidenominational chapel to play Taps at a memorial service. Although enemy activity directed against Đồng Tâm seemed atypically quiet, troops in the field were catching hell.

On July 4 a portion of the band was assigned to perform a concert at the residence of the providence chief in Mỹ Tho. Those bandsmen going boarded two deuce-and-a-half trucks, while Mister Kotterman, SFC Edmond G. LaBlanc, and several bandsmen followed in a ¾-ton cargo truck. I say "followed," because although the cargo truck made it into the DISCOM compound, it refused to start at departure time. There wasn't any time left to secure another vehicle, so as an expedient the mechanics from the 709th Maintenance Battalion hooked a chain to its front bumper and we towed it behind the bandwagon! While part of the band went to Mỹ Tho, the remainder of the band under the leadership of SFC Townley remained on Đồng Tâm to perform at a practice awards ceremony held at division HQ.

The upcoming awards ceremony at division HQ must have been a big event for the senior-grade lifers because our little convoy to Mỹ Tho was accompanied by a Huey AH-1 Cobra gunship escort (the Green Machine obviously wanted the full band intact to perform at their ceremony, which was going to be covered by the news media). The chopper picked up our convoy at Đồng Tâm's main gate and shadowed our progress by flying above us at dangerously low altitudes, slowly alternating sides of Route TL-25. About halfway to Mỹ Tho a small explosion knocked the helicopter out of the sky. Following official convoy protocol, we didn't stop to help the crew. The MPs would eventually find them. That's the way it was in the 'Nam—sometimes you had to fend for yourself until help arrived.

The province chief's residence was as luxurious a place as I'd seen in Vietnam. It was in the middle of the city and surrounded by a heavy iron fence covered with barbed wire. The compound encompassed a large area and hosted several substantial outbuildings. The main residence—an ostentatious two-story stone affair decorated in overall sparkling white with gold trim—was undoubtedly the former home of a wealthy French colonist. The structure radiated opulence in its architectural details. Most of the houses we passed driving through Mỹ Tho were borderline Asian ticky-tacky, but this place was palatial.

Soon after we arrived several of us were snagged by one of the band's multistriped lifers and assembled into a formation off the courtyard that bordered the front entranceway into the residence. The indiscriminate nature of the picking smelled of work detail, and I surreptitiously took a few steps backwards out of the formation, disappearing into a tall hedgerow. It turned out the providence chief needed a heavy grand piano moved (it was allegedly being sent to a local orphanage). I don't know why I deserted my comrades, but I did and felt none the worse for my despicable behavior!

Early the next morning the full band attended a second practice session for the scheduled noon awards ceremony at division HQ. The session was interrupted by several enemy mortars impacting near enough to scatter the attendees, including the officiating brass. Up until now the VC hadn't attacked

9. Republic of Vietnam, July 1969   201

The only occasion when the Green Machine provided security for the band was the day before a gala awards ceremony at Division HQ. The full band was motoring to Mỹ Tho for a concert performance. A Huey Cobra gunship joined our little convoy just inside of Đồng Tâm's main gate on Communal Route TL-25. It paced our movement at low altitude. Halfway to Mỹ Tho there was an explosion, followed by a puff of black smoke, and the helicopter went down (author's collection).

us during daylight hours and the highly unusual daytime mortaring caught everyone off guard. Survival instinct took precedence over military order and decorum. What ensued was a comedic helter-skelter dash to safety.

On my dash I spotted the band's big bass drum rolling unattended toward one of the drainage ditches lining the base road in front of division HQ. As the unofficial band supply sergeant, I felt enough responsibility for the instrument's care to take a running dive after it. I landed short of my objective, falling hard on my face and jarring myself into disorientation with a mouthful of poisoned Đồng Tâm dirt to boot. Some unknown trooper picked me up and manhandled me into the drainage ditch. As I've repeatedly mentioned, in the 'Nam we took care of each other. Several more incoming rounds exploded. After a spell the all-clear siren sounded and everyone sheepishly reassembled into their respective formations on the parade ground, and the practice session resumed as if nothing had happened. The big bass drum was fine, as was my trumpet, which was lying where I had set it down to

The concert at Mỹ Tho was held at the compound of the Định Tường province chief. His opulently-appointed house and sprawling property did not reflect the lifestyle of his constituents. The way he lived reminded me of a line from novelist George Orwell's *Animal Farm*, concerning how the pigs were beginning to look like people (author's collection).

chase after the drum. The awards ceremony[3] came off at noontime without further interruption. After finishing lunch the band was off to another ceremony, this one at 2nd Brigade HQ aboard the *Benewah*, which was still anchored in the middle of the Song Mỹ Tho.

The *Benewah* gig turned out to be a big 9th Infantry Division spectacle attended by generals and the news media. The Mobile Riverine Force (2nd Brigade HQ, 3/47th Infantry, 4/47th Infantry, and 3/60th Infantry battalions) was departing Vietnam on July 8 and this was their gala send-off. The reviewing stand was aboard the *Benewah* and the entire Mobile Riverine Force consisting of the three infantry battalions and over 100 river craft of the brown water navy passed in final review. The band played for what seemed like hours. After the ceremony concluded, the Navy returned us to Đồng Tâm. Once back at DISCOM the HQ company clerk told me to report to the Reliable Academy tomorrow to pick up my R&R orders. I was finally on my way to Australia (I assumed I would be departing in a couple of days, as was typical after receiving R&R orders). Hallelujah!

9. Republic of Vietnam, July 1969

As I should have expected, my joy was short-lived. At the academy I learned that although my R&R to Australia had been officially approved I couldn't go because I hadn't received the necessary immunization shots the Army required to be administered *four days* prior to departure. To further worsen matters, my R&R to Australia was the division's last trip to that destination and it was scheduled to depart on July 7, *the very next day!* The DISCOM clerk had failed to notify me of the immunization requirement! My long-anticipated R&R was beginning to look hopeless. My life again settled into glumness.

The morning I was supposed to have begun my R&R began with an early awards ceremony aboard the *Benewah*. Medals were being handed out like candy on Halloween. Following the performance and our return to Đồng Tâm I was told to get into my Class B Khakis uniform, grab what stuff I was taking on R&R, and report to the 3rd Surgical Hospital ASAP. Larry dropped me off at the hospital in the bandwagon, and I was administered the required shots. I asked about the four-day waiting period requirement and was told not to worry about that. Apparently someone had made the records look correct, not at all an uncommon practice in the Army. Although I had missed the R&R connecting flight to Tân Số Nhút Airfield, a sympathetic transportation officer managed to secure a flight for me aboard an AHC gunship headed in that direction. The helicopter was waiting for me on the hospital's medivac pad. I boarded and off we went. I was on my way to Australia!

The helicopter door gunners who made certain I was securely buckled in handed me a headset so I could listen to the chatter among the crew members as well as outside radio communications. Once aloft, the helicopter zipped along, high above treetop level. I noticed the language used by the crew didn't employ as many "fuckings" per sentence as their ground counterparts. The explicative *fucking* was the adjective of choice for the infantry— "my *fucking* sergeant, that *fucking* asshole, I have *fucking* KP," etc. Sometimes it was utilized several times in a single sentence—"Those *fucking* dinks thought they could *fucking* get through the *fucking* barbed wire." I decided these *fucking* helicopter guys were different—*they were more fucking refined.*

After we'd been aloft for a while the pilots spotted an assembly of suspicious-looking armed Vietnamese civilians moving outside a tree line. We swooped down for a closer look. In the headset I heard the pilot report the sighting as "some Little People with rifles." Definitely more refined language than I was used to hearing. The "Little People" must have been OK because the ship didn't receive authorization to fire its weapons at them. I arrived at Tân Số Nhút Airfield in time to board the flight to Australia. After a slight delay we finally took off. Leaving Vietnam soil made me feel good, so good I fell into a deep slumber. No need to worry about mortars, rockets, and snipers aboard World Airways.

After touching down in Sydney, Australia, we were bused to an R&R center in the city where we were lectured about where we could stay, what was considered appropriate behavior in Australia, what leisure-time activities were available in Sydney, local customs (don't use the thumbs-up sign—it meant something nasty to Australians), blah, blah, blah. Most of us had only round-eyed female companionship on our minds. We were emphatically instructed to look right when crossing streets (this must have been very important because all of the crosswalks I observed in Sydney had LOOK RIGHT painted on the curbing). After exchanging the money we brought with us at the prevailing rate for Australian currency, we were informed we could either purchase or rent civilian clothes (I purchased a dark-brown wool pullover with crew neck and black trousers to complement my black Army argyle socks and black Class A uniform oxford shoes—no U.S. uniforms permitted in Australia), and preregistering at an approved hotel. We were free of military control and on our own.

Before leaving the center I hooked up with another R&R trooper to share the expense of the hotel room. My new companion was savvy to the hotspots GIs frequented in Sydney to meet girls, having been primed by Australia R&R returnees in his unit. Armed with his reconnaissance data we set off for an adventurous evening of booze and babes. My initial visual impression of the Australian city women I observed on the street was that they liked to wear really short mini-skirts, not just the young svelte women but also the old, fat, ugly ones. We made our way to a bar specializing in entertaining R&R troops. The place was packed with noisy GIs—you could tell they were GIs by their closely cropped haircuts, foul language, and obnoxious behavior. I was immediately taken aback by the blatantly raw, uncensored atmosphere in the place and chose to sip my overpriced mixed drink in a reasonably quiet corner where I could just observe. The overall ambience was a bit reminiscent of what I'd encountered in the Saigon bars, except the girls weren't Asian. It hadn't taken long for one of them to spot me, and she worked her way to my corner with a cocktail waitress not far behind her. I surmised they worked in coordinated teams much like our hunter/killer helicopter outfits. I purchased the lady a drink and we chitchatted about mundane things. After several minutes she informed me I really didn't belong in this kind of establishment, that I could meet a nice Australian girl more to my liking elsewhere. She offered a few suggestions and then flittered away into the crowd of noisy obnoxious GIs.

When the working ladies appear to have your best interests at heart and suggest you leave their place of employment, it may be time to listen. I listened. After unsuccessfully attempting to locate my now-vanished roommate to let him know I was leaving, I took a cab to one of the recommended places where *nice* girls hung out. Trader Vic's was a respectable-looking restaurant on the waterfront with a large cocktail lounge attractively decorated in a South Seas island theme. Upon my entering the lounge I noticed a bunch of men loudly conversing at one end of a long bar and a bevy of relatively silent females at the opposite end. The two groups were physically separated by an unoccupied run of bar stools, which must have been a kind of social no-man's-land. I chose a stool dead center of the two groups, sat down, and ordered a drink. My social brazenness, or perhaps ineptitude, in having occupied what might have been a traditional, Australian *social buffer zone* separating male and female counterparts attracted the curiosity of several of the ladies, who began slowly shifting their position toward where I sat alone sipping my drink.

As their point lady closed on my position she asked if I was an American soldier. Apparently not many of our troops frequented Trader Vic's, so I supposed I was an oddity. After a few minutes of getting-to-know-you-type conversation, several more girls from the far end of the bar shifted over to us. I learned that Australian men typically preferred the company of their buddies, or "mates," as they called each other, to the company of their dates in social settings—boys on one side and girls on the other. It was reminiscent of my grammar school days when similar scenarios had played out during supervised dances held in gymnasiums. One of the gals, who said she was an officer in the Women's Reserve, inquired how long I'd be in Sydney, offered to take me sightseeing, and invited me to join her and her friends for dinner one evening. I asked how their boyfriends would feel about that and she said they probably wouldn't even notice. I, unfortunately, had a vision of being pounded in a back alley by half a dozen large, drunken Australian "mates."

The next morning I slept until noon. When I finally got out of bed I discovered my roommate was still asleep. I had heard about a neat place to eat that catered to American tastes and decided to try it for a late lunch. It was a pseudo-American style steakhouse with "Cattlemen" or "Texas" in its name that offered not only food but an all-girl floor show. I was seated near the stage and had an up-close view of the dancers. After the set ended one of them stopped by my table and asked if she could join me for a minute. She was pretty, and I had no objection, thinking it was the restaurant's policy to make GIs feel welcome. Although I expected the inevitable cocktail waitress, none materialized. My companion said she had taken notice of me from the stage and felt like meeting me. We talked until she had another performance.

Before she left the table she invited me to dinner at her place, saying she'd be off at five o'clock. We agreed to meet in front of the restaurant, and when the appointed time came I found her waiting for me in her dancer's costume. We hailed a cab and rode across the city to where she lived.

    Her apartment was on the second floor. It was small but tidy with kitchen, living room, and bedroom combined in one room. She said she was going to change out of her costume into something more comfortable. I assumed she meant she'd change in the bathroom, but I was incorrect. She began peeling everything off in front of me! First, off came a wig, then false eyelashes, dance tights, padded bra, and padded hips. She glanced over to where I was sitting and unabashedly assured me that the rest of her was real. Shucked of the feminine, enhancing equipment, she looked different—not bad, but different. She came to me in her panties and earrings and suggested we go to bed before dinner. It was, after all, still early. The incongruity of my situation struck me like a thunderclap. The day before yesterday I'd been dodging mortars in a godforsaken Asian land; now I had a round-eyed, sweet-smelling, naked female standing smack-dab in front of me. Although my childhood exposure to Roman Catholic doctrine had affected my proclivity toward fornication, I was no longer a virgin. But I also wasn't the stereotypical horny male always on the make. She was offering me what every soldier in combat dreamed of; I just didn't expect it to have materialized so quickly and, quite frankly, so blatantly. Fortunately for my ego she misidentified my lack of visible physiological response to her suggestion as being rooted in my trepidation in performing inadequately due to war and prolonged abstinence. She set about alleviating my concerns by exercising her tactile charms. She was obviously a very experienced young woman, certainly more experienced than I.

    We spent the next three days and nights in pseudo-connubial bliss. In between screwing sessions she went to work and I went sightseeing. We eventually discussed her emigrating to America and our living together. Things were moving fast, *way too fast*. She asked for a photo keepsake to remember what I looked like until we could be together again. I said I'd send her one from Vietnam. My R&R time in Australia was running out. On July 13 I'd have to report to the R&R station for transportation back to Vietnam. I returned to my hotel and roommate the evening before reporting. He mentioned my absence with a knowing wink. His luck hadn't been as good as mine; he had had to pay for his female companionship.

    I never sent my Australian girlfriend a photograph or even contacted her after we parted company.[4] Being with her had been nice, but I happened to spot a plastic photo-cube on the shelf below her nightstand full of snapshots of different GIs! It bothered me.

9. Republic of Vietnam, July 1969

Although I don't remember anything about the flight back to Vietnam, I do remember being shuttled from R&R Camp Alpha (the R&R in-country processing center) to Biên Hòa Army Airfield in the bed of an open deuce-and-a-half truck. I was once again attired in my snappy Class B Khakis uniform and was doing my utmost to psychologically readjust to the hostile Asian surroundings. I really didn't expect anything to happen, but I did feel uncomfortably exposed sitting in the bed of an open truck. Suddenly a volley of automatic weapons fire pierced the exhaust and clattering sounds of the noisy truck. I didn't have a weapon to defend myself. I felt the edge of panic clutching at my heart. *No cover, no concealment, and no weapon!* I was helpless, with nothing left to do but die. I was struggling with holding back my panic when another volley ripped alongside the truck. It came from a Vietnamese National in an abbreviated ARVN uniform. He was merrily firing rounds from his M-16 into the sky! It hadn't been my time to die after all, but it was a dramatic reminder of what I had returned to.

I got back to Đồng Tâm in time to change into my best jungle fatigues and join the band in a change of command gig for the 9th Signal Battalion being held a few blocks away from DISCOM. I didn't record what lifer was taking command from what other lifer. It had been the only scheduled commitment for the day and upon returning I reported to Mister Kottermann to resume performing whatever clerical tasks he needed accomplished. I learned that while I was on R&R the band had performed at an awards ceremony for DISCOM and a memorial service for the 1/84th Artillery—both held on July 7, a send-off ceremony for the 3/60th Infantry Battalion on July 8, a change of command ceremony for the 2/47th Mechanized Infantry at Bình Phước on July 10,[5] and on July 12 a practice change of command ceremony for the 9th Signal Battalion.

The gig for the homeward-bound 3/60th Infantry Battalion had included a specially written song several *lucky* members of the band had been ordered to sing. I'm glad I missed that one. Too much stateside lifer-ism was creeping into military life at Đồng Tâm. I also learned that while I was in Australia the division had deemed the bandsman MOS as critical to the withdrawal process of the division. The lifers must have wanted to depart in quick-stepping musical style because musicians certainly weren't critical to the war effort. There would be no more replacement troops (including bandsmen) coming into the division. We were informed absolutely no one could leave the band for any reason whatsoever! This turn of events had serious DEROS implications for me, especially if it continued beyond August 17.

After chow call that evening Mister Kottermann asked me to stop by the band office. I thought he had more paperwork for me to process, but instead he handed me General Orders Number 10035, dated July 11, 1969, along with a small, flat, beige-colored box. He told me to open it. While I had been screwing my brains out in Australia the Green Machine had awarded me a second Army Commendation Medal, this one with an oak leaf cluster pinned in the ribbon!

Ho, ho, ho, wasn't war hell?

July 14 summoned a big day for the division. The 4/39th Infantry Battalion was turning over their battalion HQ base, FSB Danger, to the ARVNS. The full band flew out of Đồng Tâm aboard several Huey Slicks. Aloft we resembled an eagle flight (GI parlance for a combat helicopter assault).

In ceremonial terms the turnover resembled a change of command ceremony, except there were more high-ranking brass in attendance and a spit-shined ARVN color guard. Danger was being handed over by 4/39th Battalion commander MAJ James R. Taylor to MAJ Tru Thanh of the 1st Battalion, 12th Regiment, 7th ARVN Division. After the speeches concluded the Stars and Stripes were lowered while we played "The Star Spangled Banner." Then the ARVN color guard raised their flag and we played the Republic of Vietnam

The final review of Navy Task Force 116 was held on the Mỹ Tho River across from Đồng Tâm. The reviewing stand was aboard the USS *Benewah*. The band played the seafaring ditty "Anchors Away" for what had seemed like hours. Over 100 vessels had passed in review (author's collection).

The final awards ceremony the band participated in was held at Division HQ. Everybody who was anybody in IV CTZ was in attendance. Long-winded speeches were followed by troops passing in review. It was all very colorful with unfurled banners and colors displayed from just about every single 9th Infantry Division infantry and artillery battalion still in-country (author's collection).

National Anthem. The ceremony ended with a low-altitude flyover by two jet fighters from the 7th Tactical Fighter Wing.

On July 15 the band was occupied with a morning practice awards ceremony at division HQ and later in the day the actual ceremony. The division's senior-grade bunker dwellers were generously handing out Silver Stars to each other. It seemed like every staff officer received one in recognition of their "heroic service."

In typical Green Machine command dichotomy, the critical musician status of my former roommate, Albert Denver, and I was countermanded by our receipt of special orders assigning both of us to the 3/34th Artillery Battalion.[6] This was the artillery unit that fired in direct support of mobile riverine operations. It had been deactivated along with the rest of 2nd Brigade and was now being processed out of 'Nam. On July 16 we packed our footlockers for shipment to CONUS, turned in all of our combat equipment to the DISCOM armory, and reported to 3/34th Battalion HQ, where we were given bunks in a former aviation compound bordering on the west perimeter.

FSBs Danger, Moore, and Schroeder were turned over to ARVN during July. The band performed at all three ceremonies. This photograph was taken at the practice session that preceded the actual ceremony. U.S. troops are to the left and the Vietnamese to the right (author's collection).

I was feeling pretty good about going home and early the next morning after roll call and chow I sent my parents a letter telling them not to write anymore because I was coming home! I informed them of the deactivated outfit I was now with and the probable destination of Fort Lewis in Washington State. I announced I expected to be home by the end of July.

Deactivating with the 3/34th didn't entail much duty—no KP, no shit burning, no sandbag filling, no guard duty, no anything other than hang around the compound. About the only requirement was to make roll call each morning.

On the morning of the July 18, following reveille, the VC sent a rocket over the berm. It penetrated the upstairs screen door of the barracks where I was assigned a billet, exited through the back door, and exploded on the handrail of the step landing. No one was injured, but the fellows upstairs said it swooshed down the center aisle and incredibly had missed everybody! I don't think luck had anything to do with it; I think the angels realized we'd all served our time in man-made hell and they were now watching over us.

It struck me as odd the VC had suddenly become so aggressive. I would have thought, and did think, they'd welcome the division's withdrawal. Then it dawned on me: we were housed in the former billet area of a recently relocated attack helicopter company. The dinks were after the helicopter crews that would remain on Đồng Tâm in support of future ARVN operations. Their intelligence was good, just a bit outdated. I found no comfort in the knowledge!

No more mortars or rockets came over the berm, and Albert and I safely managed the rest of the day hanging around the barracks. The weather had become so oppressively hot and humid that little relief could be had. I missed our little oscillating desk fan. After dinner, just as darkness was beginning to descend, we went to the EM showers attired in our tire sandals and towels. The showering offered some comfort from the weather, that is, until the first mortar struck near enough to set everyone in the shower on the run toward the nearest personnel shelter. Darkness had almost completely fallen and the unfamiliar compound was cloaked in deceiving shadows. We found the personnel shelter OK, but it was partially flooded with rainwater. Albert looked up and cursed. You could see the stars. *The bunker had no roof!* It was in the process of being dismantled. We ran outside and spotted the shadowy image of another bunker looming not far away. As we ran toward it bunkers along the western perimeter opened up in a blaze of deafening gunfire. More mortar rounds exploded close enough to send a shock wave of adrenaline through my body. We reached the other bunker. It had a solid wooden door secured by a heavy padlock! Mortars were now dropping everywhere around Đồng Tâm. *BOOM, BOOM, BOOM!* Over the detonations I could hear the unmistakable *AHHHHHHH* sound of an electronically fired mini-gun. Several helicopters on the opposite side of the Kinh Xáng were firing rockets. It was an all-out attack against the west perimeter. In my panic (keep in mind I was now a very short short-timer) I'd lost my sandals, my towel, and Albert. I found myself naked and alone. I dashed madly back to the partially demolished bunker reasoning that four walls without a roof were better than nothing.

After the attack ended and the all-clear sounded, I returned to the shower to rinse off. I found a towel lying on the shower steps and grabbed it. It was probably the one I had lost during the melee. I showered and toweled off, then returned to my bunk in the barracks. It had just been another day in the 'Nam.

The next morning I was called out of morning roll call and instructed to report to the company clerk. He handed me orders rescinding my transfer to the 3/34th Artillery. There were no other orders. I asked him what I was supposed to do. He shrugged his shoulders and told me to go back to my old unit.

The clerk graciously secured a ride for me in the HQ Company commander's utility truck and, after being dropped off at DISCOM, I immediately reported to Mister Kotterman, who I spotted leaving the mess hall. He was surprised to see me and asked what had happened. I related my tale of woe. He figured the Army, in typical Green Machine fashion, had flagged me for withdrawal solely because of my DEROS of August 17, which they inferred meant I had only one month left to serve in-country. I, however, had actually been in-country for only seven months and, therefore, was not eligible for withdrawal with the first increment. Some clerk had apparently discovered the error.

I informed Mister Kottermann I had no orders reassigning me back to the band, whereupon he told me not to worry; I could stay with them as long as they remained on Đồng Tâm. He said the band was eventually going to be relocated to an embarkation point with the rest of the division. Everybody was going to return to CONUS with a gala musical send-off. I asked him what he wanted me to do. He shrugged his shoulders and told me to have breakfast and then report to the band office. A lot of paperwork had backed up during the days I'd been gone, and it had to be processed!

So here I was in an active combat zone with no rifle, no helmet, no battle harness, and no orders—literally just the clothes on my back. Somehow I had fallen through the cracks of Army efficiency. Oddly enough, Mister Kottermann not only welcomed me back but also gave me Wilber West's old room at the south end of the band barracks. SSG West had DEROS'd back to CONUS at the end of June (before the critical MOS order had been issued). I found all kinds of nifty canned goods he had left behind. He must have felt the same way about mess hall chow as I did.

The one advantage that accrued from my indigent status within the division was no work details. *Hoorah!* Other than sporadic bombs falling from the sky and piles of clerical work for Mister Kottermann, I had attained a kind of military nirvana. During the morning of July 20 I wrote my parents the Army had been just fooling about my returning home earlier than expected, and they could resume writing to me using the old DISCOM address. I also warned them to expect a box from the Army full of my personal belongings. I told them to open it up and take a look. I thought they might find the black and white photograph album enclosed interesting (I had never sent home the snapshots developed by the PX).

Later that day after lunch part of the band climbed aboard three Huey Slicks and flew 20 miles to FSB Schroeder in western Định Tường Province. LTC Robert A. Sullivan, commander of the 3/39th Infantry Battalion, was turning over the FSB to an ARVN captain, Nguyen Thanh Tung, commander of the 2nd Battalion, 12th Regiment, 7th ARVN Division. Plenty of high-ranking senior-grade lifers were on hand to participate in the ceremony, including our assistant division commander, General Frank G. Gunn, and the 1st Brigade commander, COL John G. Hayes. The ceremony mimicked the earlier turnover at FSB Danger. Our flag came down and theirs went up, but there was no concluding air power flyover. The fighter jets may have been needed elsewhere.

I hadn't missed much band activity while with the 3/34th Artillery Battalion. All I'd missed was a practice and awards ceremony at division HQ on July 15, a practice awards ceremony for our provisional ACV Unit (Air Cushioned Vehicle)[7] on July 18, and on July 19 a sniper school ceremony at the Reliable Academy, followed by the actual awards ceremony for the ACV unit.

I was sorry I had missed the ACV ceremony. I knew some of the mechanics at their maintenance yard. Occasionally the band had been airlifted by Chinook from the engineering supply depot helicopter pad across the base road from the ACV maintenance area. I used to kibitz with the ACV mechanics while waiting for the helicopter to arrive. It had helped pass the time.

On July 21 the band performed another change of command ceremony for the 2/47th Mechanized Infantry at Bình Phước. It was actually part two of the earlier July 10 ceremony the band had attended while I was on R&R in Australia. MAJ William T. Muenter, who had assumed *temporary* command from LTC Douglas S. Smith, was now being relieved by the new battalion commander, LTC James R. Rowe, who had finally arrived in-country from his stateside assignment with the Pentagon. LTC Rowe and the 2/47th would remain behind in Tân An with the rest of 3rd Brigade. After we returned from Bình Phước we *didi mau'd* (hurried) over to the Division Artillery compound for a practice change of command ceremony. COL Richard M. Jennings was assuming command from COL Daniel D. Stedham.

Early that evening after evening chow call an untypically somber-looking Mister Kottermann had us form up in a circle around him, where he told us the band had been placed on combat alert. The division's roving security patrols and LPs (Listening Posts) were encountering heavy VC activity off the northern perimeter. We learned the band was given the combat responsibility of defending a guard outpost at the little-used rear entrance gate into Đồng Tâm. I hadn't even known there was a rear entrance. The bunker emplacement was outside the north perimeter astride the road at the gate. DISCOM apparently maintained a round-the-clock guard made up of slightly wounded infantrymen. They ate and slept in the bunkers. An evening attack was anticipated and it was the band's mission to bolster the guard detachment. As I listened to Mister Kottermann, cold shivers ran up and down my back.

Our approach to the outpost would be over an elevated road across a monsoon-mucky open expanse of marshland. If summoned we'd have to boogey down the road without the benefit of cover or concealment, To make matters worse, the moon was almost full. I silently prayed for rain. SSG John Franklin, who was standing next to me, mumbled something about being a short-timer (we were all short-timers) and having kids back in California. I was both scared and angry this was happening at a time when we were so close to going home. I foolishly told John if he loaned me his rifle (keep in mind I no longer had one) I'd go in his place (in view of my unassigned transient status with the band I had assumed I had the option of going or not going). Mister Kottermann gave me a long pensive glance and then announced he could risk sending only six bandsmen who played different instruments. He then asked for volunteers, and every single hand went up, including John's. The entire band was volunteering. *If we had to go, we were going together!* I noticed my pal Larry smiling. He loved this kind of stuff.

The attack never came. The VC's plans may have been thwarted by our security patrols out in the boonies beyond Đồng Tâm's perimeters. That night I was awakened several times by the sound of distant gunfire and on one occasion Four Deuces firing salvos.

At some point during the month the Green Machine had reinstated their policy of forbidding soldiers to have ammunition in their possession on Đồng Tâm. The defense of the base totally relied on the perimeter guards and the roving security patrols. All of the new company-size personnel shelters were being built with limited defensive capabilities (no firing ports). In their minds the threat of Đồng Tâm being overrun was, apparently, over. There was, however, a sinister underlying rationale behind taking ammunition away from soldiers in camp. The long-term psychological effects of six years of escalating combat, an officer corps saturated with career-oriented commanders, totally unclear military objectives, ever-increasing reliance on reluctant draftees to fill the ranks, and dwindling support on the home front displaying disdain for its soldiers had transformed USARV into a mean and disillusioned army. Too many quick-tempered troops might hurt themselves and others.

Along with the restated ammunition restriction came a new protocol classifying the seriousness of alerts. A color code was instituted to exemplify the degree and severity of our response to threats. A GRAY ALERT was the mildest form, indicating there was plenty of time to get things done, stop at the mess hall for a refreshing Kool-Aid, grab your rifle, helmet, flak vest, and shuffle over to the armory to wait in line for ammunition. A YELLOW ALERT heated things up a bit, meaning you had to cut out the refreshments and walk faster to the armory. An ORANGE ALERT signified an attack was imminent.

Now you had to hastily grab what you needed from your hooch, run like Lucifer was on your heels to the armory, and then wait in line for ammunition. I never quite grasped the significance of a RED ALERT. In consideration of the inevitable waiting line at the armory you might just as well have bent over and kissed your rosy red good-bye. Now when things went *BOOM* in the night, amidst all of the short-timer generated confusion and the normal fear of injury or death, the cry *"What color alert is this?"* echoed throughout the barracks! Despite the Green Machines threats of punishment, I continued to keep a loaded magazine hidden in my hooch and continued to accentuate the front of my flak vest with a couple of decorative copper-tipped brass cartridges slipped in the stretch webbing. No one that mattered ever seemed to notice, which was a good thing for me. Being court-martialed for having bullets in a war wouldn't have read well in my 201 file or improved my already cynical attitude toward our commanders. After seven months in the Delta, I no longer had the patience for lunatics who lived in bunkers while commanding troops who slept outside.

Besides, what could they do to me? Send me to 'Nam?

The band performed at the actual Division Artillery change of command ceremony the morning of July 22. We did it in the rain. Afterwards Mister Kottermann gave us the rest of the day off. I wiped down my trumpet and dried out my sheet music that had somehow gotten a bit soggy even though I had clamped in my trumpet's lair encased in a protective plastic holder designed to keep it dry. It had just rained too hard.

On July 23 a large contingent of the band was driven 10 miles to FSB Moore for a turnover ceremony. Normally we would have flown to Moore, but increased enemy activity in the field had diverted all rotary-wing assets to direct combat related missions. To transport us we needed the bandwagon, a second deuce-and-a-half, and the temperamental cargo truck that now seemed to be running fine. Because of the incessant rain, sheltering canvas covers had been installed over the beds of all three trucks. I took my usual sentry's position above the cab and cursed the Green Machine for exposing us to such risk. I had less than a month to DEROS and was getting too short for this kind of stuff. Larry loaned me his rifle and he took one of the Reliable Academy's M-79 grenade launchers. I stuffed my pockets with ammunition magazines and also took along a full bandolier of magazines for extra measure. Larry's pockets were stuffed with explosive and antipersonnel rounds for the M-79. Most of the roads to Moore were now paved, which eliminated the threat of subsurface land mines. All we had to worry about were CDMs (Command Detonated Mines) and ambushes. We'd be traveling on Route QL-4 most of the way. Because it was the main thoroughfare in the Mekong

Delta, it was heavily patrolled by MPs. Our chance of running into harm's way was minimal. Although I felt nervous about such a long journey by truck, I was fairly confident we'd be safe. There were certainly juicier targets available to the VC than the 9th Infantry Division Band!

Although Larry and I had prepared for the worst, nothing happened. This was the insidious nature of combat in the Delta. The lightly armed VC knew they had no chance of defeating the U.S. Army in battle. Their objective was demoralization through terror and they were accomplishing their goal far better than the U.S. was accomplishing its goal of containing communism in Southeast Asia. It was rumored the North Vietnamese communist were operating out of Laos and Cambodia.

The FSB Moore turnover ceremony involved the usual speechifying and flag lowering/raising drama. It was the final FSB in the Division's AO to be turned over and the Green Machine officially reported it in the July 30 issue of the Old Reliable News as the last of the "reliefs in place," a nebulous term which meant little to most people in the Division. FSB Moore became the HQ base camp of the 7th ARVN Division.

As each of these combat bases was turned over to the ARVN, *they* assumed the responsibility of securing their assigned areas. Several U.S. helicopter units formerly attached to the 9th Aviation Battalion would remain on Đồng Tâm to support ARVN operations, *but we were going home!*

Upon returning to Đồng Tâm the band had to hustle over to the 3/39th Infantry Battalion compound to participate in a change of command ceremony practice. The practice was immediately followed by the actual ceremony. LTC Leroy William Dyment was taking command of the battalion from COL John D. Smythe. The process of swapping commanders continued. Listening to the unending repetitive speeches made me wonder why with so many high ranking war heroes commanding Division combat assets, the VC in the Delta couldn't be eradicated.

On July 24 the 9th Aviation Battalion changed commanders. The ceremony was held at the Reliable Rotary-wing Airfield. The band had the rest of the day as well as the next day off.

July 25 began with a practice ceremony for a unit on Đồng Tâm whose identity I've now forgotten. It was followed the next day by a concert at the billet of the 6/31st Infantry, which was adjacent to the Reliable Academy, and a change of command ceremony for the 9th S&T. Although the VC kept sporadically pounding Đồng Tâm at random hours, including the daylight ones, their mortars and rockets were mostly aimed at the rotary-wing airfield. Their incessant attacks, however, did elevate the apprehension and fear at DISCOM to a fevered pitch. Troops began wearing flak vests and helmets all of the time. Some even slept in them. We were all too close to going home. I no longer had a flak vest or helmet; otherwise I would have slept in them, too!

The psychological terror factor of life on Đồng Tâm was greatly enhanced by a rumor circulating around DISCOM concerning a Vietnamese laborer who was blown to smithereens by an explosive device planted in a mess hall tray rack.[8] As the rumor went, the unfortunate contract KP laborer pulled out a tray and the rack went BOOM, immediately killing her. She must not have gotten the word about the booby trap, because the VC typically didn't harm their intelligence-gathering comrades who worked at Đồng Tâm. Although the rumor didn't include mention of which particular mess hall the tragedy occurred at, I found the scenario entirely credible.

As the month of July drew to a close, so did my record keeping for Mister Kottermann. The DISCOM parade ground in front of the mess hall was now lined with a string of CONX containers. Everyone in the band was occupied cleaning and packing unneeded band instruments, personal gear, and whatever else was leaving with DISCOM. Work details were assigned to thoroughly clean all company vehicles, including the bandwagon. We were told the vehicles would be returning with us. Most of the trucks had rust spots and holes where shrapnel had penetrated their sheet metal. We spent hours scrubbing running gear and tires only to later learn everything had been dumped into the South China Sea! Now THAT was the Army way—plenty of wasted effort and equipment. I assumed we had to be kept busy to keep the Green Machine happy!

The month ended with an awards ceremony for HHC & Band, DISCOM and a memorial service for the 6/31st Infantry on July 30 and another hoopla awards practice and ceremony at Division HQ on July 31. July marked the final monthly band commitment report I typed for Mister Kotterman. HHC & Band, DISCOM, had received their alert orders for departing Đồng Tâm, which left my status with the division rather vague.

I had 17 days until DEROS. *Way too short for this kind of uncertainty!*

10

Republic of Vietnam, August 1969

The month of August brought more rain and even more confusion concerning my assignment status within the band and division. My early-out to attend college had effectively denied me the opportunity to rotate back to The World with DISCOM. I was going to ship out as an individual, which did offer the comfort advantage of traveling to CONUS on a commercial jet flight as opposed to the Spartan discomfort of an MACV military transport. Although I remained in the division (albeit unassigned) the Green Machine must have thought I'd already departed, because on August 1 General Orders No. 11241 awarded me the Bronze Star Medal for "meritorious service against a hostile force," blah, blah, blah, but division mailed it to my HOR instead of presenting it to me at an awards ceremony, as was military protocol. Division personnel must have thought I'd departed with the 3/34th Artillery Battalion.

I received another medal on August 6. General Orders Number 11350 awarded me the Good Conduct Medal for "exemplary behavior, efficiency, and fidelity." Ah, *why not?* This one was also mailed to my HOR.

During the next several days the band participated in a few more gigs, both on and off Đồng Tâm. Nobody was keeping records anymore, so I have no recollection for whom and where we performed. Those troops withdrawing were abuzz packing equipment for the long MACV C-130 flight to Hawaii. The ten-month eligibility stipulation that had so effectively prevented my leaving with the 3/34th Artillery Battalion now had been lifted. Everyone in the division was going back to The World except, of course, the unfortunates in 3rd Brigade who would remain behind in Tan An to support 25th Infantry Division operations. On August 6 the final edition of the *Old Reliable News* was published. The featured story, "Old Reliables Return Home from War," said it all.

Amen.

10. Republic of Vietnam, August 1969

* * *

The VC, unfortunately, didn't share our euphoria for withdrawal. Every day and night they brazenly lobbed in a few mortar rounds or fired rockets over the berm. It kept our choppers buzzing around the perimeters looking for VC targets. The roving infantry patrols that up until recently secured Đồng Tâm's perimeters had been recalled and were now in their battalion stand-down billets doing PT and packing. All of the infantry elements of 1st Brigade formerly operating out of FSB Moore, Schroeder, and Danger were also on Đồng Tâm. The base was awash in humanity, which presented a juicy, target-rich political environment for the communists—their message being we hadn't really defeated them. *They* still ruled the Delta, but now in daylight as well as darkness.

The last U.S. fatality on Đồng Tâm I am aware of occurred on August 8 when SGM (Sergeant Major) Henry Lee Pippin, 37 years old and a 20-year Army veteran, died of a heart attack. He had, ironically, arrived in-country the same day as I—January 7. He had been a senior finance sergeant with the 9th Administration Company. I didn't know him.

The nine days remaining until my scheduled DEROS of August 17 seemed like a lifetime away. I had lost the edge of hopelessness born of too many close encounters with mortality. I was as nervous as a root canal candidate awaiting his turn in the dentist's chair. Although the end was in sight, I didn't want it to be *my* end. Every day Đồng Tâm's south perimeter came alive with the explosive sounds of mortar salvos from Four Deuces. My short-time jitters overwhelmed my former ability to distinguish outgoing from incoming rounds. In my present state of mind I viewed every loud BANG as a threat to my survival. At night, patrolling helicopter gunships blasted the countryside with mini-guns and rockets in a discordant cacophony of death and destruction in an all-out effort to keep Mr. Charles on his side of the perimeter. I spent as much time as I could in the personnel shelter, both day and night.

With no more musical assignments to play, the bandsman's MOS was no longer critical. A couple of musicians whose remaining time in the Army had expired left the band to depart as individuals. All band musical instruments, combat gear, and personal possessions had been securely packed for shipment in CONEX containers. On August 10 Mister Kottermann announced an official departure date of August 16. His news didn't include me, so I asked him what he thought I should do. He suggested I report to the Reliable Academy[1] and ask them, which is precisely what I did.

I discussed my situation with an academy administrative NCO who

Musical commitments for the band slowed appreciably throughout August with fewer and fewer gigs to play. The Division's 2nd Brigade had already departed Vietnam and withdrawal plans for 1st Brigade were on schedule for completion by the middle of the month. My time in 'Nam was ending, so I gave my buddy, Larry Wolf, my camera and asked him to take one final picture of me at DISCOM. I would soon be homeward bound (courtesy Larry Wolf).

10. Republic of Vietnam, August 1969

knew me from my participation as a bugler in their retreat ceremonies. He said he could cut orders getting me to the 90th Replacement Battalion in Long Bình, but once there I'd have to tell them my story. He said to come back in an hour or so and he'd have the reassignment orders cut. I went back across the road to DISCOM, gathered what items I still had in my possession, said good-bye to whomever I could find around the barracks, and reported to Mister Kottermann for the last time. He wished me well and shook my hand. I whipped up a snappy farewell salute, which he smartly returned.

My NCO acquaintance at the Reliable Academy handed me orders and a boarding pass dated August 11 for a flight aboard a U.S. Air Force 834th TAW (Tactical Air Wing) C-7A Caribou from Đồng Tâm to Biên Hòa. The academy would drop me off at the fixed-wing airfield next morning. In the meantime I was told to grab a bunk in one of the barracks—any I wanted. The academy, which until recently had processed thousands of incoming troops, was now a virtual ghost town. I'd come full circle in the division. After what had seemed like an eternity, I was finally getting out of Đồng Tâm! The 90th Replacement Battalion was my entry portal back into The World, and I rationalized that under the worst of circumstances Long Bình had to be more secure than Đồng Tâm. I relished the thought of no more bombs falling out of the sky or rockets zipping over the berm. Henceforth I'd be viewed by the Army as a transient, someone to be protected and not the other way around. It was a good feeling, my first in many months. I just had to survive a couple more nights in Vietnam.

* * *

The flight to Biên Hòa Military Airbase was blessedly uneventful. This time I deplaned under less stressful conditions than when I had first arrived in-country. The group of transients I was with was told to wait under the tent for a shuttle bus to the 90th Replacement Battalion compound. I sat on the very bench I had sat on back in January, a relatively short span of time that now seemed like it had been an eternity. My jungle fatigues, which hung loosely on my lean 175-pound frame, had faded to a drabness that bespoke my many months in-country. I spoke to no one; I just sat in silence awaiting transportation.

The bus eventually came, and I reported in at the 90th Replacement Battalion HQ. I handed the clerk my orders, and he glanced at them and inquired if I had any other orders. I gave him my copy of Special Orders Number 173, the alert order assigning me to the 90th Replacement Battalion for transfer to USATRF STA Fort Dix. He looked up at me and said I was a week early. I shrugged my shoulders and he stamped something on a piece of paper and told me to find a bunk in the transient barracks, which I, of course, did.

I thought I'd be running out my time in-country performing make-work details, as I had done when I was at Long Bình the last time. I, however, was wrong. After morning roll call the CQ found me and told me to grab some breakfast and then report to the departure point in my Class B Khakis uniform. The departure point was easy to find, it was housed in a long low building with its entrance cut into a large black-on white-sign instructing: GOING HOME—REPORT HERE—USA BOUND. I'd be shipping out to Biên Hòa Military Airfield on the first bus of the morning, my ultimate flight destination being USAOSREPLCTR, Oakland, California. I'd be going home along the same pipeline to CONUS as when I had arrived. The 90th Replacement clerk had told me the clerks at Oakland could figure out what to do with me—a situation that suited me just fine! A week of work details anywhere in the world was better than a single day in 'Nam.

I spent my last several hours in-country in the exclusive company of other returnees. Because the 90th Replacement Battalion was still actively in-processing replacement troops being assigned to the many units continuing to fight in Vietnam, we were kept physically isolated from them as if quarantined with a communicable disease. My guess was they didn't want us enlightening the NFGs about USARV. The Green Machine must have viewed us as having been *tainted* by the reality of Vietnam service. They didn't want the tainting to prematurely spread to the new guys. They could get tainted their own.

The World Airways *freedom bird* flight to Oakland took a slightly different route than my January flight from Oakland to Vietnam. On this trip the plane refueled at Yokota, Japan, as before but changed course to Honolulu, Hawaii. At the airfield we'd been informed our flight would be taking on civilians at the refueling stop in Honolulu, and we were instructed to be considerate of their status. The pilots must have thought after surviving a year in Vietnam we might—socially speaking—be somewhat coarse around the edges.

When our flight reached cruising altitude the seat belt warning lights went out, and our pretty stewardess demonstrated how to use the aircraft's emergency flotation device. She explained, in mechanical animation, the proper procedure for escape in case the plane crashed into the sea. Everyone onboard silently looked at each other. Then the plane's PA crackled: *"Gentlemen, this is your captain speaking. It is my pleasure to advise you that we have just departed Vietnamese air space."* Stunned silence was followed by a roar of exultation that reverberated throughout the aluminum fuselage of the plane! *Hallelujah, we were out of the 'Nam!* No more bullets, no more rockets, no more mortars, no more booby traps, and no more lifers messing up your life.

Approximately 20 hours later our flight landed in California. We were greeted at USAOSREPLCTR with a large WELCOME HOME sign, a fine steak dinner, and instructions not to fraternize with the troops departing for Vietnam.[2] The Green Machine didn't want us sharing our experiences with the FNGs. They would have to learn the same hard way we did.

The next morning I was fitted with a green Class A *summer weight* uniform.[3] Quartermaster Corps personnel sewed or pinned unit crests, decorations and awards, service and division citation cords, and insignia to the sleeves, breast, and lapels of my new uniform. I looked STRAC. The Army didn't waste much time with civilian social reacclimating, but they did give us an hour lecture on the benefits Uncle Sam's veterans were entitled to receive from our grateful nation. All I heard was, "No active reserve duty requirement for Vietnam draftees." *Fuckin A!* The VA (Veterans Administration) was boocoo number ONE! They even gave me a swell pamphlet entitled, *Once a Veteran*, etc., etc., etc. I figured that everything I needed to know about being a veteran I could read someday, but for now I was too happy being a civilian.

Even though I technically still had over a week left to serve until REFRAD,[4] the Army said that they didn't need me anymore, so with their blessings I went home. They handed me a dozen or so copies of Department of Defense Form DD-214, and I departed Oakland on August 13. Before any of us cleared the gate we were sternly advised we were still in the Army until the moment we removed our uniforms. Then and only then were we officially out. Until that time we were expected to behave like soldiers. Some of the guys stripped outside of Oakland's main gate! I decided to wait until I got home. Two days earlier I had been in the jungle. *I had to relearn how to behave among civilized people.*

Although the World Airways flight had taken aboard civilians at Honolulu, their numbers had been few, the flight manifest having been predominately filled by Vietnam returnees. I received my first taste of precisely how my fellow countrymen felt about Vietnam veterans during the California to New Jersey leg of the flight. I was seated next to an attractive young lady and was having a pleasant conversation with her when she asked where I was stationed. I made the mistake of telling her I was on my way home from a tour in Vietnam.[5] She stood up and found a stewardess who reseated her elsewhere! She never said good-bye or anything to me; she just moved away.

The flight landed at Newark Airport late in the wee hours of morning and to my dismay there was no taxi service available. I didn't want to wait in the airport terminal, so I told my tale of woe to a sympathetic airline counter clerk. She announced over the terminal's PA system there was a soldier returning home from war who needed a ride to Union, New Jersey. If anyone was headed in that direction would they come to the main counter. An older gentleman who had an automobile parked at the terminal said he'd be glad to take me home. We spoke little on the drive. He was headed to his home in Toms River, New Jersey. When we neared the parkway exit for Union, I told him he could drop me off on the side of the freeway and I'd walk the rest of the way home. It was only a few miles to my parents' house. Because of the lateness of the hour, I encountered no one on the sidewalks and very little vehicular traffic on the roads. The good citizens of Union rested in peace, oblivious to the ongoing horror on the other side of the world.

The darkness of early morning served to cocoon me in a shroud of complacency. I was glad to be alive and for the first time in eight months felt completely safe and at ease in my civilian environment. No VC would unexpectedly be materializing out of the landscape, and I didn't have to watch out for booby traps planted along the township sidewalks. I could now think civilian. Just as my mindset was adjusting back to my former civilian self a bush near where I was passing rattled. A cold chill of adrenaline flashed through my body! I had no weapon. I was helpless. Then a cat scurried out and darted across my path. He must have been out slumming for the night. For me Vietnam was over. I had survived. My whole life was ahead of me. I just had to keep reminding myself of that.

The last couple of miles of my journey home were without further incident, and I soon found myself standing outside my parents' house. My mom and dad had placed our nation's flag in the large living-room picture window along with a large sign that said, "Welcome Home Bob." It was very late, way past their bedtime, and my arrival was days earlier than expected. They were old, and I didn't want to frighten them by knocking on the door (I had no key). I stood outside for quite a while, alone in the darkness, gazing at the message in the living-room window. For what seemed to have been a lifetime in a different world, I had given of myself. This sign of love was all for me. My eyes watered. It was an unfamiliar sensation. I cried for joy; then I cried for all the occasions I should have cried during the past eight months, I cried for the unfinished business I'd left behind and the guys who were still a part of it....

And then I cried for myself.

11

Back in the USA

In retrospect 1969 proved to be the pivotal year of a decade of youthful, grass-roots social revolution that ultimately altered America's perception of patriotism and its established cultural values. The baby boomer generation, born of parents who had endured the hardships and horror of economic depression and world war, sanctimoniously vilified the liberties their progenitors had guaranteed for them with their blood and sacrifice. Oddly enough, the final year of this tumultuous decade ended in national optimism bolstered by an unprecedented scientific achievement. While American soldiers continued to suffer hardship, death, and disfigurement a world away, the home front reveled in sexual freedom, drugs, a good economy, and a distracting sense of pride resulting from world scientific leadership. During that wonderful July, when America went to the moon, the most-educated army it had ever fielded began disintegrating in a quagmire of political ineptitude, incompetent leadership, and home-front indifference.

My involvement with Vietnam had begun during what had been inappropriately hyped as "The Summer of Love." Coition had been confused with affection. After graduating from university in June 1967, my S-2 student draft deferment had immediately changed to A-1 eligibility. Although the law presented many options to escape military service, draft avoidance and self-exile erupted across America in high fashion. Many young males simply did not want to risk their lives or well-being for others. The chant "Hell, no, we won't go!" became the credo of an antagonistic generation of disenfranchised youths.

Although this rebellion had been little more than an extension of pubescent intolerance[1] directed against the policies of government, it matured into a cultural statement that adequately reflected the self-centered perceptions of an emerging socioeconomic middle class born of the post–World War II baby boom. Although the psychological aftermath of world economic depression and world war had compelled its survivors to vow a better life for their children, a guerrilla war of attrition in Southeast Asia, so reminiscent of the jungle warfare conducted against the Japanese in World War II, did not fulfill middle-class expectations of a better life. In Vietnam, history's greatest experiment in democracy fielded its last army of citizen-soldiers, ending a tradition begun two centuries earlier at a bridge in rural New England. Henceforth America would depend upon professional soldiers and hire mercenaries to defend its liberties and execute its political will.

The military and social events of 1968–1969 dramatically altered the common soldier's perception of combat service in Vietnam. During my eight months in-country, esprit de corps withered from a patriotic ideal of Duty-Honor-Country to an individually subscribed doctrine of survival. Many soldiers no longer sanctioned sacrificing their lives in a cause lost to questionable politics, incompetent military leadership, antagonistic societal peer behavior, and divided national loyalties. There had been, and there would continue to be, great valor and dignity in combat, but after 1969 it would be for different reasons. Soldiers now executed orders only if the objectives of the Army did not interfere with their own well-being. Commanders who did not understand or accept this reality dared not venture into the field. Over the ten years of the war, the nature of America's involvement in Vietnam eroded from an international political commitment to halt the spread of communism in Southeast Asia to what can best be described as a ritual of manhood. Late in 1969 the universal draft was replaced by a general lottery. This unfortunate change of government policy psychologically implied losing and bad luck for the chosen. As the army of the 1960s continued to be withdrawn piecemeal from Vietnam, those remaining in-country understandably valued the tangible aspect of self-preservation above the intangible notion of Duty-Honor-Country.

Initially I didn't talk much about Vietnam. I tried to put it all behind me. I was overjoyed to have survived the experience. I, like my fellow citizens, watched the dinnertime combat footage on the evening news with disinterest. It wasn't my war anymore and the people in my life really didn't want to talk about it or hear about it. We all, however, felt the horror of the Kent State University incident.[2] *My heart* went out to the handful of ill-trained, beleaguered Ohio Army National Guardsmen, who, while attempting to disengage from an overwhelming force, felt the desperate need to cover their withdrawal with suppressive fire.[3] I quickly learned the societal inappropriateness of my reaction. We were supposed to sympathize with the irrational horde of students who thought they were privileged to attack the sovereign State of Ohio. For years I speculated about the outcome had it been a squad of USARV infantry being stoned at Kent State.[4] Police serve and protect; soldiers kill. Both carry weapons, but each responds differently to threats.

Bitterness began festering in my heart toward my countrymen who had the impudence of mind and spirit to have drafted me into a charnel and then hold *me* in contempt for what *they* had forced me to do.[5] I began to talk about Vietnam. It amazed me how people resented hearing what I had to say. Social drinking loosened my tongue, and the pervasive wall of common indifference I encountered encouraged me to speak excessively and at times obnoxiously. Even individuals I considered friends became inconsiderate of my service to this country. Many a time I vowed to myself that I would never speak of Vietnam again. I, however, could not dismiss it from my thoughts.

The bitterness I felt toward my fellow citizens eventually matured into cynicism. Their collective attitude toward the Vietnam War and its participants was outrageous. Well-meaning but ignorant people advised me to put Vietnam behind me. The implication was that my military service to America was shameful. "Block it out, Bob. Forget it. Move on with your life." Others actually doubted my service and its quality. They judged my loquaciousness by the stereotypical, fiction-inspired combat veteran who never talked about the war because of the undisclosed horrors he had endured. *"Cat got your tongue?"* Unfortunately there exists no norm to qualify horror or standard to quantify its immediate effect and ultimate effect upon the individual psyche. Humans perceive, process, and cope with fear—the resultant of horror—in a fashion compatible with their individual intellect and emotional disposition. This is why some excel in threatening environments while others wither. Experience and training can artificially alter the natural perception of horror, but then fear accumulates in the memory and invites future psychological shock.[6]

It took many years for me to realize it wasn't the telling that caused distress but rather the psychological and emotional state of the recipient listener. Risking one's life for the well-being of another or a conceptual value remains beyond the intellectual understanding of the average American citizen. We are a nation of self-centered consumers. We deny God, we deny the sanctimony of marriage, we deny, we deny, we deny. Vietnam taught different lessons.

My war experience remains as much a part of my life now as it was then. There isn't a day that goes by wherein a smell, a sight, or a sound doesn't trigger a memory and, for an instant, I am back in the Delta. Sometimes in the early morning while rousing from sleep, I awaken thinking I am still there, confusing the past with reality. But, no, I know I am home. Here I have a family and relationships that are worth any man's or soldier's sacrifice. There all I had was an intangible concept of Duty-Honor-Country to steel my resolve and keep my faith with those who over the decades of history had defended America from its enemies, both perceived and real. Not much to risk life and limb for, and, yet, *perhaps it had been everything.*

Nearly half a century has unfolded since I left Vietnam. The hawks, doves, hippies, and war protestors of the 1960s have, for the most part, calmed down and faded back into the great mass of mainstream American society, their days of political awareness and protesting, like my days of soldiering, having expired. The wars America now engages in[7] are, similar to Vietnam, distant wars, but now without the complication of an involuntary draft, which tends to bring the intimate realities of war closer to home. Social unrest and anarchy no longer rage across the land, and young men no longer burn their draft cards in protest and anger. Graphic televised evening footage of the horror of combat no longer dominates the nightly news as it did during the late 1960s and early 1970s. We are at peace with the inviolability of our economy and our insatiable appetite for consumerism. Distant wars fought in alien lands are not a major public concern. On the surface all is well in America.

When I departed for Vietnam in January 1969, I had been an ingenuous romantic enamored with the rhythm of words and the synergy they created when combined with musical notes. I loved poetry and literature. For eight frightening months I made music with the 9th Infantry Division Band, and when I closed the lid of my trumpet case that last time on Đồng Tâm it was forever. I returned home in August 1969 a *realist* who no longer appreciated the synergy of words and music.

For me the music had faded.

Glossary

USARV Acronyms and GI Vernacular Expressions

ACV   Air Cushioned Vehicle
AG   Adjutant General (Corps)
Agent Orange   A powerful herbicide used to defoliate land areas
AHC   Assault Helicopter Company
AHSC   Assault Helicopter Support Company—CH-47 Chinook medium-lift helicopter company
AIT   Advance Individual Training
AO   Area of Operation
Áo Dài   A slit-side tunic worn by Vietnamese females over the traditional pajama outfit
APB   Amphibious Propelled Barracks—a Navy LST modified to quarter Army troops
ARVN   Army of the Republic of Vietnam, our indigenous allies
ASAP   As Soon As Possible
AUS   Army of the United States—draftee
Baby-San   GI slang for Vietnamese child
BCT   Basic Combat Training
Boo-Coo   GI aberration of the French beaucoup, meaning much or great in amount or quantity
Boom-Boom   Vietnamese prostitute's term for sexual intercourse
Boondocks   The field, also "the boonies"
Boonie Rat   An infantryman
The Boonies   In the field
BOQ   Bachelor Officer Quarters
Brown Water Navy   U.S. Navy personnel and equipment operating within the borders of South Vietnam, so named for the muddy brown color of Vietnamese canal and river water
Bush Cap   A soft, floppy, wide-brimmed hat worn in the field, or boonies
CAB   Combat Aviation Battalion
CAG   Combat Aviation Group

CDM   Command Detonated Mine
Charlie   Term for Viet Cong irregular soldiers taken from the Army phonetic Victor Charles; also "Mr. Charles"
Cheap Charlie   Vietnamese expression for GI who is not liberal with his money
Chieu Hoi   Vietnamese for a Viet Cong political repatriate
CIB   Combat Infantry Badge
CIDG   Civilian Irregular Defense Group—local Vietnamese militia
CO   Commanding Officer
COL   Colonel—the highest level colonel displaying an eagle rank insignia (nicknamed "bird" or "full" colonel)
CONEX   Container Express—steel container used to ship bulk items
CONUS   Continental United States
Count Down Calendar   A reverse calendar tracking a GI's remaining days in Vietnam, each expiring day being crossed off daily
CPT   Captain—identified by a vertical two-bar insignia
CQ   Charge of Quarters
CS   Combined Service Battalion
CSM   Command Sergeant Major, highest ranking sergeant in the Army with three stripes over three rockers and a star within a wreath centered between the two
CTZ   Combat Tactical Zone. Vietnam was divided into four major operational regions: CTZ I, CTZ II, CTZ III, and CTZ IV
DI   Drill Instructor
Didi Mau   Vietnamese for "hurry"
Dinky Dou   Vietnamese for "crazy"
DISCOM   Division Support Command
DMZ   Demilitarized Zone—the demarcation line between North and South Vietnam
Eleven-Bravo (11B)   Basic infantry MOS designation
EM   Enlisted man
1LT   First Lieutenant—highest-ranking lieutenant identified by a single vertical silver bar
First Sergeant   A rank and position displaying three stripes over two rocker stripes with a diamond centered between the two, superior in position to a SFC
Fragging   The assassination of an unpopular NCO or officer, usually in the heat of battle and by a fragmentation grenade so as not to miss the target
Freedom Bird   The airplane transporting soldiers out of Vietnam on REFRAD or DEROS
Friendly Fire   An occurrence when a U.S. unit mistakenly fires upon another U.S. unit
FSB   Fire Support Base—a semipermanent fortification manned by artillery and infantry
FSPB   Fire Support Patrol Base—a permanent fortification manned by artillery and infantry

Glossary

FTA Fuck the Army—a popular enlisted soldier's sentiment stenciled on equipment or inked on bush caps and helmet covers
Fuckin' A Expression meaning something good has happened
GI Government Issue, meaning a U.S. soldier
Gig A civilian musician's term, meaning a performance
Green Machine The Army command hierarchy
Ground Pounder Infantryman
Gung Ho A GI who is super enthusiastic about the military
HHC Headquarters & Headquarters Company
Hooch A Vietnamese dwelling or a GI's sleeping quarters
HOR Home of Record
HQ Headquarters
In-Country Serving within the borders of the Republic of Vietnam
Indian Country In the field or boonies
KIA Killed in Action
Kinh Vietnamese word meaning "canal"
Klick One kilometer (3,280.84 feet)
KP Kitchen Patrol
LAWS Light Antitank Weapons System—a shoulder-fired rocket primarily used in Vietnam by U.S. troops to destroy enemy bunkers
Lifer A career soldier or volunteer
Little People The Vietnamese
LP Listening Post—troops hidden outside a camp perimeter to listen for enemy activity
LRRP Long Range Reconnaissance Patrol, pronounced "lurp"
LST Landing Ship Tank—a World War II era Navy ship originally designed to nose up to a beach and land heavy rolling equipment and troops
LTC Lieutenant Colonel—lowest-ranking colonel identified by a silver oak leaf insignia
LZ Landing Zone—helicopter landing site for unloading troops
MAAG Military Assistance & Advisory Group—the precursor of MACV
MACV Military Assistance Command Vietnam
MAJ Major, usually a staff rank identified by a bronze oak leaf insignia
Momma-San A married Vietnamese woman
MOS Military Occupational Specialty
MP Military Police
MPC Military Payment Certificate; military money
MRF Mobile Riverine Force—U.S. brown water Navy operating in conjunction with 2nd Brigade, 9th Infantry Division
The 'Nam Republic of South Vietnam
NCO Noncommissioned Officer—the ranks of corporal and sergeant
Newbie Nicer way of identifying a New Fucking Guy
NFG New Fucking Guy—derogatory term for recent arrival

NG   National Guard—prefix to Army service number identifying soldier as a National Guardsman
NVA   North Vietnamese Army
0-Two-Bravo (02B)   MOS designation for trumpet player
OCS   Officers Candidate School
PA   Public Address System
PAL   Pacific Air Lift—air service that transported packages between Vietnam and the United States
PBR   Patrol Boat River
PFC   Private First Class, second-grade private identified by one stripe
POL   Petroleum Oil Lubricant—a petroleum storage facility
Police Call   Work detail organized to remove trash from a designated area
Popping Caps   Firing the M-16 rifle, derived from the toy cap-gun sound made by the .223 round
POW   Prisoner of War
PSP   Perforated Steel Plate; a sheet of metal with drainage holes primarily used in runway construction
PT   Physical Training
PX   Post Exchange
PZ   Pickup Zone—a helicopter landing site for loading troops
RA   Regular Army—prefix to Army service number identifying soldier as a volunteer
Rach   Vietnamese word meaning "stream"
R&R   Rest & Recuperation or Rest & Recreation
Rear Area   A place relatively secure from enemy action, usually inhabited by REMFs
RECON   Reconnaissance
REFRAD   Released From Active Duty
REMF   Rear Echelon Mother Fucker—derogatory term used by field troops to describe combat support troops functioning in rear areas
RE-UP   Reenlisting for another tour of duty
RF/PF   Regional Forces/Popular Forces—Vietnamese civilian defense troops, called "Ruff Puffs" by GIs
ROTC   Reserve Officers Training Course
RPG   Rocket Propelled Grenade—an enemy shoulder-fired weapon used to knock out U.S. bunkers and other fortifications and equipment
SAC   Surveillance Airplane Company (Army); Strategic Air Command (Air Force)
S&T   Supply & Transportation—a combat support function
Saddle up   Prepare to depart
Saigon Tea   A faux alcoholic beverage purchased by GIs at cocktail prices and served to bar girls working in Saigon bars
Saigon Warrior   A combat support troop assigned to the Saigon Capital District

Glossary

2LT Second Lieutenant—lowest-ranking lieutenant identified by a single, vertical, gold bar
SFC Sergeant First Class—three stripes above two rocker stripes
SGG Staff Sergeant—three stripes above one rocker stripe
SGM Sergeant Major—three stripes above three rockers with a star centered between the two
SGT Buck Sergeant—three stripes
Shit Hook A CH-47 Chinook medium-lift helicopter
Short A euphoric state of mind held by those nearing their DEROS date tempered by the fear of being a causality
Short-Timer A GI nearing his DEROS date
Slick A Huey UH-1 troop transport helicopter
Smoke 'em Shoot them
Sông Vietnamese word meaning "river"
SOP Standard Operating Procedure
SP-4 Specialist Four—a technician's rank equivalent to corporal
SP-5 Specialist Five—a technician's rank equivalent to buck sergeant
Stand Down A short respite from combat duty
STOL Short Take Off & Landing—an aircraft specifically designed to land on short runways
STRAC Strategic Army Command; a term meaning super-sharp soldier
Swagger Stick A small wooden baton, sometimes ornately carved, often carried by short-timers to indicate their status
Tango Boat A flat-bottomed World War II–era Navy landing craft modified with armored superstructure to transport infantry. The nickname, "Tango," comes from the Army's phonetic pronunciation of the alphabetic preface of the boat's hull number, example T-100
TAS Tactical Airlift Squadron—United States Air Force
TAW Tactical Air Wing—United States Air Force
Tết Vietnamese lunar New Year celebration traditionally occurring in February
TDY Temporary Duty
TO&E Table of Organization & Equipment—guide to what type of unit gets what personnel and equipment
201 File A soldier's personnel record that follows him from one duty station to another
Ultimate Weapon U.S. Army adulation popularized in Basic Combat Training to designate a trained soldier
U.S. United States—the country and also the prefix used on Army service numbers identifying a soldier as a draftee
USAF United States Air Force
USAOSREPLCTR United States Army Overseas Replacement Center
USARV United States Army Republic of Vietnam

USATRF STA   United States Army Transfer Station
USO   United Servicemen's Organization
VC   Viet Cong
WAC   Women's Army Corps
White Mice   Officers of the Republic of Vietnam National Police
WIA   Wounded in Action
The World   United States of America
WO-3   Chief Warrant Officer Pay Grade 3
WO-4   Chief Warrant Officer Pay Grade 4
WP   Will Proceed
XO   Executive Officer, second in command to CO

Vietnam Era Phrases

Hurry up and wait   Self-explanatory
It don't mean nothing   Uttered by GIs to assuage bad news or disappointment
What are they going to do, send me to 'Nam?   Meaning Vietnam service is as bad as it can get
Read it and weep   Typical statement made by NCOs when handing out orders

Chapter Notes

Preface

1. This wide range of numbers is the result of whose government you believe; the correct number is most likely somewhere in between.
2. Technically Vietnam wasn't a war, having never been declared one by Congress.
3. The depth, breadth, and ferocity of Mekong Delta waterways varied from lazy slow-moving waters during the dry months to raging torrents in monsoon season that could sweep the legs out from under a soldier carrying a 70-pound combat load and easily overwhelm him.
4. Unless, of course, a soldier was already morally predisposed to killing or ordered to do so, as was the case at My Lai, where soldiers were faced with either firing their weapons at civilians or subjecting themselves to very serious mutiny charges that could result in imprisonment or a firing squad.
5. Known as "lifers" by conscripted soldiers who were not as career oriented as their volunteer counterparts.
6. The theme song of mid 1960s Broadway musical *Man of La Mancha*, with the score written by Mitch Leigh and the lyrics by Joe Darion.
7. Throughout this book pseudonyms have replaced the actual names of common soldiers to protect their privacy. The names of senior-grade officers and politicians are actual names, as are the names of the 9th Infantry Division soldiers who died defending America's interests in the Republic of Vietnam.
8. As is the case with the total number of Vietnamese killed during the war, the ratio of support to combat troops varies widely and has been recorded by some to have been as high as 14 to 1. In all likelihood it varied throughout the war as the needs of the military changed to accomplish different objectives.
9. Some Vietnam veterans may object to the use of the adjective "elite" to describe a military band, since it was used by the military to describe Special Troops (specifically the Green Berets).

Introduction

1. 1939–1945.
2. Late in 1941 President Franklin Delano Roosevelt and British Prime Minister Winston Churchill announced their wartime intention of decolonizing the world in an agreement titled "The Atlantic Charter." Immediately prior to President Roosevelt's demise in 1945 he began wavering on total decolonization, which his successor, President Harry S. Truman, took into account in his postwar decolonization policies.
3. The "Enclave Theory," ironically, hadn't worked for the French in Vietnam either; unfortunately, senior U.S. Army planners had failed to notice this and American soldiers ultimately paid the price.
4. Operations Cambodia, 1970, and Lam Son 719/Dewey Canyon II, 1971.
5. A nickname sometimes used in reference to the scientist who developed the atom bomb at Los Alamos, New Mexico, under the direction of J. Robert Oppenheimer.
6. Buffalo Bob Smith was the likeable host of television's comedy/variety Howdy Doody (*It's Howdy Doody Time*) show for children, which was nationally televised between 1947 and 1960.
7. John Wayne, the stage name of Marion Mitchell Morrison, was an American actor known for his cinematic staunchness in the face of adversity. For three decades he had been an icon of heroism and the defender of American cultural values for young boys having starred in such military film classic as *She Wore a Yellow Ribbon*, *The Horse Soldiers*, and *Tales of the Green Beret*.

8. A reference to the famous British fighting formation of the 19th century where soldiers would group into a four-sided formation a few ranks deep. The front rank would fire their weapons upon command and then fall back between soldiers in the rear ranks to reload while, at the same time, the nearest rear rank moved forward to take position and fire. It had been a very effective combat formation.

Chapter 1

1. A weekly television adventure drama portraying two young men traveling across the United States in a Chevrolet Corvette. The series aired between 1960 and 1964 and revolved around two main characters: Tod Styles, played by Martin Milner, and Buz Murdoch, played by George Maharis (replaced in 1963 by Vietnam returnee Linc Case, played by Glen Corbett).
2. During May 1965 the 173d Airborne Brigade became the first Army combat unit sent to South Vietnam. It was followed in July–August by three brigades of the 101st Airborne Division. The first *full division* to be deployed was the 1st Cavalry Division (Airmobile), which began arriving in August 1965.
3. An accolade used by the United States Army Training Center Infantry Fort Dix, New Jersey, to describe a soldier who has successfully completed basic combat training.
4. The "71" refers to the overall category of CLERK, the "H" specifically PERSONNEL MANAGEMENT, and the "30" SKILL LEVEL based upon pay grade.
5. During the mid 1950s the Army switched from brown leather boots to black leather.
6. A wad-cutter is a blunt-nosed bullet, also know as a dum-dum if used under hostile circumstances.
7. The late SP-4 George Lee, Jr., Americal (23d Infantry Division), KIA September 17, 1968.
8. A euphemism for Army super lifer.
9. The late SP-4 James Randall Jones, 23d Infantry Division, KIA October 7, 1968, and the late CPL Joe Travis Russell, 9th Infantry Division, KIA October 9, 1968.

Chapter 2

1. Prior to January 15, 1969, the Class B Khakis uniform had been the only authorized dress for travel between Vietnam and the United States. After January 15 enlisted men up to and including the rank of First Sergeant traveling between Vietnam and the United States on military or contracted flights were required to wear a clean serviceable set of jungle fatigues. The wearing of jungle fatigues was optional for sergeant majors, warrant officers, and officers.
2. When U.S. troops initially arrived in South Vietnam all sewn-on uniform patches were embroidered in distinctive colors for recognition. Name tapes were black on white, rank stripes and eagles were yellow gold on olive drab, unit crests were multicolored, and the "US Army" tape was yellow gold on olive drab. These bright, highly visible patches soon proved to be a liability in combat, well serving the enemy as aiming points. Midyear of 1966 all color sewn insignia on jungle fatigues began being replaced by *subdued* black on olive drab patches. The following year the subdued rank patches were replaced by small, black metal, pin-on, collar insignia to confuse enemy snipers who sought out high-ranking targets. These changes took months to effect, resulting in a mishmash of overlapping patch styles.
3. Americal (23d Infantry Division) was the Army's solitary *named* division. The name had been instituted during World War II when Americal became the Army's first (and only) division formed outside of territorial United States. Americal had been assembled from Army units on New Caledonia who supported U.S. Marines fighting on Guadalcanal. The name was a combination of the words America and Caledonia.
4. Air America was the name given the airline operated by the Central Intelligence Agency in Vietnam.
5. A rugged, gasoline-fueled two-and-one-half-ton truck that served as a basic platform for troop motor transportation and a variety of specialized bed-mounted equipment.
6. A bird colonel is Army slang for a senior grade officer rank immediately below the rank of general. The prefix bird originated in the design of the colonel insignia, an eagle with spread wings. The rank is also known as a full colonel to distinguish it from the lesser, or "light," lieutenant colonel.
7. A kilometer is a metric measure of distance equaling 3,280.84 feet, or .6 of a mile.
8. Infantry squads in Vietnam were smaller than their World War II counterparts due to the elimination of the mortar section from the squad makeup and a never-ending shortage of manpower. The typical squad size in Vietnam was between six and eight troops.
9. A sapper is a combatant whose mission is to destroy enemy fortifications and infrastructure with explosives.

Chapter 3

1. A hooch was 'Nam troop jargon for a soldier's living quarters. It was also used to describe a Vietnamese peasant farmer's dwelling.
2. The lieutenant who had picked me up at the Reliable Airfield also had a military driver's license, but he wasn't part of the band; he was just a band groupie doing the bandmaster a favor.
3. The 266th Army Band, the only numbered Army Band to serve in Vietnam, was stationed in Saigon at the Armed Force Band Headquarters and Band School located in the Thủ Đức District. The Armed Force Band Headquarters and Band School was responsible for administering the budget and musical supplies for all bands in Vietnam.
4. In an uncaring environment Bummer had become the symbol of the band's humanity and affection. During mortar or rocket attacks, when aerial bombs were exploding all about, the cry *"Where's Bummer!"* could be heard above the din of combat.
5. Regardless of age, only soldiers in pay grades E-6 and above were authorized to purchase hard liquor at the base liquor store, hence the term "Class Six Store."
6. The exotic-by-combat standards playtime amenities at Đồng Tâm served two purposes: entertainment to boost morale for the troops and a political snub to the enemy, the latter being a visual statement implying that while they lived in hardship we lived in luxurious comfort *on their turf*.
7. The regulation baseball cap was a uniform accessory intended to appeal to the enlisted soldier's sense of familiarity. Baseball had once been America's most popular sport, so much so that during World War II questions about baseball facts had been used to determine friendlies from foe in uncertain situations. The Army hierarchy in Vietnam had, unfortunately, been behind the times; they should have issued football helmets.
8. At the start of the Vietnam War there were 18 overall Selective Service classifications that either delayed or exempted young men from the draft. As the war progressed several of the subclassifications within these overall classifications were redefined or eliminated.
9. The slip-on webbing harness that supports ammo pouches, hand grenades, gas mask, pistol holster, first aid kit, canteens, etc.
10. Provincial Route TL-25 ran along the north bank of the Sông Mỹ Tho between the city of Mỹ Tho and the hamlet of Sùng Hiếu.
11. A descending monthly calendar with a soldier's number of days remaining in-country replacing actual dates.
12. Police call entailed forming troops into a battle line and having them advance across a designated area picking up cigarette butts and other trash. The work detail was commonly referred to as "policing the area."
13. As a general rule, Vietnamese civilians were not allowed on Đồng Tâm during combat alerts or the evening hours. The Vietnamese civilians catering to the needs of senior-grade officers may have been an exception to this rule.
14. The duration of the Korean War was from June 25, 1950 to July 27, 1953.
15. At some point during the war Foremost Dairies set up an in-country processing plant in the Thủ Đức District of Saigon.
16. Private First Class (PFC) Robert Joseph Gniadek and PFC Joseph Louis Reagle.

Chapter 4

1. It was possible to triangulate the flight path of incoming mortar rounds on radar because mortars are indirect fire weapons that launch shells high into the air in an almost vertical arc before descending to target.
2. The Erector set manufactured by the A.C. Gilbert Company consisted of miniature gears, girders, bolts, and nuts that could be assembled into bridges and other structures that were limited only by the imagination of the assembler.
3. Long Định was a little over 13 kilometers (about 8 statute miles) from Đồng Tâm.
4. One day while a few bandsmen were having an informal jam session on the bandstand improvising a tune, a Vietnamese laborer was spotted slowly walking in the DISCOM compound. This in itself was not an unusual occurrence, but this fellow had been walking in what appeared to be calculated tangents between buildings while visibly counting to himself. Mister Johns was informed and he immediately reported the worker's bizarre behavior to the MPs. Upon their arrival they interrogated the man and after finding a pencil sketch of the compound on his person took him away.
5. Pre- by just by a couple of months; I was born late in 1945. The baby boomer generation is considered to have occurred between 1946 and 1964.
6. The old, politically insensitive Action Army of the 1960s favored the use of gender associated terms to describe anything less than what it deemed macho male.

7. Artillery is the King of Battle.
8. The EM Club bar only served 2.4 percent alcohol beer troops called "panther piss" or "near beer" to minors. To those of legal age, a locally brewed rice beer called "Ba Moui Ba" (pronounced Ba-Me-Ba) and labeled "33" was available—each bottle tasted a little different!
9. The round landed in the Reliable Academy billet area across the road, a hundred feet or so from the bandstand, instantly killing Master Sergeant Walther Scott Hamner, who had just arrived in-country five days earlier on February 18.
10. The M-151 Military Utility Tactical Truck was notorious for its independent four-wheel suspension that could tuck under during jerky sharp turns, turns which were commonplace in combat when trying to avoid unpleasantness.
11. A fragging is the assassination of a superior under the guise of combat, typically with a *fragmentation* grenade.
12. There were also some of the older-style cloth sandbags still in use.
13. The 9th Infantry Division had been labeled a "draftee division" by division commander Major General Julian J. Ewell (commanding general, February 25, 1968 through April 2, 1969).

Chapter 5

1. A clerk with the NCO rank of corporal was unusual. I later learned this particular clerk was a slightly shot-up infantryman running out his in-country time at DISCOM, too wounded to hump the bush and too healthy to go back home.
2. SP4 Richard Strode Mark, HQ Company, KIA February 23, Đồng Tâm.
3. SP-4 Irwin Beyda, SP-5 Joe Ben Stuart, and SP-4 Burt Joseph Meyer, Jr., KIA February 28, Đồng Tâm.
4. Although Dipherio was listed as the location for the 3/39th Infantry Battalion memorial ceremony in the official "Memo for Colonel Hanket—Band Commitments for March 1969," it's likely an error. There is no record of a site called Dipherio in IV CTZ.
5. Renamed "Schroeder" in March.
6. The herbicide Agent Orange was widely used by the 9th Infantry Division to defoliate vegetation throughout the Mekong Delta.
7. A GI double negative expression to assuage the psychological impact of bad news.
8. There were seven divisional bands and a single numbered Army band serving in Vietnam, which entailed about 340 musicians if all the bands were operating at full strength (which they never were, with the possible exception of the numbered band, which consisted entirely of professional musicians).
9. A Huey UH-1 "Slick" was a rotary-wing troop transport that got its nickname from it smooth, unencumbered-from-weaponry *slick* appearance. It did not mount the external rocket pods, Xenon lights, and gun turrets of its brother UH-1 gunships.
10. Nicknamed "Shit Hook" by 'Nam troops.
11. Division intelligence reports of a VC battalion in the area may have been accurate; unbeknownst to Đồng Tâm's roving infantry patrols or the division, a battalion could easily have kept out of sight in the enemy's vast network of secret underground tunnels.
12. Precisely what an Honor Guard Ceremony was now eludes me, although I suspect it had something to do with division colors.
13. 2400 hours to 0400 hours, i.e., midnight to 4:00 A.M.
14. Rumor had it that an earlier senior adviser, who now happened to be the commander of one of our division's infantry battalions, hadn't appreciated the name Crum and had tried to get it changed to something he felt was more appropriate.
15. A captured VC had divulged information concerning a coordinated regional attack against several Mekong Delta installations, including Đồng Tâm.
16. Being denied ammunition on a combat-active base situated deep in enemy-controlled territory is just one symptom of the lunacy that permeated the command structure of the 9th Infantry Division during 1969. The general discontentment of the troops and the lightning-fast anger reflex some displayed might have led commanders to surmise that if ammunition was generally available to the troops at Đồng Tâm they might hurt each other or perhaps their commanders.
17. *Newark (NJ) Evening News*, March 26, 1969, p. 3.
18. David Haskill Hackworth, *Steel My Soldiers' Hearts*, p. 280.
19. Officers were authorized to display rank pins on their baseball caps. Airborne troops were authorized to display only the airborne insignia on their caps.
20. The Combat Infantry Badge was a special distinction awarded only to infantrymen who had engaged the enemy in battle or had been with a unit actively pursing the enemy on the ground. This badge utilized individual stars to denote each war of participation.

21. He hadn't been entirely crazy. On one occasion while I was taking a break during KP duty I had overhead him counseling a very young, transient infantry officer in the DISCOM mess hall. This officer was troubled about his responsibility in commanding troops in combat. He kept throwing increasingly harrowing combat scenarios at the old sergeant and asking him what he should do. Finally, in desperation the old veteran admonished, "If everything you do fails, then try to die like a man."

22. I never understood the logic of demolishing the far more accessible bunkers at each end of the barracks in favor of one large central shelter that was much farther away.

23. The pile of dirt was destined to fill in the roof of the new personnel shelter, which meant in its state of completion it had afforded no protection from incoming mortar or friendly howitzer rounds.

Chapter 6

1. Departure ceremony practice, the actual departure ceremony, awards ceremony, general's party, and general's farewell ceremony.

2. Held for SP-4 Edward Barr, A Company, 15th Engineer Battalion, KIA March 30.

3. Also known as a communications shack.

4. Scary rumors always circulated around Đồng Tâm about guards falling asleep while on duty and having their throats cut by stealthy VC insurgents. The rumors were undoubtedly manufactured by the Green Machine to scare perimeter guards into staying awake and alert.

5. Pronounced "Loach" by GIs.

6. President Franklin D. Roosevelt's Atlantic Charter of 1941 echoed former President Woodrow Wilson's desire to decolonize the world. Ho Chi Minh, president of the Democratic Republic of Vietnam, interpreted the Atlantic Charter as a promise from President Roosevelt of freedom for the people of Vietnam from French colonial rule. During President Roosevelt's final year in office, he began backing away from total decolonization of the world, specifically as it applied to Vietnam.

7. Our advice to the French during this period had been to draw the enemy into conventional battle, which they succeeded in doing. It ended with French forces being unequivocally defeated at the Battle of Diện Biên Phủ in 1954.

8. The MACV predecessor organization, MAAG—Military Assistance & Advisory Group—hadn't had the authority to deploy regular army troops

9. During 1968 forty-three National Guard and reserve units were mobilized for one-year tours in Vietnam. Upon receiving their alert orders for deployment these units were found to be ill-trained and not ready for combat duty. In 1969, after retraining, they were deployed to Vietnam to support infantry operations. All of the deployed National Guard and reserve units were withdrawn later in the year. In total, 94 National Guardsmen lost their lives in Vietnam. There were no reserve fatalities.

10. There was no infantry stationed in Saigon. The only permanent U.S. troops on duty in the city were office types and MPs. Saigon was treated as a separate CTZ.

11. I didn't understand his logic on this one. Perhaps he meant during an evening mortar attack, which occurred more often than not, but the mess hall was usually closed before darkness descended.

12. The ranks of major and lieutenant colonel could also serve in the field but typically in administrative or command positions with some officers opting to join their troops during critical missions.

Chapter 7

1. COL Crittenberger would lose both his command and life on September 17, 1969, when the helicopter he was aboard collided with its gunship escort.

2. A "Duster" was a Korean War–vintage, two-barreled, anti-aircraft weapon mounted on a Walker Bulldog tank chassis that rapidly fired explosive shells. It was a devastatingly effective weapon when used against enemy soldiers.

3. A swagger stick is a short staff—typically 18 inches long and ornately carved of wood—that is deeply rooted in military history as an unofficial symbol of authority. In Vietnam its use was modified to signify a short-timer.

4. This was the slogan the Army used on recruitment posters and in its advertisements of the era.

5. The Mekong Delta had been historically dubbed "The Land of the Nine Dragons," not for mythical creatures of yore but for the nine branches of the mighty Mekong River that split off the main river in the Delta.

6. A flat-bottomed World War II landing craft modified with armored superstructure to transport infantry. The nickname, "Tango," came from the Army's phonetic pronunciation of the alphabetic preface of the boat's hull number, e.g., T-100.

Chapter 8

1. Loosely paraphrasing William Wordsworth's poem, "I Wandered Lonely as a Cloud." The actual line reads, "When all at once I saw a crowd, a host, of golden daffodils."
2. I probably shouldn't have saluted. I had been outfitted in full combat gear, serving as band security for this trip, and according to Army protocol should have brought my rifle to present arms—maybe that had been what prompted the Marine lifer's scowl.
3. The Huey UH-1B helicopter was an underpowered Army castoff the Navy had rebuilt into an all-weather, night-flying, heavily armed fighting platform used in support of Brown Water Navy operations.
4. The official monthly "Memo for Colonel Hanket—Band Commitments for June 1969" erroneously listed the concert as having occurred in Cần Thơ.
5. My test scores *were* mediocre.
6. The bird terminology refers to the design of the rank insignia, an eagle with outstretched wings, and not the officer's intelligence quotient, i.e., bird brain.
7. Other passengers and crew killed aboard the Slick were CPT David Randall Mackey, MAJ Dana Wesson Mitchell, CPT Donald William Dietz, MAJ William Terrell McNair, LT Richard Atwood Snowdon (pilot), WO-1 Robert P. Mayer (co-pilot), SP-5 Gary Lee Haught (door gunner), and SP-5 William Andrew Fitch (door gunner). Also lost were both Cobra pilots, Warrant Officers Gary James Davis and Theodore Van Skiles.
8. Official records of monthly band activities, as reported to battalion HQ by both Mister Johns and Mister Kottermann, sometimes conflict with my weekly reports to Mom and Dad.
9. Định Tường Province was divided into seven districts: Giáo Đúc, Cái Bè, Cai Lậy, Long Đình, Châu Thành, Bên Tranh, and Chợ Gạo, each under the auspices of a senior-grade U.S. Army District Military Advisor.
10. The band had probably been loaned out to another division and the troop was most likely an element of the 7th Cavalry, 1st Cavalry Division.

Chapter 9

1. Soldiers wore two tags around their necks, one on a long metal necklace that resembled an old-fashioned ceramic light fixture pull chain and the second on a shorter extension loop—one tag for record keeping and the other to remain with the body for identification at graves registration.
2. Lucky Larry had rented a wife for a week!
3. Vietnamese General Cao Van Vien, Chief Joint General Staff, presented the division with his country's highest unit valor award, their Cross of Gallantry with Palm and their Unit Citation Streamer of the Civic Action Medal with Oak Leaf.
4. After enduring the harshness and brutality of Vietnam for over six months, the sweetness of female companionship and the unexpected sex had shaken up my sensibilities. Vietnam had, at the time, been my reality and by comparison had caused my feelings toward a normal male-female relationship to be greatly enhanced, a relationship that stressed life and happiness over death and survival.
5. MAJ William T. Muenter had taken temporary command of the 4/47 Mechanized Infantry Battalion from LTC Douglas S. Smith until Smith's replacement could complete his stateside assignment and arrive in-country.
6. The orders were printed on mimeograph paper that has browned almost to illegibility. Much of the document can no longer be read.
7. The 9th Infantry Division was the only division in Vietnam to operate Air Cushioned Vehicles. Four vehicles came from the U.S. Navy. During my time at Đồng Tâm the unit bore the name "Air Cushioned Vehicle Unit (Provisional)." When assigned to the Division's 3rd Brigade during August 1969, it was renamed the "39th Cavalry Platoon," which might have be an overstatement of its assets. Only one vehicle remained operational.
8. The Bakelite compartmentalized meal trays the Army used instead of separate dishes were stacked vertically in wooden racks located at the entrance to the food serving area. Hungry troops would enter the area, slide out a tray, and proceed to the serving counter.

Chapter 10

1. The Reliable Academy processed both incoming and outgoing troops in the division and had limited authorization to issue local orders.
2. Out-processing troops were kept physically isolated from in-processing troops to the extent a solid seven-foot-high fence at the airfield ramp kept the two groups separated almost to the portable stairway leading up into the aircraft.
3. When I had departed for Oakland in January I had been wearing a green Class A *winter*

weight uniform, which looked the same as the summer weight uniform but was cut of heavier cloth.

4. Although my DEROS had been approved for August 17, my REFRAD to attend school had been approved for no earlier than August 24. In view of this the Army had deducted one week's compensation from my final paycheck.

5. Because of the widespread animosity being shown Vietnam returnees by civilians on the home front, the Army unofficially advised all returnees *not* to wear their uniforms in public!

Chapter 11

1. A popular sentiment chanted by rebellious youthful Americans of the era had been "Don't trust anyone over 30."

2. May 4, 1970.

3. During this period the National Guard mostly comprised young men lawfully avoiding active military service. They had little crowd-control training and no combat experience. They were essentially ill-suited to deal with what transpired at Kent State University.

4. The American soldiers of the Vietnam War, while cantankerous to their commanders and their orders, developed a strong bond of unit pride and identification that melded into brotherhood. These soldiers would have held their ground—together as one in victory or defeat.

5. To the extent the government is elected by the people and in theory represents their wishes.

6. A mental health syndrome, often affecting survivors of chaos, that the medical profession has labeled Post Traumatic Stress Disorder.

7. Specifically the long-drawn-out wars in Afghanistan and Iraq.

Bibliography

Documents

Commanding Officer, HHC & Band, DISCOM, approval for early separation to attend school, dated June 11, 1969.

834th Air Division Tactical Airlift, Southeast Asia Airlift System, Boarding Pass for flight from Đồng Tâm to Ben Hoa, August 11, 1969.

Headquarters 9th Infantry Division, General Orders No. 4392, award of the Army Commendation Medal, dated April 12, 1969.

Headquarters 9th Infantry Division, General Orders No. 10035, award of the Army Commendation Medal—First Oak Leaf Cluster, dated July 11, 1969.

Headquarters 9th Infantry Division, General Orders No. 11241, award of the Bronze Star Medal, dated August 1, 1969.

Headquarters 9th Infantry Division, General Orders No. 11350, award of the Good Conduct Medal, dated August 6, 1969.

Headquarters 9th Infantry Division, Special Orders No. 16, assigned to HHC & Band, DISCOM, dated January 16, 1969.

Headquarters 9th Infantry Division, Special Orders No. 165, assigned to USATRFSTA Fort Dix, NJ, WP October 20, 1969, dated June 14, 1969.

Headquarters 9th Infantry Division, Special Orders No. 173, assignment to USATRFSTA Fort Dix, NJ, WP August 13, 1969, dated June 22, 1969.

Headquarters 9th Infantry Division, Special Orders No. 174, Special Orders No. 165, assignment to USATRFSTA Fort Dix, NJ, amended, dated June 23, 1969.

Headquarters 9th Infantry Division, Special Orders No. 310, promotion to SP-5, dated February 27, 1969.

Headquarters 9th Infantry Division, Special Orders No. ? [mimeograph orders are only partially legible due to overall foxing], assignment to the 3/34 Artillery Battalion, WP July 21, 1969, dated July 20, 1969.

Headquarters U.S. Army Personnel Center, Oakland, California, Special Orders No. 223, release from active duty August 13, 1969, dated August 13, 1969.

Letters sent from Vietnam to family members and friends.

Memo for Colonel Hanket—Band Commitments for March 1969.

Memo for Colonel Hanket—Band Commitments for April 1969.

Memo for Colonel Hanket—Band Commitments for May 1969.

Memo for Colonel Hanket—Band Commitments for June 1969.

Memo for Colonel Hanket—Band Commitments for July 1969.

Selective Service System, Order to Report for Induction, dated October 18, 1967.

Selective Service System, pamphlet, *Selective Service and You…*, February 18, 1963.

Selective Service System, Student Certificate, dated October 1, 1965.

Seton Hall University, letter of acceptance into graduate program, June 4, 1969.

United States Army Flight Training Center Fort Stewart, Letter Orders No. 856, TDY to attend 1968 Service Rifle and Service Pistol Instructor Clinic, WP OA September 30, 1968, dated September 13, 1968.

United States Army Flight Training Center Fort Stewart, Letter Orders No. 891, TDY to Jacksonville, Florida, to render military honors for the late George Lee, WP OA September 28, 1968, dated September 26, 1968.

United States Army Flight Training Center Fort Stewart, Special Orders No. 249, assignment to USARV, dated November 1, 1968.

Voice recordings sent from Vietnam to fiancée.

Books

Bowman, John S., ed. *The Vietnam War: An Almanac*. New York: Bison Books, 1985.

Dougan, Clark, and Stephen Weiss. *The Vietnam Experience: A Nation Divided*. Boston: Boston Publishing, 1983.

_____. *The Vietnam Experience: Nineteen Sixty-Eight*. Boston: Boston Publishing, 1983.

Hackworth, David H. *Steel My Soldiers' Hearts*. New York: Rugged Land, 2002.

Kelly, Michael J. *Where We Were in Vietnam*. Central Point, OR: Hellgate, 2002.

Lipsman, Samuel, and Edward Doyle. *The Vietnam Experience: Fighting for Time*. Boston: Boston Publishing, 1983.

Maga, Timothy P. *The Complete Idiot's Guide to the Vietnam War*. Indianapolis: Alpha, 2000.

Stanton, Shelby L. *The Rise and Fall of an American Army*. Navato, CA: Presidio, 1985.

_____. *Vietnam Order of Battle*. Mechanicsburg, PA: Stackpole, 2003.

Newspapers

Newark (NJ) Evening News. "Red Mortars Blow Up 500 Tons of US Ammo," March 26, 1969, p. 3.

Old Reliable News. Vol. 3, nos. 2–31. Republic of Vietnam, 9th Infantry Division, 1969.

Index

Abrams, Gen. Creighton 110
Advanced Individual Training (AIT) 25–27, 36, 42, 47
Agent Orange 68, 99
Air America 43
Air Cushion Vehicle Provisional (ACV) 213
ANH Steam Bath Massage Parlor 132
AP Tan Than 162
AP Tan Tri (Giao Duct) 186
Army of the Republic of Vietnam (ARVN) 71, 78, 79, 93, 100, 102, 109, 110, 127, 131, 133, 134, 135, 145, 155, 156, 160, 168, 177, 185, 194, 207, 208, 210, 211, 212, 213, 216
Army of the Republic of Vietnam Units (ARVN): 7th ARVN Division 109, 110, 208, 213, 216; 9th ARVN Division 109; 21st ARVN Division 109; 213th ARVN Artillery Battalion 100, 102, 145

Basic Combat Training (BCT) 21, 23, 25, 26, 85, 97
Ben Luc 134
Ben Thranh 157
Ben Tre 169
APB-35 USS *Benewah* 153, 154, 163, 165, 175, 199, 202, 203, 208
Bien Hoa 38, 39, 40, 43, 44, 92, 207, 221, 222
Bien Hoa Province 38
Binh Duc 122, 190
Binh Phuoc 185, 191, 195, 207, 213
Brigades of the 9th Infantry Division: 1st *Recondo* Brigade 103, 153, 157, 213, 219, 220; 2nd *River Raiders* Brigade 51, 77, 153, 154, 156, 163, 169, 199, 202, 209, 220; 3rd *Go Devils* Brigade 134, 148, 149, 180, 181, 183, 213, 218

Cai Lay 103, 104, 144, 172
Cam Ranh Bay 40, 61, 144
Camps: Alpha 207; Evans 157; Long Binh Junction 38, 40; Panther 191, 194, 195; Robert Bethune 185; Scott 162, 184;
Can Tho 98, 100, 102, 145–147, 155, 175, 176, 180, 182, 183, 196, 197
Canals: Kinh Chet Say Cu 156; Kinh Xang 68, 78, 79, 189, 211

Cao Lanh 109–112
Cho Bung 142
APB-36 USS *Colleton* 153
Commanding Officers: Abrams, Gen. Creighton 110; Eckhart, Maj. Gen. George S. 69; Ewell, Maj. Gen. Julian J. 50, 120, 121; Gunn, Brig. Gen. Frank L. 50, 51, 108, 213; Hanket, Col. Arthur P. 88–89, 143, 176, 190, 191; Hayes, Col. John G. 104, 213; Hollis, Maj. Gen. Harris W. 121, 168, 180, 188; Hunt, Ira A. 104, 180; Westmoreland, William C. 92, 110, 128; Zumwalt, Adm. Elmo R., Jr. 177–178
Compounds: Crum 109, 110; Eakin 155; Shannon-Wright 69; Tiger II (Tiger's Lair) 156, 169

Dinh Tuong 43, 186, 202, 212
Division Support Command (DISCOM) 50, 58, 59, 60, 62–64, 67–71, 73–75, 77, 82, 85, 87, 88, 90, 93, 95, 97, 98, 102, 107, 108, 112, 114, 115, 117–120, 122, 128, 131, 132, 142, 144–146, 149, 151, 152, 154, 161, 162, 164, 165, 175, 176, 180–182, 188, 190, 193, 198–200, 202, 203, 207, 209, 212, 213, 216–218, 220, 221
Đồng Tâm 43–45, 49, 51, 53–56, 58, 60, 61, 63, 65–72, 74, 75, 77, 78, 80, 82, 83, 85, 86–91, 95, 96, 98–107, 110–112, 115–117, 120–122, 125, 130, 131, 133, 135–137, 141, 142, 143, 145, 149, 150, 152–154, 156–159, 161–165, 167–169, 172, 174–176, 179, 180, 182, 183, 185, 186, 188–190, 193, 196, 198–203, 207, 208, 211–214, 216–219, 221, 228

Eckhart, Maj. Gen. George S. 69
834th Tactical Air Wing (TAW) 221
80th Army Band 30, 34, 49, 103, 154
84th Artillery 1st Battalion 152, 187, 207
86th Engineer Battalion 148
11th Artillery 1st Battalion 106, 145, 186
Ewell, Maj. Gen. Julian J. 50, 120, 121

15th Combat Engineer Battalion 74, 78, 98, 120, 121, 148, 183
5th Armored Cavalry 157, 168, 196, 197

245

Index

51st Maintenance Company 176
52nd Signal Group 146
Fire Support Bases (FSB): Danger 186, 187, 191, 193, 208, 210, 213, 219; Dizzy 187; Moore 103–106, 121, 125–127, 129, 167, 168, 180, 210, 215, 216, 219; Schroeder (formerly Dirk) 125, 126, 144, 145, 155, 158, 165, 167, 168, 172, 184, 188, 210, 212, 219
Fire Support Patrol Bases (FSPB): Binh Phuoc (Camp Panther) 191; Rach Kien 184, 193; Tan An 134, 149; Tan Tru (Camp Scott) 162, 184
First Recondo Religious Center 127, 145, 165
535th Tactical Air Lift Squadron (TAS) 170
536th Tactical Air Lift Squadron (TAS) 170
Foremost Dairies, Inc. 74
Forts: Benjamin Harrison 27, 28, 30; Benning 32, 33; Dix 21, 23, 25, 36, 41, 73, 85, 183, 188, 221; Leonard Wood 25, 26, 35, 36, 189; Stewart 28–35, 39, 41, 49, 54, 94, 103, 107, 117, 154
44th Special Tactical Zone 109–111, 113
47th Infantry 4th Battalion 164, 202, 208
47th Infantry 2nd Battalion 104, 191, 194, 196, 207, 213
47th Infantry 3rd Battalion 156, 202
Four Deuces Mortar Platoon 49, 56, 77, 86, 214, 219
4th Artillery 2nd Battalion 104, 149, 158, 164, 191, 195
Gunn, Brig. Gen. Frank L. 50, 51, 108, 213

Hanket, Col. Arthur P. 88–89, 143, 176, 190, 191
USS *Harnett County* 134
APB-35 USS *Benewah* 153, 154, 163, 165, 175, 199, 202, 203, 208; APB-36 USS *Colleton* 153; APB-39 USS *Mercer* 153, 154, 172; APB-40 USS *Nueces* 153–154
Hayes, Col. John G. 104, 213
Headquarters and Headquarters Company & Band, DISCOM (HHC & Band) 58, 95, 162, 181, 217
Hollis, Maj. Gen. Harris W. 121, 168, 180, 188
Hunt, Ira A. 104, 180

Infantry Divisions: 5th Infantry 157; 23rd (Americal) Infantry 42; 25th Infantry 181, 218

Kien Hoa Province 156

Long An Province 148, 161, 165, 181
Long Binh 39, 40, 43, 221, 222
Long Dinh 78–81

APB-39 USS *Mercer* 153, 154, 172
Military Assistance Command Vietnam (MACV) 42, 73, 92, 109, 110, 128, 218
Military Payment Certificate (MPC) 42, 71, 74
Mobile Riverine Force (MRF) 47, 154, 164, 169, 202

My Tho 133, 157, 159, 160, 170, 179, 199, 200, 201, 202
My Thaun 104

National Police 136, 159, 170, 185, 190, 194
Naval Support Activity Detachment at Binh Thuy 176, 177
Naval Support Activity Saigon at Ben Luc 134
Naval Task Force 116 47, 208
Navy Ships: USS *Harnett County* 134; APB-35 USS *Benewah* 153, 154, 163, 165, 175, 199, 202, 203, 208; APB-36 USS *Colleton* 153; APB-39 USS *Mercer* 153, 154, 172; APB-40 USS *Nueces* 153–154
90th Replacement Battalion 38–41, 42, 43, 44, 45, 90, 221, 222
91st Combined Services Battalion 182
93rd Engineer Battalion 120
9th Artillery 106, 120, 179, 180, 213, 215
9th Aviation Battalion 160, 175, 216
9th Medical Battalion (Detachment) 148, 198
9th Military Police Battalion (MP) 57, 88, 89, 98, 99, 114, 134, 160, 188, 194, 200, 216
9th Signal Battalion 176, 185, 207
9th Supply & Transportation Battalion (S&T) 162, 165, 216
North Vietnamese Army (NVA) 26, 157
APB-40 USS *Nueces* 153–154
Numbered Units: 2nd Artillery 5th Battalion 148; 3rd Surgical Hospital 56, 66, 117, 142, 190, 198, 203; 4th Artillery 2nd Battalion 104, 149, 158, 164, 191, 195; 5th Armored Cavalry 157, 168, 196, 197; 9th Artillery 106, 120, 179, 180, 213, 215; 9th Aviation Battalion 160, 175, 216; 9th Medical Battalion (Detachment) 148, 198; 9th Military Police Battalion (MP) 57, 88, 89, 98, 99, 114, 134, 160, 188, 194, 200, 216; 9th Signal Battalion 176, 185, 207; 9th Supply & Transportation Battalion (S&T) 162, 165, 216; 11th Artillery 1st Battalion 106, 145, 186; 15th Combat Engineer Battalion 74, 78, 98, 120, 121, 148, 183; 16th Infantry 1st Battalion 185; 17th Cavalry 3rd Squadron 1st Aviation Brigade 183; 22nd Replacement Battalion 40; 29th Artillery Battalion Headquarters Company 148; 31st Infantry 6th Battalion 104, 183, 198, 199, 216, 217; 34th Artillery 3rd Battalion 180, 188, 209–211, 213, 218; 39th Infantry 2nd Battalion 98, 126, 144, 168, 186; 39th Infantry 3rd Battalion 98, 150, 152, 153, 180, 212, 216; 39th Infantry 4th Battalion 117, 186, 187, 193; 44th Special Tactical Zone 109–111, 113; 47th Infantry 2nd Battalion 104, 191, 194, 196, 207, 213; 47th Infantry 3rd Battalion 156, 202; 47th Infantry 4th Battalion 164, 202, 208; 51st Maintenance Company 176; 52nd Signal Group 146; 60th Infantry 2nd Battalion 162, 189; 60th Infantry 3rd Battalion 49, 77, 163, 172, 174, 199, 202, 207; 60th Infantry 5th Battalion 184, 185, 192–194, 196; 73rd

Index

Surveillance Company-Army 170; 77th Artillery 6th Battalion 98, 100, 102, 145, 146; 80th Army Band 30, 34, 49, 103, 154; 84th Artillery 1st Battalion 152, 187, 207; 86th Engineer Battalion 148; 90th Replacement Battalion 38–41, 42, 43, 44, 45, 90, 221, 222; 91st Combined Services Battalion 182; 93rd Engineer Battalion 120; 114th Attack Helicopter Company (AHC) 69; 147th Assault Support Helicopter Company (ASHC) 170, 171; 162nd Attack Helicopter Company (AHC) 149, 164; 164th Combat Aviation Group (CAG) 175, 180; 191st Attack Helicopter Company (AHC) 95, 98; 199th Light Infantry Brigade 42; 214th Combat Aviation Battalion (CAB) 168, 169; 307th Aviation Battalion 196, 197; 535th Tactical Air Lift Squadron (TAS) 170; 536th Tactical Air Lift Squadron (TAS) 170; 709th Maintenance Battalion 160, 161; 834th Tactical Air Wing (TAW) 221
147th Assault Support Helicopter Company (ASHC) 170, 171
114th Attack Helicopter Company (AHC) 69
191st Attack Helicopter Company (AHC) 95, 98
199th Light Infantry Brigade 42
164th Combat Aviation Group (CAG) 175, 180
162nd Attack Helicopter Company (AHC) 149, 164

Operations: Big Switch 100, 102, 145, 146; Enterprise 148; River Raider I 154; Water Trap 51

Pacific Air Lift (PAL) 117
Phong Dinh Province 146
Phuc Toy Province 169
Provinces: Bien Hoa 38; Dinh Tuong 43, 186, 202, 212; Kien Hoa 156; Long An 148, 161, 165, 181; Phong Dinh 146; Phuc Toy 169

Rach Kien 183, 184, 193, 194
Reliable Academy 43, 46–56, 58, 67, 70, 88, 105, 106, 114, 120, 125, 131, 132, 145, 153, 154, 160, 162, 168, 176, 179, 186, 193, 196, 202, 203, 213, 215, 216, 219, 221
Reliable Fixed-Wing Airfield 48, 87, 91, 111, 155, 221
Reliable Rotary-Wing Airfield 69, 95, 96, 196, 216
Rivers: Song Bassac 176; Song Ben Tre 156; Song Co Chien 69; Song My Tho 16, 47, 51, 54, 68, 99, 132, 154, 159, 163, 172, 189, 199, 202, 208; Song Vam Co Tay 134, 162; Song Vam Co Dong 134, 135

Saigon 40, 61, 72, 74, 78, 85, 101, 116, 130, 131, 133–140, 141, 149, 169, 170, 171, 185, 204
Schofield Barracks 117
2nd Artillery 5th Battalion 148

709th Maintenance Battalion 160, 161
17th Cavalry 3rd Squadron 1st Aviation Brigade 183
77th Artillery 6th Battalion 98, 100, 102, 145, 146
73rd Surveillance Company-Army 170
16th Infantry 1st Battalion 185
60th Infantry 5th Battalion 184, 185, 192–194, 196
60th Infantry 2nd Battalion 162, 189
60th Infantry 3rd Battalion 49, 77, 163, 172, 174, 199, 202, 207

Tan An 134, 148–150, 162, 165, 168, 180, 181, 213, 218
Tan Hiep 134
Tan Tru 161, 162, 180, 189
Tan Tich 109, 111
3rd Surgical Hospital 56, 66, 117, 142, 190, 198, 203
31st Infantry 6th Battalion 104, 183, 198, 199, 216, 217
34th Artillery 3rd Battalion 180, 188, 209–211, 213, 218
39th Infantry 4th Battalion 117, 186, 187, 193
39th Infantry 2nd Battalion 98, 126, 144, 168, 186
39th Infantry 3rd Battalion 98, 150, 152, 153, 180, 212, 216
Thoi Son *(VC Island)* 51
307th Aviation Battalion 196, 197
29th Artillery Battalion Headquarters Company 148
22nd Replacement Battalion 40
214th Combat Aviation Battalion (CAB) 168, 169

United States Army Overseas Replacement Center at Oakland (USAOSREPLCTR) 36, 37, 222, 223
United States Army Republic of Vietnam (USARV) 34, 35, 43, 47, 68, 73, 91 93, 110, 117, 125, 153, 214, 222, 226

Viet Cong (VC) 26, 47, 48, 51, 52–56, 58, 66, 67, 68, 71, 73, 75–77, 81–83, 85, 86, 87, 91, 92, 94–96, 101–103, 107–109, 114–119, 121, 122, 125, 127, 130, 132–136, 141, 150–152, 156, 160, 164, 167, 176, 178, 179, 185, 190, 200, 210, 213, 214, 216, 217, 219, 224
Vietnamese American Association 131, 136, 137
Villages and Cities: AP Tan Than 162; AP Tan Tri (Giao Duct) 186; Ben Luc 134; Ben Thranh 157; Ben Tre 169; Bien Hoa 38, 39, 40, 43, 44, 92, 207, 221, 222; Binh Duc 122, 190; Binh Phuoc 185, 191, 195, 207, 213; Cai Lay 103, 104, 144, 172; Cam Ranh Bay 40, 61, 144; Can Tho 98, 100, 102, 145–147, 155, 175, 176, 180, 182, 183, 196, 197; Cao Lanh 109–112; Cho Bung 142; Long Binh 39, 40, 43,

221, 222; Long Dinh 78–81; My Tho 133, 157, 159, 160, 170, 179, 199, 200, 201, 202; My Thaun 104; Rach Kien 183, 184, 193, 194; Saigon 40, 61, 72, 74, 78, 85, 101, 116, 130, 131, 133–140, 141, 149, 169, 170, 171, 185, 204; Tan An 134, 148–150, 162, 165, 168, 180, 181, 213, 218; Tan Hiep 134; Tan Tru 161, 162, 180, 189; Tan Tich 109, 111; Thoi Son *(VC Island)* 51; Vinh Kim 68, 69; Vinh Long 69, 149; Vung Tau 61, 144, 168–172

Vinh Kim 68, 69
Vinh Long 69, 149
Vung Tau 61, 144, 168–172

Westmoreland, William C. 92, 110, 128
World Airways 38, 204, 222, 223

Zumwalt, Adm. Elmo R., Jr. 177–178

www.ingramcontent.com/pod-product-compliance
Ingram Content Group UK Ltd.
Pitfield, Milton Keynes, MK11 3LW, UK
UKHW041937140426
5217IPUK00014B/518